Countdown to Your Perfect Wedding

01/15/2009

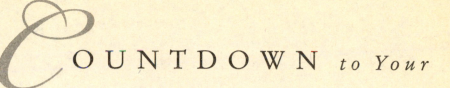

Countdown *to Your* Perfect Wedding

FROM ENGAGEMENT RING TO HONEYMOON,
A WEEK-BY-WEEK GUIDE TO PLANNING
THE HAPPIEST DAY OF YOUR LIFE

JOYCE SCARDINA BECKER

St. Martin's Griffin ❧ *New York*

www.stmartins.com

Developed by Literary Productions

Illustrations on page 79 by Jennifer Angilello of All about the Dress

Library of Congress Cataloging-in-Publication Data

Becker, Joyce Scardina.
Countdown to your perfect wedding : from engagement ring to honeymoon,
a week-by-week guide to planning the happiest day of your life / Joyce Scardina Becker.—
1st St. Martin's Griffin ed.
p. cm.
ISBN 0-312-34845-2
EAN 978-0-312-34845-8
1. Weddings—Planning. 2. Wedding etiquette. I. Title.

HQ745.B425 2006
395.2'2—dc22
2005044414

10 9 8 7 6 5 4 3

CONTENTS

ONE'S WEDDING DAY is a magical occasion that is bigger than life itself. Having attended several weddings by the tender age of six, I became quite the expert on them early in life. I saw many weddings that appeared to be similar in style. Bridesmaids adorned with pillbox hats and veils walked down the aisle; immediately after the "I do's," reception meals consisting of cake and coffee were served in the church hall, which was usually decorated with large, white, paper bells.

When my oldest sister, Gerry, got married in 1959, I knew something was very different. Bridesmaids danced the night away in Audrey Hepburn, duchess satin, fuchsia dresses, champagne flowed from fountains, and dramatic ice sculptures embellished the buffets. It was a grand occasion orchestrated by Miss Lauretta Parker, who was also known as "the Wedding Secretary." You see, my mother had the brilliance of hiring the very first wedding planner in San Francisco to stage Gerry's special day.

Did the influence of this occasion rub off on me? You bet! I knew right away that I, too, wanted someday to be a wedding planner. This book reflects my passion for weddings and my lifelong experience as a successful event planner and designer. As you read through the following chapters, you will discover the keys to planning the perfect wedding through the eyes of someone with firsthand knowledge on the subject. I've been at this for more than twenty-five years, and I live and breathe wedding planning every day. It's my life and my passion.

In *Countdown to Your Perfect Wedding,* I guide you step-by-step, week-by-week through this wonderful process. This book will enable you to become your own personal wedding planner. I also tell you what to look for in a professional, if you opt to go this route instead.

Unlike the weddings of yesteryear, today's brides and grooms express themselves in surprising new ways. For many couples, the wedding celebration is an investment in their future and an expression of their taste— a rite of style passage, if you will. Never before has planning the wedding become so complex and the details of the wedding been noticed by so many. Even the men are noticing, as more and more grooms are becoming actively involved in the wedding-planning process.

Nothing is more joyful than planning this celebration of a lifetime as a couple. When my husband, Dana, proposed to me in 1993, we were married just six months later! It didn't take us a lifetime to plan our wedding, and yours won't either. All you need is an understanding of the planning process and someone to guide you through it. The key to a successful wedding-planning experience is to identify the tasks that need to be performed, know how to organize them in an orderly fashion, and then execute them in the right way. That's exactly what this book shows you how to do.

To bring order to your planning process, *Countdown to Your Perfect Wedding* is divided among the items you need to address over the course of fifty-two weeks. If you are a year away from your wedding, you can cover one chapter each week. Of course, if you have more or less than a year to plan your wedding, you can slow down or speed up the process accordingly. In every chapter, I give you innovative ideas, real-life anecdotes from couples I've worked with, and valuable advice from leading wedding experts—including myself—who have dazzled brides, grooms, and their guests around the world.

The trick is to make the result—your fabulous wedding day—run like a seamless, perfectly timed production that looks effortless to your guests. For that to happen, all elements of the wedding—the guest list, the location, the food and beverages, flowers, decor, lighting, and so much more—must be expertly choreographed ahead of time. There is just no substitute for attention to detail and planning.

The process of planning your wedding may seem a bit overwhelming at first, especially if you are performing this task while also working a full-time job or carrying a full load of classes in college. But trust me: It can be a lot of fun, if you allow it to be.

Whether you're planning a traditional or nontraditional wedding, and regardless of whether you have one year, six months, or less, *Countdown to Your Perfect Wedding* will walk you through the necessary planning steps in an organized and informative way so you can get to the altar on time—and in great shape.

So let your wedding dreams become a reality. Together, we'll plan a spectacular wedding day just for you that's far beyond your wildest imagination.

Countdown to Your Perfect Wedding

Savor the Proposal

PERHAPS HE POPPED the question along the azure shores of Hawaii. Or maybe you asked him while dining at one of the fanciest New York restaurants. Either way, a wedding always begins with the proposal.

I remember my first proposal from my husband, Dana. (Yes, there were two!) Dana was the best man at a friend's wedding. Flying home on a first-class upgrade from Seattle to San Francisco, the champagne bubbles must have pickled his brain. Unrehearsed, he proposed to me in flight! I was so excited that the second we got on the ground I called my best friend and asked her to be a bridesmaid. By the time we arrived home, all the bubbles had burst, and the proposal was withdrawn. Lesson learned: Savor the moment, but keep it private in the beginning. Three months later, exactly a year from the day we met, Dana proposed again over a five-star meal. This time, we didn't officially announce our engagement until a month later at a party we hosted together.

My advice, therefore, is to revel in your engagement, but don't tell everyone until you have had time to take it all in and discuss the details between the two of you.

If either of you has children from a prior relationship, set aside some private time to share the news with your children. News like this can be confusing to kids, especially little ones. It's important to assure your children that they will remain your top priority throughout your engagement and marriage.

Traditionally, a man first asked a woman's father for her hand in marriage before proposing. If you haven't exactly followed tradition, it is an excellent idea to share the good news with the bride's parents shortly after you've popped the question. It's never out of style to have good manners. If possible, make the engagement announcement to the bride's parents in person. If this isn't possible, a phone call is the next best option. (Don't even think about e-mail.) Be sure to tell the groom's parents soon after. If both sets of parents have not met yet, and it's convenient to do so, now's the time to get together and celebrate, perhaps at a dinner or family weekend.

Beyond that, this is enough notifying for now. I get into the "complete" announcement of your engagement a couple of chapters down the road. If the weekend is approaching, head out of town to a favorite destination you enjoyed while you were dating and chill out. If you can spare the vacation time, take a couple of workdays off, too. It's time for you simply to savor the moment and celebrate your engagement quietly together. There will be plenty for you to do in the coming weeks. For now, just enjoy yourselves and your new engagement.

Select an Engagement Ring

ALTHOUGH MANY OUTDATED wedding traditions have vanished in the twenty-first century, one that may endure forever is the engagement ring. When your friends and relatives find out you're engaged, it is the first thing they ask about and want to see. If you feel the need to make a statement about your engagement, this is your big chance. (Incidentally, this step often comes before the previous one, which is why I put them back-to-back.)

Another enduring rule of wediquette: It is still the groom's responsibility to purchase this symbol of love for his lovely bride. But guys, unless you are clairvoyant or have a perfect understanding of your future wife's taste in jewelry, you may not want to take on the burden of buying the ring without consulting her first. (After more than ten years of marriage, I can honestly say that my husband still doesn't have a clue when it comes to the kind of jewelry I like.) A more contemporary approach is for couples to shop for the ring together, have the bride identify her favorites, and then let the groom make the final purchase on his own.

Let's say you're a guy who's big on upholding tradition, and you want to pleasantly surprise your gal by springing a ring on her as you pop the question. What's the best way to pick one out that you know she'll love? Brian Merkley, owner of Merkley Kendrick Jewelers in Louisville, Kentucky, suggests seeking the assistance of close friends of your bride-to-be "who can be trusted to keep their mouths shut."

Regardless of how you choose to approach the buying process, it's important to educate yourself about engagement rings before opening your wallet. After all, this is one of the most significant purchases you'll ever make.

Let's take a look at the kinds of engagement rings that couples are buying these days. While most jewelers offer a mind-boggling array of choices, Marilyn Monroe's famous refrain is likely to live on forever—diamonds truly are a girl's best friend. According to Mel Wasserman of Zwillinger & Company in San Francisco, diamond engagement rings outsell all other types by 20-to-1 (sapphires and rubies come in a very distant second and third). Given this overwhelming popularity, I address diamond rings exclusively in this chapter, although many of the general concepts regarding diamonds can be applied to other precious stones as well.

A Diamond Primer

UNLESS YOU'VE JUST crawled out from under a very large rock, you have probably already heard about the "4 Cs" of diamonds— carat, clarity, color, and cut. But what does this mean to you, the purchaser? Simply put, the 4 Cs, taken together, determine the overall value and beauty of a diamond (and should determine its price as well). If you focus on just one or two Cs while searching for your perfect engagement ring, you may end up with a diamond that isn't worth its weight in cubic zirconium. So it's definitely worth your while to study the 4 Cs before you start shopping.

Carat

This is simply the weight of the diamond. A 1-carat diamond weighs 200 milligrams. To complicate matters, jewelers invented a "points" scale as an alternate measurement of a diamond's weight (mostly for stones weighing less than 1 carat). There are 100 points to a carat, so a diamond weighing ¾ carat is a 75-point diamond. Without trying to sound like your high school algebra teacher, let me summarize: 1 carat = 100 points = 200 milligrams.

Don't confuse the *carat* weight of a diamond with *karat*, which is a measurement of the purity of gold. (Notice the difference in spelling.) I talk more about karats later.

If you are out shopping and want to verify a stone's carat weight, ask the jeweler to weigh it while you watch. First, make sure that the scale registers zero when there is nothing on it. Then, after the unmounted stone is placed on the scale, take the number of milligrams indicated and divide by 200 to get the number of carats. Don't make the mistake of looking for the biggest rock at the smallest price. You will likely get a stone with substandard clarity, color, and cut—and it will probably look cheap, too.

Clarity

Clarity is a measure of the number and extent of the flaws in a diamond. In general, the fewer the flaws, the more valuable the diamond. Since the word "flaw" has a negative connotation, jewelers and gemologists came up with a pleasant-sounding euphemism: They refer to flaws as *inclusions* (as in, there's other stuff *included* in this rock besides pure diamond).

There are several methodologies used to measure clarity, but the Gemological Institute of America (GIA) has developed a scale that is the most widely used and respected. The GIA scale rates diamonds as flawless (FL), internally flawless (IF), very very slightly included (VVS), very slightly included (VS), slightly imperfect (SI), and imperfect (I). There are further subdivisions within these grades, which are intended to provide a more precise definition of clarity. Here are practical definitions for each category:

- **FL**   Completely flawless, very rare and worth a king's ransom.
- **IF**   Internally flawless; only external flaws are present, which can be removed by further polishing the stone.
- **VVS1 and VVS2**   Only a trained gemologist can detect inclusions with a 10-power microscope. If an expert can see an inclusion from the top of the diamond, it is classified as a VVS2. But if an expert can detect flaws only when viewing the bottom of the stone, then it is a VVS1.
- **VS1 and VS2**   The average consumer can see flaws with a ten-power microscope, but it takes a while to spot them (around ten seconds or so).
- **SI1 to SI2**   The average consumer can immediately see flaws with a ten-power microscope but not with the naked eye.
- **I1 to I3**   Flaws can be seen with the naked eye. For stones rated I2 and I3, a minor league umpire can see the flaws, even without his glasses. Consider avoiding these diamonds.

To get a better understanding of clarity, ask a jeweler if you can look at several diamonds under a microscope before making a purchase. A reputable jeweler takes the time to show you different stones under the microscope and is even willing to point out their flaws so you can learn how to detect them by yourself.

According to Brian Merkley, there are several tricks of the trade that disreputable jewelers may employ: They use a loupe to demonstrate clarity characteristics. Clarity characteristics are much harder to see with a loupe than a microscope. Or they use the improper magnification level to demonstrate clarity characteristics. Inclusions should be viewed at ten-power magnification. If viewed under a lesser magnification, they don't seem as significant.

Another pitfall to avoid is the "clarity-enhanced" diamond. This is an artificial process used to fix the flaws on an otherwise good stone. Although a clarity-enhanced diamond can be made to look nearly flawless, the enhancing process makes the stone more brittle, reducing its durability and therefore its long-term value. Be sure to confirm with your jeweler that the stone you are considering is not clarity-enhanced.

For Brides on a Budget

In some respects, clarity is the least important of the 4 Cs when purchasing a diamond. Since an SI2 diamond is indistinguishable from a VVS1 to the naked eye, consider a lower-clarity diamond as a cost-saving alternative. After all, when you are showing off the ring to family and friends, it's unlikely that someone will whip out a microscope to check for flaws.

Color

The color of a diamond refers to the degree of "yellowness" that can be seen. A perfect diamond is completely colorless, which also makes it the most expensive.

The most widely used and accepted system for measuring color was developed by the GIA. With the GIA scale, color is alphabetically rated from D (totally colorless) to Z (yellow). In order for a diamond to receive a prestigious (and expensive) "colorless" designation, the GIA requires that it receive a D, E, or F grade. The average color for engagement ring diamonds in the United States is G or H; colors ranging from I through L are more affordable. Grades of M and below should not be considered for engagement rings.

To judge the color of a given diamond, jewelers place the diamond in question alongside a reference set of stones with known color grades. The jeweler then makes a qualitative assessment by determining the closest match. When shopping for a diamond, it's a good idea to ask the jeweler for a reference set of stones so you can judge the color for yourself. To do this, it is crucial to see the diamond unmounted. Place the diamond you're interested in next to the reference stones, facedown on a white piece of paper, and compare the color of the stones until you get the best match.

The type of band and setting you choose for your engagement ring can greatly affect your selection of color for the diamond. If you decide to mount the stone on a platinum or white gold setting, consider a diamond in the D–G range, because the yellowness of lower grades will be more noticeable. Conversely, according to Alex Angelle of the GIA, the appearance of a diamond of a lower color grade, which might otherwise show a tint of yellow, could be improved by mounting it on yellow gold.

Cut

Cut is probably the most important of the 4 Cs. That's because, according to the American Gem Society (AGS), it can affect the value of diamond engagement rings by 25 to 50 percent. However, cut can also be the most confusing of the 4 Cs, since it sometimes refers to the shape of the stone, its proportions, or the workmanship of the actual diamond-cutting process.

There are two basic types of cuts: the step cut and the brilliant cut. (There are also many variations within those two basic cuts.) The step cut has parallel facets that usually span the length or width of the stone. If the facets are rounded off on the corners, this is a variant of the step cut called the emerald cut. The step cut is often preferred by women who want a more glassy, elegant look.

Round shape, brilliant-cut diamonds are the most popular today because they provide the most "sparkle" when sized properly. This cut has triangular facets that surround the stone and a flat top called a *table*. In a properly proportioned brilliant-cut diamond, all of the light entering the diamond reflects within the stone and is cast back through the table, giving it maximum brilliance and fire. If the stone is too shallow or deep, some light escapes through the bottom part of the diamond, giving the appearance of shadows.

For all diamonds that it inspects and grades, the GIA issues certificates that contain data about the physical characteristics of the diamond, including color and clarity ratings, and statistics concerning the cut. Two important statistics are the table percentage and depth percentage. These are ratios comparing the depth and table to the width of the diamond. An appropriate table size should be between 53 and 64 percent of the width, and a proper depth percentage ranges between 58 and 64 percent. Anything outside this range means the diamond is too deep or too shallow. When checking out diamonds, you want the GIA certificate to give at least a "Good" rating for both statistics.

THE SETTING

WHILE THE EMPHASIS on engagement ring shopping is rightfully placed on the stone, you can't properly display your dazzling diamond without choosing an appropriate setting. Most brides select a prong-style setting to maximize the diamond's sparkle. The most important choice in selecting a prong setting is whether to get four or six prongs. Four prongs show off more of the diamond, but six prongs hold the diamond much more securely. If you plan to wear the ring all the time, six prongs are highly recommended to avoid losing the stone.

There are many other types of settings that do not use prongs. Some use pressure to keep the diamond in place, while others form a "channel" where the diamond is inserted. Your personal sense of style should guide you in selecting any of these alternative settings.

THE BAND

THE FINAL ELEMENT of your engagement ring is the ring itself. By far, the most common materials chosen for engagement bands are platinum and gold. Although your choice is ultimately a matter of personal style, here are a few facts about each metal.

Gold

For ages, gold has been the most popular metal in jewelry making. But because pure gold is soft and bends easily, it is usually alloyed with nickel, copper, and/or zinc to make it stronger. The purity of gold is measured in karats. A 24-karat ring is made of pure gold, whereas a 14-karat ring is 58.3 percent gold. Most gold jewelry sold in the United States is 14 karats, while 18-karat jewelry is more popular outside of the United States

Platinum

Platinum is rarer than gold and costs four times as much. To many people, however, platinum is worth the added expense because it is an extremely "hard" metal, and it will never tarnish. A three-digit number marked on the band indicates the purity of platinum. For example, "950 platinum" means the band is made of an alloy of 95 percent platinum and 5 percent other metals (usually palladium or iridium).

When Money Is No Object

If you can afford it, choose the highest quality diamond you can find—one that scores high in each of the 4 Cs. Couples with unlimited budgets often place added emphasis on size, picking a diamond that is 3 carats and above. And they select a platinum band for its added durability, unless they prefer the look of gold.

PURCHASING POINTERS

NOW THAT I'VE covered the basics of engagement rings, I want to offer some suggestions on how to make the purchase like a savvy shopper.

Where to Shop

Although online shopping has become more popular, even for diamond rings, I recommend going to brick-and-mortar stores for this purchase. Every diamond is unique, and you should have the opportunity to see and feel a purchase this important. Also, most reputable jewelry stores have an "upgrade policy" that allows you to trade in the diamond you buy for a more valuable stone in the future. Most Internet sellers do not offer this policy.

Begin by identifying jewelers in your area that have been in business for a long time, say, at least ten years. Contact the local chapter of the Better Business Bureau (www.bbb.org) to see if any complaints have been registered against them and, if so, whether these complaints were satisfactorily resolved. Then call the store and ask if they offer an upgrade policy.

How to Shop

Once you have compiled a list of reputable jewelers in your area, visit all of them, if you have the time. At a minimum, shop at three. That way, you see a wider variety of styles, and you can compare prices.

Make sure the jeweler has certificates for all of the diamonds, preferably from the GIA or AGS. These certificates provide an independent, objective analysis of the 4 Cs. Once you find a desirable diamond, ask to see its certificate and review the data carefully to verify the quality of the gem.

Don't assume that the listed price is set in stone (no pun intended). Some stores have negotiable pricing. After you have found a few diamonds that interest you, ask the jeweler whether he or she can do any better on the price. Even if you have your heart set on one particular diamond, try to act as if you are considering other possibilities. According to Fred Cueller (aka "the Diamond Guy") of Diamond Cutters International, once you have selected a ring and agreed on the purchase price, you should request that the final sale be contingent upon the opinion of an independent appraiser.

When making the purchase, use a credit card if possible. That way, if there is a problem with the ring, you can dispute the charge and your credit card company can help resolve the problem. If the store you are dealing with does not accept credit cards, that is a very large red flag and you should leave immediately. All legitimate jewelers take plastic.

Jerry Ehrenwald of the International Gemological Institute recommends obtaining insurance after you have purchased the ring. Your homeowner's or renter's insurance may not provide sufficient protection. Submit a copy of your sales receipt and the grading certificate to your insurance company, and include a photo of the ring. This ensures a fair replacement value if the ring is lost or stolen.

Finally, never lose track of the reason why you're buying an engagement ring. Your love for your fiancée should have absolutely nothing to do with the price you pay for the ring. Instead, this symbol of your commitment is to be enjoyed together and shared with family members, friends and, someday, your children.

HELPFUL HINTS

Once you have purchased a diamond ring, it is important to clean it regularly to maintain its sparkle. Jerry Ehrenwald shares an old "family recipe":

1. *Place your ring in a pot.*
2. *Cover with water to twice the height of the jewelry.*
3. *Add 1 teaspoon of granular electric dishwasher detergent and place the pot on the stove.*
4. *Bring the water to a boil for 3 to 5 minutes.*
5. *Turn off the heat and let the pot cool off naturally.*
6. *DO NOT remove the ring until it is fully cooled, as dramatic temperature changes can sometimes damage diamonds.*
7. *When the pot and ring are cool enough to touch with your hand, rinse the ring over a collander with tap water.*

Announce the Engagement—but Not the Date

YOU'RE ENGAGED AND on cloud nine. Your parents are just as thrilled about your engagement as you two are. Now it's time to tell the rest of the world.

Close relatives—including grandparents and siblings—should be the next to know. Your parents may be so excited that they already notified them before you can get to it. But Grandma and Grandpa, even your bratty teenage brother, still want to hear it from you as well.

If one or both of you are divorced with children, it's also wise to inform your ex of your plans. A phone call is fine if you're on speaking terms. Otherwise, a short letter will suffice. Either way, your ex should get the news from *you*, not your children, so that your kids aren't put in a position of having to answer questions about your wedding plans.

As far as your friends are concerned, I would break the news right now only to close friends whom you're absolutely certain you will invite to the wedding. If you go out of your way to notify friends, especially this soon after the proposal, they're going to start assuming that they will receive a wedding invitation later on.

Decide Whether to Have an Engagement Party

TO PARTY OR not to party? That is the question, and the answer is not as obvious as it might seem at first. The traditional engagement party hosted by the bride's parents has taken on a new twist. Today's engagement parties can be given by anyone, including the wedding couple themselves. From beach clambakes to sumptuous cocktail soirees and everything in between, the engagement party can certainly set the tone for the months ahead. However, having an engagement party is neither obligatory, nor should it be expected.

If you are going with tradition and the bride's parents are hosting a party, guests can be invited either by phone or written invitation, depending on how much time you have to pull the party together. The official engagement announcement is made during a toast given by the bride's father. Of course, the groom's father or other friends may also want to join in on the fun and toast to your happiness as well.

If you decide to host your own engagement party, you can spice it up by making it a "surprise" party. In that case, forget everything I already said about notifying family and friends—and keep a lid on it. You'll need to dream up a good phony excuse for having this party. Otherwise everyone will probably be suspicious and not particularly surprised when you and your sweetie get up to make the big announcement. Whether or not you attempt to surprise your guests, make sure you don't invite anyone to the party who won't subsequently be invited to the wedding. You don't want any unpleasant surprises down the road.

According to Emily Post, who (literally) wrote the book on etiquette, the only people who might give you an engagement present are very intimate friends or relatives—a godparent, your absolutely best friend. These are the same people who will likely spend a bundle on your wedding present. I think once is enough. So on the invitations to your engagement party—whether printed or verbal—it is a nice touch to add, "No gifts, please."

The Engagement Announcement

ACCORDING TO TRADITION, just prior to hosting a party in your honor, the bride's parents announce your engagement in the local newspaper. Whether or not you have an engagement party, publishing the news of your engagement in your hometown papers, as well as the cities where you live and work, is a fun way to spread the word.

Every newspaper has its own set of protocols for submitting engagement announcements. Some encourage photos, while others run only text. Some charge a fee; others run them for free. Call the newspaper's lifestyle or community editor to obtain information on submission requirements, deadlines, and fees.

Next, consider how you want your announcement to be worded. Most announcements include basic background information about the two of you: your full names, where you were each educated, where you work and live, and your parents' names. (See "Helpful Hints" below for more information.) You can also include information about club memberships, community or school associations, and military service. Unless you have already decided that you absolutely must get married on a particular date, indicate that "no date has been set for the wedding" in your announcement.

HELPFUL HINTS

If you do not have a way with words, you may be interested in the "standard" verbiage for engagement announcements recommended by etiquette experts. If you want to invoke tradition and have your announcement come from the bride's parents, here is an example to follow:

Mr. and Mrs. William Henderson of Minneapolis, Minnesota, announce the engagement of their daughter, Victoria Ann, to Mr. Richard James Thompson, son of Mr. and Mrs. Robert Thompson of Des Moines, Iowa. No date has been set for the wedding. *(If this announcement were being printed in a Minneapolis newspaper, it would not need to indicate that Mr. and Mrs. William Henderson live there.)*

There are multitudes of different family situations, which can lead to many variations on the standard wording of an announcement. Here is an example where the bride's father has been divorced and remarried:

Mr. and Mrs. William Henderson of Minneapolis announce the engagement of Mr. Henderson's daughter, Victoria Ann, to Mr. Richard James Thompson, son of Mr. and Mrs. Robert Thompson of Des Moines, Iowa. Miss Henderson is the daughter of Ms. Carol Stevenson of Chicago. No date has been set for the wedding.

If you want to break from tradition and make your own announcement, but you still want the wording to follow conventional guidelines, here is one suggestion:

Victoria Ann Henderson of St. Louis, Missouri, Loan Officer for Commerce Bank, is to be married to Richard James Thompson, medical student at Washington University. Ms. Henderson is the daughter of Mr. William Henderson of Minneapolis and Ms. Carol Stevenson of Chicago. Mr. Thompson is the son of Mr. and Mrs. Robert Thompson of Des Moines, Iowa. No date has been set for the wedding.

Many newspapers allow you to submit engagement announcements electronically through their Web sites, and you can e-mail a digital photo as well. While this option is certainly very convenient, it usually requires that you fill out a standard form on the Web site, so there is little flexibility in how your announcement can be worded. If you want some artistic freedom, the best approach is to print your desired text, double-spaced on a standard-sized sheet of paper, and send it to the newspaper via snail mail. At the top of the page, put the name and telephone number of a local family member who can be contacted to verify the information.

After receiving your announcement submittal, the newspaper may take a while to print it—sometimes as long as one month. The paper's staff is usually unable to tell you exactly when the announcement will run, so if you want to see it in print, you'll probably have to spend a few minutes each day skimming through the paper until it's finally published.

Your Wedding Web Site

MOST CONTEMPORARY COUPLES are techno-savvy. Some even found their soul mate in cyberspace. Others are just plain Internet addicts. For those people, the trendy choice for announcing their engagement is to build a new Web site together. Major "wed sites" like *The Knot* and the *Wedding Channel* offer easy-to-create personal pages that will help keep your guests informed on the details of your wedding. Once you've created a site, you can e-mail your friends and family a link to its URL. But in case you have any acquaintances who are computer illiterate, you should have the wedding Web site in addition to, not in lieu of, an announcement in the newspaper.

When Money Is No Object

Although somewhat outdated, the use of formal announcement cards is a beautiful and elegant way to spread the word of your engagement. Your local stationery store can help you select an appropriate announcement card and have it printed for you. One drawback of these cards, aside from the expense, is that they force you to decide on your guest list at this early stage of your engagement, because you don't want to send an announcement to anyone you're not also inviting to the wedding. But if you're not worried about the budget, you can afford to invite everyone you know to your wedding, anyway—right?

Decide Whether or Not to Hire a Professional Wedding Planner

YOU PRESUMABLY BOUGHT this book in order to plan your own wedding, so your first temptation might be to skip over this chapter entirely. Because I am a wedding planner myself, I willingly acknowledge that I may not be totally unbiased about this subject. But you don't have to take my word for it. According to *Modern Bride*, more than 50 percent of all couples today enlist the services of a wedding planner. Therefore, my first suggestion is that you carefully weigh the pros and cons before making a decision, especially if you want a perfect, you-don't-have-to-worry-about-a-thing day!

Why Hire a Wedding Planner?

WITH MYRIAD DETAILS to handle, wedding planning can be very time-consuming, and spare time is often in short supply for engaged couples who are busy establishing professional careers or attending school. You should consider hiring a wedding planner if

- you don't have at least 12 hours a week to devote to planning
- you're having a destination wedding
- your idea of being creative is copying a wedding that you saw in a bridal magazine
- you've previously planned parties where you spent all your time in your kitchen
- you have large stacks of papers on your desk, messy drawers, untidy closets, and leftover fast food in your car

Aside from saving you that precious element of time, there is another fundamental reason why wedding planners can be a tremendous benefit to you: They are experts at what they do. The more complex the details of your wedding, the greater the level of skills required to make your wedding day flawless. So, for the same reasons that people hire professional accountants to do their taxes, people also hire professional planners to plan their weddings. The only difference is that weddings are so much more fun than taxes!

What a Wedding Planner Can Do for You

SUCCESSFUL WEDDING EVENT management requires an understanding of multiple disciplines—including knowledge of food and beverages, flowers, audiovisuals, invitations, entertainment, photography, transportation, videography, and wedding cakes. A solid track record of planning hundreds of weddings, maintaining quality relationships with many vendors, and keeping current with trends separates the pros from the novices. This experience provides the foundational knowledge for the certified wedding planner to effectively assist you with

- the research, design, planning, and coordination of your wedding
- budgeting and financial management
- site selection
- recommending appropriate vendors that fit your taste and budget
- scheduling appointments with vendors
- providing cost analysis of vendor proposals
- understanding hospitality law and effectively negotiating contracts
- organizing the logistics of planning in a timely fashion
- understanding that timing is everything
- developing a detailed timeline that works for your ceremony, cocktails, and reception
- providing floor plans drawn to scale
- on-site management for your wedding day—overseeing all activities to ensure a flawless execution

Types of Wedding Planners

I HAVE BEEN using the term "wedding planner" thus far to describe my occupation, but we really don't have a consensus about what to call ourselves. Some of the other titles my esteemed colleagues use include architect, consultant, coordinator, designer, director, producer, and stylist. These differing designations are not just ingenious marketing pitches. They usually reflect a special expertise that the planner possesses. Below is a general explanation of the different kinds of planners, the services they offer, and what to look for in hiring them:

- Typically a **wedding planner** or **producer** embraces your style and vision and orchestrates a wedding from start to finish. The wedding producer puts together the perfect team of vendors for you and manages all details of the entire wedding. For these services, you can expect to pay anywhere from $15,000 to $50,000. A wedding planner/producer should have received professional training and a degree in event management, hospitality management, and/or hotel and restaurant management at a university, or a certificate in meeting planning, special event management, or wedding management from an accredited institution. The wedding planner must also be an expert in wedding etiquette, protocol, and ethnic customs, with the flexibility to understand each couple's uniqueness. Finally, the wedding planner should bring a sense of calm to the planning process and wedding day, be devoted to details, be a friendly multitasker, and be totally resourceful.

- A **wedding consultant** or **coordinator** is for the couple that wants to take an active role in planning their own wedding yet is looking for a "coach" to help them along the way. The consultant or coordinator furnishes vendor referrals and sets up appointments but usually is not present with you at the various meetings. The consultant or coordinator also typically schedules the wedding day activities and is on-site to manage the wedding. Customary fees for a wedding consultant range between $5,000 and $20,000.

- A **wedding designer, stylist,** or **architect** is focused on fostering your personal wedding vision. These professionals inspire you with clever design ideas to make your wedding look sensational. Typically, they charge between $15,000 and $50,000 for their services. The wedding designer/stylist/architect should have formal training in a relevant field, such as floral design, interior design, graphic design, or fashion design. Carefully examine the wedding designer's portfolios and other

materials that demonstrate how he or she has designed prior weddings. Design elements should be consistently woven through every
aspect of the wedding from the save-the-date card to wedding programs, tablescapes, favors, and decor. Confirm what elements of the
wedding were actually conceptualized by the wedding designer and
not a graphic artist or florist. Also, because the wedding designer
needs to understand your personal preferences in order to design a
wedding that reflects your tastes, he or she should be asking *you* lots
of questions to begin to understand what's important to you.

For Brides on a Budget

If you decide that you want to forge ahead and plan your wedding by yourself, you can always change your mind if you get into troubled waters and
hire a wedding planner later on. Many wedding coordinators even offer "day
of" service. But let me make this clear: There is no such thing as a "day of
planner." This term is widely misunderstood and misleading because no wedding planner of sound mind, experience, and education would simply show up
on the day of your wedding and expect everything to flow flawlessly. Instead,
at a minimum of thirty to forty-five days before your wedding, the planner
should

- review all of your wedding vendors' contracts
- inspect the ceremony and reception site
- develop a detailed timeline and floor plans to be sent to wedding vendors
  two weeks before the wedding
- prepare a separate, abbreviated wedding party schedule to be sent to parents and all attendants two weeks before the wedding
- reconfirm logistics with all vendors
- oversee the wedding rehearsal and be on-site on your wedding day

Providing this service usually requires thirty to forty-five hours, considerably more than simply showing up on the day of your wedding. Expect to pay
$3,000–$6,000 for anyone who's qualified.

Selecting a Wedding Planner

TO FIND A qualified wedding planner, check out nonprofit professional associations such as the International Special Events Society (www.ises.com) for a list of current members in good standing. You can also ask the catering departments of the top hotels in your area for a list of wedding planners they recommend.

After you have found some prospective planners, and gotten a warm fuzzy feeling during your initial phone conversation, here are some questions to ask during a face-to-face interview:

- Do you have a business license and business insurance?
- How long have you had your business?
- What did you do before having your business?
- What is your educational background?
- Do you have a college degree? If so, what was your major?
- Have you pursued continuing education in event management or design? If so, where?
- Do you belong to any professional associations? Have you served on the board of these associations?
- Are you a certified wedding consultant? If yes, what certification program?
- How have you established vendor relationships?
- Do you have letters of recommendations from other vendors?
- When reviewing their portfolio, ask who was responsible for the conceptualization of the design. Who implemented the design?
- What are the steps you take to plan a wedding?
- Can I see a staging guide? Timeline? Floor plans?
- How do you charge? What does your fee include? Do you receive fees from any of your vendors?
- How many weddings do you plan a year?
- Describe the weddings you typically plan.
- Can you work with our budget and create our vision?
- Will you be present at the wedding rehearsal and wedding day?
- Are there any additional staff and costs?

Finally, when interviewing wedding planners, there needs to be good chemistry between you. An effective wedding planner must clearly understand your needs and articulate your visions. Besides that, your wedding planner will be your best new friend up through your wedding day (and maybe long beyond your wedding as well). It is, therefore, imperative that you are comfortable working together—and, most important, having fun!

At the beginning of this chapter, I suggested that you consider the pros and cons of hiring a wedding planner. It's now time to talk about the con: cost. Although a planner can help you avoid costly mistakes, there is no guarantee that he or she will save you money overall (despite what some planners suggest in their marketing blurbs). In addition, wedding planners who are also experts in design charge more for this service. In any event, a planner always saves you time. You need to subjectively place a value on your time and decide if the value of your time, plus the added value of the planner's experience, is worth the price.

HELPFUL HINTS

Be wary of consultants who charge for their services as a percentage of the total wedding cost. With this kind of arrangement, there is no incentive for the planner to save you money, because a reduced wedding cost results in reduced fees for the planner. The fairest way for planners to charge for their services is either an hourly rate or flat fee.

Also be careful of wedding planners who represent only one particular vendor, such as a reception site, florist, or caterer. They may be taking kickbacks from these vendors.

Prepare a "Staging Guide"

YOU'RE ALMOST READY to begin the actual planning of your wedding. But before you get started, it's important to be organized at the outset of the planning process. Otherwise, you'll soon find yourself swimming in a sea of paperwork that only a government bureaucrat would enjoy. The easiest way to keep things under control is to have a system for filing and storing all the papers you will accumulate in the coming weeks. Whether it's correspondence with vendors, notes that you make during meetings, or fabulous photos of other weddings that you find in bridal magazines, you should keep all of these documents in a single but well-organized collection. That way, you have everything at your fingertips when you need it.

What's the easiest way to deal with wedding paperwork? Some brides-to-be use those pretty opaque pastel plastic accordion folders, which look great but are impractical. Because all the papers, pages, and documents regarding each of your wedding categories are all clumped together in a cramped folder, it makes finding specific documents difficult. Instead, I recommend an old-fashioned three-ring binder for holding and organizing your documents. You can easily carry it around with you (sans your high school boyfriend's initials scribbled all over the cover), then store it on a bookshelf when you're not planning your wedding. In the professional field of event management, this binder is known as a "staging guide." That's really the way you should view this process: You are the producer of one of the most important days in your life. Like a theatrical production, you will need your gathered information to guide you.

By the time your big day arrives, your staging guide should contain a complete written description of the requirements, specifications, and instructions for *all* aspects of the wedding. Copies of contracts, letters, room setup diagrams, timelines, and checklists should also be included. The name, address, phone, fax, e-mail address, and cell phone number of key people involved with your wedding should all be listed, along with their areas of responsibility and any other related information. Include everything you possibly can about the people who will be producing your special day.

I'm getting a bit ahead of myself. For now, you first need to purchase the following items (all of which can be readily obtained from the nearest office supply store):

- A three-ring binder. To allow enough room for all of your documents, I recommend a 3-inch binder.
- A three-hole paper punch.
- About 35 dividers, with tabs that you can label, so you can keep your papers properly organized inside your staging guide.
- A package of three-hole-punched clear plastic business card holders, so you can have an organized system of keeping track of all of the business cards you will undoubtedly acquire.
- A packet of clear plastic 8½ × 11 sheet protectors. (These are helpful for papers that don't hole-punch well.)

Once you've stocked up on your staging guide supplies, it's time to label your tabbed dividers. In general, the tab titles should correspond to the specific types of vendors and documents that will be used. Here is a list of tab labels that I recommend:

Budget, Actual Costs, Payment Schedules	Lighting
	Musicians—Ceremony
Cake	Musicians—Reception
Calligrapher	Officiant
Caterer-Beverages	Photographer
Caterer-Food	Reception Location
Ceremony Location	Registries/Gifts
Ceremony Program	Rehearsal Dinner
Design	Rental Items
Favors	Timelines
Florist	Transportation
Gown, Veil, and Shoes	Tuxedos and Groom's Attire
Guest List	Valet Parking
Hair and Makeup	Vendor List
Honeymoon	Videographer
Hotel for Guests	Wedding Party
Invitations	Wedding Planner

In the chapters that follow, I explain what each tab label means and what kind of documents you would typically place in each of these sections of your staging guide. Don't be daunted by the length of the list.

You will soon see how all of the listed categories fit together seamlessly to create your perfect day.

Depending on the particulars of your wedding, you may not need some of these tabs. For example, if you have your reception at a hotel, you won't have separate beverage and food caterers. The hotel's banquet staff handles both. In that case, you don't need a "Caterer/Beverages" divider in your staging guide, and you can simply remove it.

Note that the tab labels I recommend are listed in alphabetical order. I always find that this is the easiest way to place the dividers into the binder. If you use any other sequence, Murphy's Law will prevail, and you will have trouble locating the section you're searching for when you need it most.

Initially, as you begin the planning process, keep all of the papers you accumulate in your staging guide. As you start making decisions and selections, some of the documents you originally collected will no longer be relevant. For example, you may look at several wedding magazines and tear out lots of photos of designs you like, but later on come up with a specific design concept for your wedding. At that point, photos of designs that you will not be using with your chosen concept are no longer important, and you can toss them. Periodically weed out papers in this manner to keep your binder from bursting at the seams—and prevent you from looking like a bridal packrat.

That said, you should keep certain documents even if they are not obviously being used for your wedding. For instance, if you obtain proposals from two different cake bakers, keep both proposals even after you have decided which one to hire. If your chosen baker doesn't work out, you still have a Plan B baker, and it will be easier to line up your backup if you have kept their proposal.

Now that you have constructed your staging guide, you're ready to begin building a perfect wedding. Remember that your binder is your bridal bible, so it's important to keep it organized and up-to-date in the weeks ahead.

Design the Day of Your Dreams

WHAT IS THE best way to create a wedding that has your own signature design on it? In my experience, a wonderful walk down the aisle always begins with the couple's hopes and dreams for their wedding day. The key is to transform those dreams into design concepts.

You can design a wedding around almost anything that reflects your heritage, personalities, and lifestyle. While designing the wedding of your dreams may sound like a daunting chore, it's not nearly as complicated as brain surgery, and it's a lot less painful, too. Using some creative brainpower, you can develop personalized wedding designs on your own. If you want to stamp your unique style on your nuptials, you need to turn your dreams into a workable plan.

Below I offer my Six Steps to Dreamy Designs. As you work through the steps, put any notes you take or papers you collect into your new staging guide under the "Design" tab.

1. **Use visualization.** What do you want guests to say about your wedding? What feeling do you want them to experience? Try to visualize in detail the look and feel you want to convey at your wedding from beginning to end. Write down your ideas. This is pretty easy for brides who have been dreaming about their wedding day ever since they began playing with Barbie. But, ladies, please give Ken a chance to contribute his two cents' worth on this subject, too.

2. **Inspiration points.** One of the best ways to find new ideas for your wedding is to hit trendy neighborhoods where people are living tomorrow's styles. Take a voyage of discovery into the hottest restaurants for food and beverage ideas for your wedding. Explore chic shops for decor accessories, welcome gift ideas, and favors. For an infallible eye on what's hot, check out www.splendora.com and www .dailycandy.com.

   Other creative juices can flow from . . .

- your favorite bridal magazines, as well as fashion, interior design, and architecture magazines
- visiting art galleries
- attending live performances of the ballet, opera, or theater
- seeing the latest blockbuster movie or renting an oldie
- attending a home-decorating tour
- studying merchandising and window displays (my favorite stores are Williams-Sonoma, Pottery Barn, Cost Plus, and Pier 1 Imports)

Become aware, engage all of your senses, and take your digital camera for lots of photo ops.

3. **Write about yourself.** Weddings are intimate occasions. You are inviting family and friends to a unique personal moment in your life to have a wonderful time. Give as much of yourselves as possible. Show your true personalities. Begin by preparing a brief autobiography of yourself, listing such things as your ethnic background, where you grew up, where you have lived, where and how you met your fiancé, and your current occupation. Next, make a detailed list of your favorite things in life: colors, movies, hobbies, books, restaurants, sports, music, and so on. Also make a list of things you dislike. You and your fiancé should each prepare your own lists separately.

4. **Shape your vision.** With a glass of your favorite beverage in hand, calmly sit down together and identify common items on your lists that you both feel strongly about (positively and negatively). Also take a look at all those fabulous photos you took on your voyage or revisit the bridal magazine photos that you love. Dream big! Don't shoot down ideas before they are allowed to develop. Don't be bound by the time of day, season, or location for your design concept. And don't worry about the how-tos for implementing the design concept. You can always leave that to the pros. You can build a theme around anything, so begin to narrow down all the possibilities from ideas that you have generated until you can select one concept or theme for your wedding.

5. **Start and finish with a flourish and utilize the five senses.** Incorporate your theme into the first communication about your wedding, such as your save-the-date card or invitation. Continue to thread elements of your theme throughout the wedding—all the way to your last dance or final getaway. The most powerful way to experience your theme is to

see, hear, touch, smell, and taste it. When choosing a theme, make sure it can be communicated through not only the invitation but also your decor, music, food, beverage, tabletops, and vignettes.

6. **Keep it a secret.** I know you're excited about your wedding and all the wonderful creative ideas you are thinking. However, don't tell all and spoil the surprise. Just like a great movie, you would never want to tell your best friend the whole story and then suggest she see the film. Don't reveal all of your creative design ideas to your family and friends. Save many surprises for your guests to keep them on the edge of their seats throughout the planning process and at the wedding. On your stellar day, let them experience the Oscar-winning performance while you savor the standing ovation.

ONE COUPLE'S STORY

An escape from the ordinary all-red Asian wedding, I designed a delicious palette of colors honoring Jennifer's Chinese and Gary's Japanese heritages.

What began as a paper origami kimono fold was later transformed into a dazzling custom-designed letterpress ensemble, a silk kimono, and a dragon design. A captivating collection of pieces in gray slate and persimmon red—the save-the-date card, invitation, wedding program, escort cards, and menus—created a sense of anticipation and drama.

"One Night of Love" and "Un bel dì" from the opera *Madama Butterfly* floated from the instruments of the string quartet as the bridesmaids gracefully entered the ceremony area in their silk charmeuse cheung sams, traditional form-hugging Chinese dresses. Jennifer, escorted by her mother and father, glided magically down the breathtaking marble staircase in her Jin Wang obi-pleated gown, as Gary waited adoringly below. Jennifer and Gary joyfully exchanged their vows flanked by two Japanese springlike "trees," consisting of tall, growing yellow-green hala leaves, combined with a cluster of Leonidas roses, and a burst of saffron oncidium orchids.

The Old Federal Reserve banking hall, a stately, elegant palace fit for the Ming Dynasty, was selected for their reception. Upon arrival, guests were welcomed with butler-passed saketini's, tea-smoked duck in rice flour crepes, and lemongrass-braised pork siu mai. To achieve a dramatic effect, a striking combination of lighting, ice, and dupioni green and hot pink silk fabric dressed up an architectural display of "iced shots"—cold soup sips in hot colors, including chilled fresh pea puree with sweet shrimp and Thai basil; lobster, yellow tomato and ginger gazpacho; and chilled beet with horseradish and salmon caviar.

Creatively adorned to capture the essence of the Orient, three manzanita branch "trees" presented guests with their escort cards. Perched in a low mahogany box filled with fuchsia dahlias, red magic roses, and black stones, the escort card was hung in a whimsical and enchanting interactive way to assist guests to their seats. The tables were named after revered Asian virtues, such as benevolence, energy, tranquillity, and honor, showing respect for the bride's and groom's ancient heritages.

In the "banking temple," where dinner was served, the decor was a dazzling display of ethnic color and culture—bold and edgy, square and round, East meeting West, complete with alternating colors of Bali clay linens and topaz olive seat cushions at round tables, and Toshi celadon linens with pumpkin topaz cushions gracing square tables. The dinner menus were carefully positioned inside obi-folded napkins, which were placed atop bronze leaf and Italian hand-sponged copper chargers. Combining all the flowers of the day—yellow oncidiums, rust roses, fuchsia dahlias, red berries, green cymbidiums—the centerpieces were breathtaking!

A sumptuous dinner presentation began with "A Trio of Tastes," including eggplant mousse with miso and tomato served in Asian spoons; lobster, plum, and shiso spring roll with plum soy; and terrine of shiitake mushrooms with five-spice-scented foie gras. A striking black Savoy dinner plate artistically displayed the second course of tamari-glazed black cod fillet. And it was a standing ovation for the roasted shichimi-rubbed beef tenderloin, presented on the Martinique spoked black plate, for the entrée.

Each rite, each detail of the day, was one more silken tie that bound Jennifer and Gary together. Inspired by personality and ethnicity, the perfect ending to the evening included green tea ice cream served in mini–sesame waffle cones and yin-yang shortbread cookies. A chiffon wedding cake of mango mousse, adorned with cherry blossoms and surrounded by polished river rock, made a dramatic statement and a delicious dessert. And as a departing farewell, guests were sent off with Chinese to-go boxes filled with the couple's favorite candy, to provide sweet dreams for their happy ending.

Jennifer and Gary's wedding was a true Asian fusion—two lives, two worlds, two cultures that were joyfully joined on this auspicious day.

Make a Guest List and Check It Twice

NOTHING IS MORE important in your initial steps of wedding planning than getting a grip on your guest list. The number of guests you invite greatly affects the cost of your wedding, as well as many decisions you make. For instance, you can't select a site for your reception until you know how many people you expect to have there on your big day. Otherwise, you may be stuck in a place that's too large or, worse, too small for your group. So before you go running off in search of a hot spot for your celebration, you need to sit down and figure out who's invited to the party.

By now, Mom and Dad have probably announced their intention to invite some of their friends. You may become a bit perturbed as you visualize a gang of gate-crashing geezers busting in on your big bash. But please remember the Golden Rule of Life which, applied to weddings, goes something like this: "He (or she) who provides the gold gets to make the rules." So if you're expecting your parents to donate to your worthy cause, you should also expect to see their best buddies snapping photos as you're walking down the aisle (with their film cameras, of course). If it's any consolation, this is your one great opportunity to tell your parents what to do, as they need to compile their guest lists too.

Deciding Whom to Invite

THIS IS ONE of the most difficult questions facing couples and parents everywhere, and there are no simple answers.

First, take a few moments to review the wedding visions that you two came up with in the previous chapter. Perhaps the type of wedding you're envisioning makes sense only as a grand gala with many guests, or maybe it's best suited for an intimate gathering of fewer than 50.

Next, as you're flipping through your address book to identify potential invitees, I recommend that you place them into one of three simple categories: Yes, Maybe, and No. Every couple's situation is unique, so there are no clear-cut criteria for categorizing your guests that apply in all cases. In general, though, don't feel obligated to invite people you are not close to. A wedding is no place for mere acquaintances. Here are some guidelines to consider, even though they may not exactly fit your unique circumstances:

Yes
your parents
your dearest friends whom you see regularly
your grandparents
your brothers and sisters and their spouses
aunts, uncles, and cousins you see frequently

Maybe
new friends you have made within the past couple of years and see regularly
old friends you used to see frequently but now see only a few times a year
neighbors you grew up with and/or see regularly
coworkers you enjoy working with and see socially after work
relatives you see occasionally

No
all other coworkers
distant relatives (both in genealogy and location)
old friends you send holiday cards to each year but otherwise don't see

Again, these are just general suggestions. If you want a small wedding, you probably won't need to go beyond the Yes category to finalize your guest list. Or, if you win the lottery next week, all of your Maybes can immediately be converted to Yeses. Assuming you have a finite supply of money, take another look at the Maybes on your list after you have begun to establish a budget (which is covered in Week 9).

HELPFUL HINTS

Another often agonizing aspect of the guest selection process is deciding what to do with children. Basically, you have three choices: (1) You can welcome children with open arms; (2) you can decide to have an adults-only wedding; or (3) you can hire a child-care service to provide "wedding day care" for the kids. It is not an option to allow some fam-

ilies to bring their children while excluding kids from other families. This only engenders resentment among the families whose children were left off the guest list.

Beyond that, there are no right or wrong answers when it comes to children at weddings. This is a personal decision based on your personal preferences. One thing to keep in mind: While many children are very well behaved, if you decide to have a one-hour nuptial mass for your ceremony, it is not realistic to expect all of them to sit quietly for that length of time. You need to ask yourself if you're sufficiently smitten with the pitter-patter of little feet to tolerate some pitter-pattering by the pews while exchanging your vows.

How to Create the Guest List

IN MY EXPERIENCE, the best way to compile and keep track of your guest list is to use a spreadsheet program like Microsoft Excel. This approach gives you the most flexibility in the long run, because you will be using the guest list for many purposes during the planning process. If your parents are compiling their own guest lists, you can easily merge them together into one master spreadsheet.

Some of you techno-wizards may find this exercise as simple as opening your Palm Pilots, BlackBerries, or e-mail contacts, then downloading, converting, importing, or otherwise zapping your acquaintances into a spreadsheet. Those of you who break into a cold sweat at the sight of a computer may view this as a daunting task. (I believe that the bride and groom should both take an active role in planning their wedding. Since so many guys seem to have an extra "computer chromosome" in their genetic makeup, this may be the perfect time to get your groom in the game.) Regardless of your level of electronic expertise, the time you save by putting your guest list into a spreadsheet format ultimately far outweighs your investment of time to create this file.

How should you set up your spreadsheet? Input information for each guest in a row across the spreadsheet, and there should initially be several columns of data to be filled in. Specifically, I recommend that you create the following column headings for now (you will be adding more later):

1. Salutation (the formal title for the guest(s), Mr. and Mrs., Ms., Dr., etc.)
2. First Name (for a more formal wedding, use the husband's first name for addressing the married couple; also, use legal given names instead of nicknames—e.g., "Richard" instead of "Rick.")

3. Last Name (you want to have the last name as a separate column so that you can organize your list alphabetically)
4. Other Names (children, the other member of a couple living together, etc.)
5. Address (don't use abbreviations—write out "Street," "Avenue," and so forth in full)
6. City
7. State (again, no abbreviations)
8. Zip
9. Invited by (an optional column that allows you to keep track of whether a guest is being invited by you, your fiancé, your parents, or your fiancé's parents)
10. Inviting to Wedding? (Yes, Maybe, or No)
11. Number of Adults Inviting
12. Number of Children Inviting (assuming you decide to invite children)

Below is a hypothetical example of Amy & Rich's wedding guest list:

As you're filling in your spreadsheet, it is very important to have the correct spelling of all first and last names, titles, and addresses. So just like Santa Claus, make your list and check it twice. If you become aware of guests who move, get married themselves, or have other changes to their contact information, update your spreadsheet immediately.

Once all of the information has been input into the computer, including the guest names being supplied by your parents, sort the data by the "Inviting to Wedding?" column (using the "Data Sort" command). All of your Yeses will appear toward the bottom of the spreadsheet. (The computer sorts in alphabetical order, so in this case, the Yeses will appear last, after the Maybes and the Nos.) You can now easily calculate the total number of adults and children who are Yes and Maybe.

Salutation	First Name	Last Name	Other Names	Address	City	State	Zip	Invited by	Inviting?	# Adults	# Children
Mr.	Eric	Andersen		512 West Griggs Avenue	Pittsburgh	Pennsylvania	15202	Rich	Maybe	1	
Mr. and Mrs.	Elmer	Backmeister		251 74th Street	Huntington Beach	California	92646	Rich's Dad	Maybe	2	
Ms.	Leah	Baker	Mr. Joseph Swan	39 Clearview Drive	Sevickley	Pennsylvania	15143	Amy	Maybe	2	
Mr. and Mrs.	Ronald	Boucher		156 Edgemere Avenue	Dover	Massachusetts	02030	Rich	Maybe	2	
Mr.	Tommy	Brennan		49 Elm Street	Alameda	California	94501	Amy	Maybe	1	
Mr. and Mrs.	Scott	Cash		15 Colonial Road	Columbus	Ohio	43214	Rich's Mom	Maybe	2	
Mr. and Mrs.	Paul	Cottrell		6 Conick Lane	Medford	New Jersey	08055	Amy	Maybe	2	
Ms.	Liza	Crawford		705 Killington Court	Johnstown	Pennsylvania	15904	Amy	Maybe	1	
Mr. and Mrs.	Douglas	D'Antonio	Christina	21 LeGrange Place	Coral Springs	Florida	33071	Amy's Parents	Maybe	2	1
Miss	Meredith	DePinto		514 Hayfield Court	Mystic	Connecticut	06355	Rich's Mom	Maybe	1	
Ms.	Patsy	Dunn	Mr. Carl Brown	649 North 3rd Avenue	Brighton	Massachusetts	02135	Amy	Maybe	2	
Mr. and Mrs.	Robert	Elvenz	James and Stacey	344 Grable Road	Ridgefield	Connecticut	06877	Amy's Parents	Maybe	2	2
Mr. and Mrs.	Raymond	Eickhag		3300 Neuhaming Boulevard	Demarest	New Jersey	07627	Amy's Parents	Maybe	2	
Mr. and Mrs.	Alfred	Greco		501 Delancey Street	Payson	Arizona	95541	Rich's Dad	Maybe	2	
Mr. and Mrs.	Daniel	Gregg		200 West 60th Street	Indianapolis	Indiana	46208	Rich's Mom	Maybe	2	
Mr. and Mrs.	Harry	Harris		286 Moulton Street	Gilbertsville	Kentucky	42022	Rich's Mom	Maybe	2	
Mr. and Mrs.	Jeffrey	Hartigan		200 West 60th Street	Vacaville	California	95688	Rich's Dad	Maybe	2	
Mr. and Mrs.	Stan	Hergert	Josephine	546 East Boston Post Road	Florham Park	New Jersey	07932	Rich's Mom	Maybe	2	1
Mr.	Sylvester	Hoang	Ms. Allison Glover	675 Franklin Road, #127	Reno	Nevada	89509	Rich	Maybe	2	
Miss	Karen	Hottenstein		8010 Evergreen Lane	West Palm Beach	Florida	33412	Amy's Parents	Maybe	1	
Mr. and Mrs.	Raymond	Ross		480 Country Road 480	North Oaks	Minnesota	55127	Rich's Dad	Yes	2	
Mr.	Cecilia	Pupsoti		10177 La Vonne	Woodburn	Oregon	97071	Amy	Yes	1	
Mr.	John	Schifano		3796 E. Guthrie Mt. Road	Vancouver	Washington	98663	Rich	Yes	1	
Mr.	Louis	Schiller		7933 S.E. 140th Place	Portland	Oregon	97266	Rich	Yes	1	
Mr.	Helen	Skinner		449 Madison Street	Gladstone	Oregon	97027	Amy	Yes	1	
Mr. and Mrs.	Allen	Spencer		2020 Market Street	Batavia	Illinois	60510	Rich's Mom	Yes	2	
Mr. and Mrs.	Thomas	Straka		Post Office Box 268	Portland	Oregon	97201	Rich's Dad	Yes	2	
Mr. and Mrs.	David	Tomasik		426 Dudley Avenue	Estacada	Oregon	97023	Amy's Parents	Yes	2	
Mr. and Mrs.	Allison	Tonio		43 Sleepy Hollow Drive	Narberth	Pennsylvania	19072	Amy	Yes	2	
Dr. and Mrs.	Gary	Vezzi		22795 S.V. Utelq Road	Newton Square	Pennsylvania	19073	Rich's Mom	Yes	2	
Miss	Alice	Westwood		1230 Greenbriar Place	West Linn	Oregon	97068	Amy	Yes	1	
Mr.	Elizabeth	Williams		4029 S.V. 22nd Drive	Newberg	Oregon	97132	Amy	Yes	1	
Mr. and Mrs.	Peter	Wittington		5717 S.E. Monterey Avenue	Manitou Springs	Colorado	80829	Amy's Parents	Yes	2	
								GRAND TOTAL		245	30
								Number of Yes's		167	14
								Number of Maybe's		77	7

Congratulations! You've made it through a very difficult but very important exercise. Print out your sorted guest list, mark today's date, and file it under the "Guest List" tab in your staging guide. (At least that part was easy!)

Last, I want to comment on a guest list concept that is frequently brought up in bridal magazines and books. Many etiquette experts embrace the employment of A and B (and sometimes even C) lists, which they have you manipulate almost until the moment you walk down the aisle. Basically, the concept is first to invite guests on your A list, then extend an invitation to a B-rated guest whenever someone from the A list sends regrets.

I don't agree with this approach, because I believe a B-list guest who gets invited shortly before the wedding will not be naive enough to feel honored by such an untimely invitation. Furthermore, this approach is based on a fundamentally flawed premise that you should have a fixed number of guests at your wedding. If your final actual guest count is somewhat less than your hoped-for amount because a few people can't make it, fine! You'll be able to spend a bit more time with each of the guests who do show up, and your bar bill will probably be lower too. Is that so terrible?

By the time you finish the chapter on budgeting, you will reassign all of the Maybes on your current guest list to either the Yes or No category. At that point, the number of guests to invite to your wedding is determined, leaving you to focus on other important matters.

Narrow Down the Big Day to a Season, but Not a Date

NOW THAT YOU have a pulse on your head count, the next questions are where and when to wed. Today there are more places and times to tie the knot than ever before. The decision about the location for your wedding is crucial, because this becomes the canvas on which you apply your design ideas and visions.

Begin by thinking globally and clear your mind of any preconceived ideas about where you should have your wedding. The typical starting point is to consider your hometowns. However, since many couples no longer reside where they grew up, perhaps a favorite destination can be an alternative. A true destination wedding is one where the complete wedding party and all the guests travel (sometimes thousands of miles) to a resort, hotel, bed-and-breakfast, or private estate to take part in several days of unforgettable celebrations including the wedding itself.

Choosing the right topography for your wedding is more of a science than an art. It requires careful analysis, playing the part of Sherlock Holmes, to choose a site that best suits your needs. Before venturing too far, consider the elementary needs of your guests. After all, it won't be much of a party if no one shows up! Ask yourself these questions:

- Where do most family and friends live?
- How far do you think they are willing to travel?
- How much can they afford to spend to come to your wedding?
- Would your family and friends prefer a city experience?
- Are sightseeing and nightlife important to them?
- Would your family and friends prefer a resort and a more recreational experience?

Now start to visualize the atmosphere for your wedding. Is it a captivating marble stone Beaux Arts structure, or a breathtaking 360-degree panoramic view of cresting waves? Or does a mansion graced by Persian carpets, crystal chandeliers, silk wall coverings, and eighteenth-century furniture speak to you? Look at the lists below and try to imagine yourself in each of these kinds of locations. Both you and your fiancé should go through the exercise separately. Circle any of the venue types that interest you.

Animalistic
Animal farm, park, ranch,
　or sanctuary
Aviary
Stable
Zoo

Childlike
Amusement park
Carousel
Children's museum
Doll museum
Fairgrounds

Food Thoughts
Apple orchard
Bakery
Banquet hall
Brewery
Cooking school
Galley
Restaurant
Winery

Lights, Camera, Action
Circus
Comedy club
Drive-in movie theater
Former movie location
Historical movie theater
Motion picture production
　studio
Professional theater—lobby or
　onstage

Lodging/Bed-and-Breakfast/Hotel
Bed-and-Breakfast
Country inn
Hotel

Museums
Aquarium
Art museum
Automobile museum
Aviation museum
Historical society
　museum
Natural history
　museum
Planetarium
Science museum
Sports museum

Musical
Bandshell in a park
Opera house
Recording studio
Symphony hall

Nature
Arboretum
Beach
Cavern
Christmas tree farm
Garden (botanical, rose)
Greenhouse
Meadow/pasture
Park (city, state, or national)

Regal
Castle
Grand ballroom
Lobby in a beautiful building
Mansion

Rustic
Barn
Dude ranch
Historical landmark
Summer camp

Sporting
Baseball field
Basketball court
Country club
Football field

Ice-skating rink
Racetrack
Roller-skating rink
Ski resort
Tennis court/club
Yacht club

Transportation
Aircraft carrier
Aircraft hangar
Cruise ship
Double-decker bus
Hot-air balloon
Paddle wheel
    steamboat
Railroad train
Sailboat

What choices did you both circle? What choices do you both feel the strongest pull toward? Now start to consider specific geographic areas. Ask yourself if your favorite types of venues exist

- in or near where you live now?
- in the town where you grew up?
- in your fiancé's hometown?
- in your favorite vacation spot?

Regardless of the region you have in mind, there is another important question you need to consider: Is there enough lodging in this area to accommodate your out-of-town guests? Do some quick research to make sure this won't be a problem.

Think through all these questions carefully, and you should start to come up with some solid ideas for geographic areas and types of venues.

'Tis the Season

DO YOU IMAGINE a spring celebration with an unbelievable bouquet of colors bursting forth, or do you envision a patchwork of autumn reds, golds, and greens? No one says you have to be a June bride. In fact, according to the Condé Nast Bridal Study Group, the most popular marrying months are May through October. Weddings can be celebrated year-round, and having one in a less popular month or season might be less of a load on your purse strings.

Here's a listing of the percentage of weddings by the month throughout the year:

January	4%
February	7%
March	8%
April	8%
May	10%
June	10%
July	11%
August	11%
September	10%
October	10%
November	6%
December	7%

Give yourself extra time to plan ahead if you are thinking about holiday weekends for your wedded bliss. You'll be in competition with a jillion other wedding couples for these desirable dates: Memorial Day, Fourth of July, and Labor Day.

Other dates to avoid are religious or national holidays: Martin Luther King weekend, Presidents' Day weekend, Palm Sunday, Passover, Lent, Easter weekend, Rosh Hashanah, Yom Kippur, Thanksgiving, Christmas Eve, and Christmas Day.

If you long for an outdoor wedding, investigate when the weather is most favorable in your preferred geographic area(s). Go to www.weatherplanner.com for assistance. If your wedding visions involve colors associated with a particular season, this may also influence your choice of a time.

Beware of busy seasons when costs may escalate. A florist may raise the bar on pricing at Valentine's Day, Mother's Day, and Christmas. At resorts during high season, the weekends may be untouchable, unless you are willing to pay top dollar. If you're pondering the idea of a destination wedding and your guests are ready, willing, and able to travel, does it matter to them whether it's a Wednesday night wedding instead of a Saturday? If you are willing to consider the off-season, you can find some favorable savings from being in a buyer's market. You are the buyer, after all.

Once you have weighed all these factors, you should be able to zero in on a geographic area, type of venue, and season. Now go back to your guest list spreadsheet and add two more columns:

13. Number of Adults Likely to Attend
14. Number of Children Likely to Attend

In these last two columns, record your own assessment of whether you think a particular guest will come to your wedding if invited. Consider the time of year you have chosen and the distance he or she would have to travel to come to your wedding, as well as his or her current state of health. If you believe the guest will attend, enter the same number of adults and children in these columns as you did in the previous "Number Inviting" columns. If you think the guest is unlikely to show up, enter a zero in each of these columns. (A quick tech tip: The "Copy" and "Paste" commands in Excel make adding the two new columns a breeze. Just copy and paste the numbers and totals from the two previous "Number Inviting" columns into your new "Likely to Attend" columns. Then all you need to do is input zeros for those guests who are unlikely to attend.) If some of the names on your spreadsheet came from your parents, ask them to perform a similar evaluation for those names.

After you have compiled this data, calculate the total number of guests who are "Likely to Attend" for both your Yeses and Maybes. To give you a reality check, typically about 10 to 20 percent of invited guests are unable to attend a wedding. If your estimate of "Likely to Attend" falls outside of this range, consider whether the circumstances of your celebration are unusual enough to justify your calculations. Once you're satisfied that your estimate is reasonable, reprint your spreadsheet and put it in your staging guide. (You can toss the previous printout.)

Create a Budget

FOR SOME TIME now, your wedding dreams have been sailing along on a collision course with the reality of how much they will actually cost to implement. You're now going to navigate your dreamboat into the Bay of Reality, allow that collision to happen, and find out whether you have a massive shipwreck on your hands, or just an inconsequential bump as you dock at the pier.

The Price of Your Dreams

MOST NEWLY ENGAGED couples have no idea how much a wedding costs. So let's first come up with a ballpark figure for your matrimonial visions.

According to 2004 data from the Condé Nast Bridal Group, the average wedding cost in the United States is $22,300. For you statistical aficionados, there is a very large standard deviation associated with that average. It includes everything from elopements, where the marriage license and justice of the peace are the only expenditures, to lavish "celebrity weddings," whose budgets can exceed the gross national product of half the world's countries.

Relying on national averages to set your own wedding budget has another shortcoming. There are tremendous differences in costs across the country. Where I live, in San Francisco, the cost of living is more than twice the national norm. In many other major cities, prices are also significantly higher than "average." So the price you end up paying depends largely on whether you want to wed in Midtown Manhattan or Manhattan, Kansas.

Typically, the cost of a nice but not over-the-top wedding in a major metropolitan area like New York, Los Angeles, Chicago, or San Francisco is around $500 per person. So if you have 100 guests at your wedding, you're looking at a minimum of $50,000.

To begin to figure out how much your wedding might cost, it's time for some number crunching. Pull out your guest list and look at the column labeled "Number of Adults Likely to Attend." For the time being, add together the Yeses and Maybes from this column to get a total possible guest count. Then multiply this total number of guests by the $500 per person figure I mentioned above. This will give you a total amount measured in "San Francisco dollars," so you need to adjust this number to reflect the cost of living where you're getting married. On Microsoft's MSN Web site, there is an excellent page to help you make this currency conversion. It's located at http://houseandhome.msn.com/pickaplace/comparecities.aspx.

Let's do some math. From the example in the last chapter, Amy and Rich have estimated the following number of adults as likely to attend their wedding:

94 Yeses + 61 Maybes = 155 potential total adults

They plan to have an elegant dinner reception at a luxurious historical mansion in Charleston, South Carolina. My estimate for their wedding budget is

155 guests × $500 per guest = $77,500

This is the minimum amount I would budget for the wedding if it were held in San Francisco. Using the MSN Web site to adjust these figures for the cost of living in Charleston, the estimate becomes $38,953, as shown in the illustration below.

Since this is just a rough estimate, and there are always unanticipated expenses, I would round up this calculation to $40,000.

You now have a first pass at your budget estimate. I hope it's not a number that makes you pass out.

The Cash in Your Stash

IT'S TIME TO determine whether you can afford your dream wedding. You need to realize up front that you're not required to fund your festivities on your own. Nor should you conclude that it's okay to selectively invoke tradition by sticking your parents with the entire bill. Instead, paying for a wedding in today's world often requires teamwork. In a survey conducted in 2002, the Condé Nast Bridal Group found the following answer to the question "Who pays for the wedding?"

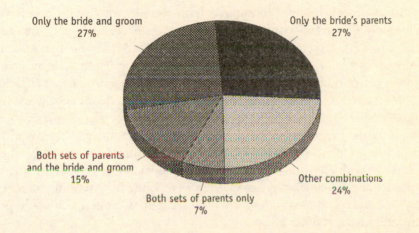

Only the bride and groom
27%

Only the bride's parents
27%

Both sets of parents
and the bride and groom
15%

Both sets of parents only
7%

Other combinations
24%

So in almost half of the weddings across the United States, more than one party contributes.

With this in mind, first determine what amount of personal savings you can afford to spend on your wedding. If you're like most couples, it may not cover the initial budget estimate you have just calculated. Then it's time to go to your parents and your fiancé's parents with your hat in hand to find out how much they are willing or able to contribute to the cause. Open a wedding checking account exclusively for paying the nuptial bills, then pool your resources. If you've scraped together enough dough to cover your rough budget, congratulations! Change all the Maybes on your guest list spreadsheet to Yeses and skip over the next section.

Cutting Back to Reach Reality

IF THE COMBINED contributions of yourselves and your parents still don't get you to your dream budget, it's time to start making painful decisions about how to scale back your celebration.

In my opinion, the first thing to cut are the Maybes on your guest list. Go back and recalculate your budget using only the Yeses who are likely to attend. If this reduced number of guests results in a budget you can live with, you can move on to the next section ("Breaking It Down and Keeping It Under Control").

Some of you may be enraptured with the idea of having a baseball stadium–sized crowd cheering you on as you exchange your vows, so you're balking at the notion of cutting your roster. But keep in mind that in order to meet your budget, you may need to keep that baseball theme going at your reception by serving a gourmet meal of hot dogs and Cracker Jacks.

What should you do if you've cut all the Maybes from your guest list and you still don't have enough greenbacks? Consider having your wedding at an off-peak time. Generally speaking, the most expensive time for a reception is on a Saturday evening in the summer, as this is when wedding venues and vendors are in greatest demand. If you are willing to consider less popular alternatives, such as having your wedding on a Friday or Sunday, or having a luncheon instead of a dinner, you could potentially save some big bucks.

If all else fails, you may have to consider a lower-priced venue than you had originally envisioned. Think of wedding providers similar to the experience of staying in a hotel. Are you looking for a five-star Ritz-Carlton or a Four Seasons experience? Would you be happy at a Sheraton Hotel, or would a Holiday Inn Express do? There are differing levels of wedding service providers at different prices. Whatever you do, remember that a wedding does not have to be expensive to be fabulous. Creating a wedding with innovative vision—such as a warehouse loft with a jazz trio, chic cocktails and small plates—can be more memorable than the traditional five-course sit-down dinner—and less expensive, too.

Breaking It Down and Keeping It Under Control

MANY BRIDAL MAGAZINES and Web sites offer guidelines for budgeting by providing suggested percentage breakdowns for various vendor categories. These breakdowns are not very helpful until you have actually established an overall budget, but you can put them to use now if you wish. Here is one way to divvy up your funds (and I included approximate dollar amounts based on Amy & Rich's $40,000 wedding):

Ceremony	2%	$800
Reception Site and Catering	46%	$18,400
Cake	2%	$800
Flowers	8%	$3,200
Gifts and Favors	2%	$800
Gown and Attire	7%	$2,800
Invitations and Printed Materials	3%	$1,200
Musicians	7%	$2,800
Photography	7%	$2,800
Transportation	2%	$800
Videography	4%	$1,600
Miscellaneous/Reserve	10%	$4,000

Keep in mind that these percentages are just guidelines, so you don't need to feel bound by them. In fact, your personal tastes should influence how much you allocate to each category. For instance, if you love music and want to hire the very best band around, you can allocate more money to your musicians and correspondingly less to the other vendors.

Regardless of how you disperse your funds, our old friend the spreadsheet is the best way to track your expenses. I recommend that you list all of the vendor categories in the first column of a spreadsheet, then add two columns labeled "Original Budget" and "Current Estimate." The "Original Budget" column contains the pie chart/percentage allocations of your overall budget that you have just calculated. (In fact, let Excel do the calculating.)

For now, copy the values from the "Original Budget" column into the "Current Estimate" column, so that they are equivalent. Later on, when you start contacting potential vendors and receive cost proposals from them, you can put the proposed prices in the "Current Estimate" column. Once you have signed a contract with a vendor, make sure you record the actual contracted price in the "Current Estimate" column. If you find yourself going over budget for a particular vendor category, you may need to cut back or eliminate other items in order to keep your bottom-line amount the same.

You also want to expand the level of detail in your budget spreadsheet as you move through the planning process, by breaking down the broad categories into specific expenditures. Below is a detailed list of items that you could conceivably include in a final itemized budget.

AMY & RICH'S WEDDING BUDGET		
	Original Budget	Current Estimate
Cake	$800	
Cookies/Desserts/After Dinner or Favors		
Edible Place Cards/Escorts' Cards		
Groom's Cake		
Preceremony Sweets		
Wedding Cake		
Ceremony	$800	
Candles/Candelabras		
Ceremony Site Fee		
Marriage License		
Officiant		
Flowers	$3,200	
Ceremony Site		
Aisle Decor		
Aisle Runner/Carpet		
Altar Arrangements		
Chuppah/Mandap/Canopy		
Last-Row Decor		
Pew/Chair Treatments		
Personal Flowers		
Bridal Bouquet		
Bridesmaids' Bouquets		
Fathers'/Grandfathers'/Relatives' Boutonnieres		
Flower Girls		
Groom's Boutonniere		
Groomsmen's Boutonnieres		
Mothers'/Grandmothers'/Relatives' Flowers		
Readers		

		Ring Bearers		
		Ushers' Boutonnieres		
	Reception Flowers			
		Accessory Pieces/Entrance/Ledges/ Mantels/Tables/Stairs		
		After-Dining Lounge Areas/Tables		
		Bar Arrangements		
		Cake Tables		
		Chair Treatments		
		Cocktail Tables		
		Dessert Stations		
		Escort Card Table		
		Guest Book Table		
		Head Table Centerpieces		
		Hors d'Oeuvres Stations		
		Table Centerpieces		
Gifts and Favors			$800	
	Gifts			
		Bride and Groom Exchange		
		Bride's Attendants		
		Groomsmen and Ushers		
		Parents		
		Pre- or Postwedding Parties' Hosts		
		Readers		
		Welcome Baskets		
	Guest Favors			
	Wedding Rings			
		Bride		
		Groom		

Gown and Attire		$2,800	
	Apparel/Bride		
	Alterations		
	Gown		
	Hair/Makeup		
	Hat/Headpiece/Veil		
	Gloves		
	Going-Away Outfit		
	Jewelry		
	Lingerie		
	Manicure/Pedicure		
	Shoes		
	Apparel/Groom		
	Cuff Links/Studs/Accessories		
	Cummerbund		
	Formalwear/Tuxedo/Suit		
	Hair		
	Manicure/Pedicure		
	Shoes		
	Tie		
Invitations and Printed Materials		$1,200	
	At-Home Card		
	Calligrapher		
	Ceremony Card		
	Direction/Transportation Card		
	Engagement Announcement		
	Envelopes		
	Escort Card		
	Graphic Designer		
	Guest Book and Pens		

Invitations			
Menu			
Place Card			
Postage			
Postmarriage			
Premarriage			
Printer			
Reception Card			
Response Card and Envelope			
Save-the-Date Card and Accommodation Cards			
Thank-You Cards			
Wedding Programs			
Miscellaneous/Reserve		**$4,000**	
Cake Knife/Server/Toasting Flutes			
Hotel Accommodations			
	Attendants		
	Bride and Groom		
	Guests		
	Parents		
Personal Improvement			
	Plastic Surgery		
	Teeth Whitening		
Pre- and Postwedding Events			
	Clothing		
	Engagement Party		
	Food/Beverage		
	Honeymoon		
	Hotel/Cruise		
	Luggage		

		Passport		
		Rehearsal Dinner		
		Transportation/Flights/Car Rentals		
	Tips			
	Wedding Insurance			
	Wedding Planner			
		Assistant(s)		
		Consulting		
		Design		
		Overnight Accommodations		
		Travel		
Musicians			$2,800	
	Ceremony Music			
	Cocktail Music			
	Dance Lessons			
	Entertainment			
	Reception Music			
Photography			$2,800	
	Albums			
	CDs			
	Engagement Session			
	Labor			
	Negatives			
	Overnight Accommodations			
	Processing			
	Proofs			
	Reprints			
	Travel			

Reception Site and Catering			$18,400	
	Beverages			
		Beverage Company		
		Catering Company Beverages		
		Self-Purchased Beverages		
	Catering			
	Child-Care Providers			
		Cake-Cutting Fee		
		Food/Labor/Gratuity/Service Charge/Tax		
	Facility Rental			
	Rental Company			
		Accessories		
		Air-Conditioning/Heat		
		Audio and Video Equipment/ Ceremony and Reception Microphones/ LCD Projector and Screen		
		Barware		
		Candelabras		
		Chairs		
		Chargers		
		China		
		Chocolate Fountains		
		Coat Racks and Hangers		
		Dance Floor		
		Flatware		
		Hedging/Trees		
		Lighting		
		Linens		
		Lounge Furniture		
		Piano Rental		

		Portable Restroom		
		Security		
		Sound System		
		Stage		
		Stemware		
		Table Lamps		
		Table Numbers		
		Tables		
		Tenting		
Transportation			$800	
	Pre- and Postwedding Airport Transportation			
	Rehearsal and Rehearsal Dinner			
		Guests		
		Parents		
		Wedding Party		
	Wedding Day			
		Bride and Groom		
		Guests		
		Parents		
		Wedding Party		
Videography			$1,600	
	Commemorative Video Presentation			
	DVDs			
	Labor			
	Rehearsal/Rehearsal Dinner			
	Travel and Overnight Accommodation			
TOTAL Budget			$40,000	

Decide on a House of Worship (or Not)

BEFORE YOU CAN find the ideal space for your wedding, you must decide whether you want to have a religious or civil ceremony. Revisit your wedding dreams and focus on where you envision the "I dos" taking place. Do you see yourself in your hometown church? A grand cathedral? An adorable little chapel in the countryside? Or an enchanting outdoor location? Whatever your vision, it should be uppermost in your mind as you search for your perfect place.

Rules and Regulations

CIVIL CEREMONIES IN the United States are governed by legal requirements determined by each state. In most states, judges, mayors, and county clerks are authorized to perform marriages. Other officiants, such as nondenominational ministers or laypeople, are usually required to obtain a license from the state in order to conduct a civil ceremony. There are no particular restrictions on where civil ceremonies can take place.

Religious ceremonies are performed according to the covenants of the specific faith or denomination. If your religious affiliation is Roman Catholic, Eastern Orthodox, or Episcopal, marriage is considered a sacrament. Therefore, in order for your wedding to be considered "legitimate" in your faith, it must take place in a church of your religion. On the other hand, most Protestant denominations do not consider matrimony as a sacrament, and although they welcome religious weddings within their hallowed halls, they also permit ceremonies to be performed elsewhere. Similarly, Jewish weddings need not occur at a synagogue (but they should never take place on the Sabbath—from sundown Friday to sundown Saturday).

Sanctified Sites

MANY COUPLES, ESPECIALLY those with strong religious convictions, have always pictured their ceremony in a place of worship. Other nearlyweds may not be regular churchgoers but find spiritual inspiration for their marriage in an enchanting historical chapel or cathedral.

If you and your fiancé are of the same faith, the only choice you need to make is the specific location for your denomination. The old tradition was for the bride to be married in her hometown church. If that doesn't fit your vision, pick a place that does. If you already have a particular geographic area in mind for your reception, you should obviously search for a church of your faith in that same area.

If you and your partner are not of the same religion, but you want to tie the knot in a place of worship, you have three basic options:

1. **Choose one faith.** This works best if one of you feels very strongly about getting married within your religious affiliation and the other does not have a strong preference.
2. **Choose a "neutral" denomination.** For example, the Unitarian-Universalist church embraces elements of both Christianity and Judaism, and therefore is attractive to interfaith couples. Alternatively, many communities have nondenominational churches that welcome people of all religious beliefs.
3. **Pick one religion to host the ceremony, but balance both faiths by having two clergy members officiate.** It can often be challenging, however, to find officiants who are willing to be coparticipants in this manner.

Other Options

TODAY, MANY BRIDES and grooms are exchanging vows in other locations besides a house of worship. Couples who choose this course are not necessarily opting for a civil ceremony. Rather, they are selecting a venue that best fits their personal preferences. They can then determine how much religion they want to bring into their service.

If you are not stuck on having a church ceremony, there are often significant advantages to exchanging vows at the same location as your reception. First, your guests do not need to travel to two separate locations and they need to find only one place to park. Second, your reception can begin immediately after the ceremony, so the excitement from your nuptials can carry through the rest of the celebration without interruption. Third, many sites charge a flat fee for the entire day, so there is little or no additional cost for having a ceremony there.

However, it is not always desirable to have your ceremony and reception at the same site. In order for a site to be serviceable for both segments of your celebration, it is essential that it have separate spaces for both. You don't want your guests to be able to see the reception area from where your ceremony is taking place. It spoils the element of surprise that makes a wedding so engaging. Also, if a dual-purpose site offers anything less than 6 hours for your wedding day, seriously consider taking your ceremony to another location. You don't want your guests to feel as if they're being rushed through the festivities.

Finally, if you do choose a church or any other kind of separate location for your ceremony, you don't want the energy of your fabulous day drained by a grueling pilgrimage to your reception location. For that reason, it is best to have your ceremony and reception sites within a 20-minute drive of each other.

Tips for Ceremony Site Searching

THE YELLOW PAGES (either the hard copy or online version) can greatly aid your search for an appropriate house of worship; or check out www.worshiphere.org. You should also be able to get some good leads from the Chamber of Commerce and the Convention and Visitors Bureau in your chosen geographic area.

Once you have a list of prospective ceremony sites, first drive by to see if they are architecturally appealing to you. Stop and look inside if the doors are open. Keep in mind that the more charming the church, the more holy hurdles you may encounter on a trip to their altar. Often, the biggest obstacle is finding availability at a time that works for you, because you're not the only one wanting to get married there. Also, churches typically give priority to their own parishioners, and some flat-out refuse to allow outsiders into their inner sanctum.

After you've done the drive-bys, narrow down your list to your top three choices. Phone them in your order of preference to find out if they are available for weddings. An extra dose of diplomacy is required here because selecting a church is not like shopping for a new pair of shoes. Respectfully inquire about their policies, procedures, and restrictions by asking the following questions:

- Do I have to be a member of your congregation in order to have my wedding at your church?
- How many people does your church hold? (Or if you're considering a site without pews, ask about the square footage of the ceremony area—you need at least 10 square feet per guest.)
- What dates do you have available for a wedding ceremony? (Give them a time frame that you're considering.)
- What times during the day do you allow weddings to take place?
- Do you require that we use a clergy member from your church?
- What requirements do you have regarding marriage preparation programs and/or counseling sessions?
- What are your policies and restrictions regarding photography and videography?
- What kinds of floral arrangements and decor are permitted? Are candles permitted?
- What are your policies and restrictions regarding music and musicians?
- What policies do you have regarding attire for the wedding party and guests?
- Do you have a parking lot for guests? If so, how many cars does it hold? If not, where do your parishioners usually park?
- What is your fee for the officiant and use of the church?

The responses you receive, as well as the responder's level of warmth and friendliness, may cause you either to change the order of your choices or reduce the number on your list.

Now call your first choice again to schedule an appointment. During your meeting, here are a few more questions to ask:

- How many other weddings are scheduled for the same day(s) that we are interested in? What time(s) are they scheduled for?
- How much time is allowed for our florist to set up?
- How much time are we allowed for photos inside the church before or after the ceremony?
- What choices do we have regarding our processional?
- What choices do we have regarding readings?
- Can we face our guests during the ceremony?
- Can we write and recite our own vows?
- Is amplified music permitted? If so, does the church have a built-in sound system?
- At the end of the ceremony, are there any restrictions on tossing or releasing items outside the church?

If the appointment with your preferred church leaves you with reservations about getting married there, schedule a meeting with your second choice. Otherwise, stick with your first pick. If your chosen site has a number of possible wedding dates that appeal to you, ask them to place a "hold" on your first choice and make a note of the other dates available. You don't want to definitively decide on your date now (unless there's only one choice), because you haven't looked at reception sites yet.

Select a Reception Site

THERE IS NOTHING that gets a bride more excited—or anxious—than embarking on a search for a suitable reception site. While it may be the most important decision you'll have to make, you don't need to go chasing after a venue like a wild goose. Instead, I recommend a levelheaded, two-step approach to finding the perfect place.

Step 1. Screen Your Sites

FIRST, BEFORE RUNNING off to look at locations, do some focused research from inside the comfort of your own computer. The Internet provides the best mechanism for screening sites that might meet your needs and wants. You can start with major wed sites, such as The Knot, Modern Bride, and the Wedding Channel. There are also many helpful regional wedding Web portals and directories. From there, you can jump to the Web sites of individual properties.

Most venues that regularly host weddings have a gallery of photos to showcase their spaces. As they say, a picture is worth a thousand words. For those sites that look good, also stop to read their words to get as much additional information as possible.

If you're seeking an unconventional location, or if the sites you find on wedding Web portals don't float your boat, try a more direct online search for your dream location using major search engines like Yahoo! and Google. For example, if you want to get hitched at a dude ranch in Montana, just enter "weddings dude ranch Montana" as your search criteria. Soon, you and your dude will be galloping down the aisle.

Step 2. Visit Your Favorite Venues

WHILE THE INTERNET can help you identify potentially perfect places for your reception, you need to get up close and personal with these sites before making a final decision. When checking out your possible choices, there are tons of questions that you want to get answered. I provide a checklist at the end of this chapter to help you get those details thoroughly covered. Before we get to that, there are three fundamental issues that you should focus on as you search for the right site.

VISION

FIRST AND FOREMOST, does this venue still fit your wedding vision now that you're seeing it live? Keep in mind that a site may not look exactly like the photos you saw on the Web. An empty room looks drastically different from an online image where it was all decked out with decor. Or, if you're visiting an outdoor site during the off-season, remember that the bare bushes you see now may be in full bloom by your wedding day. In these situations, you need to use your imagination to envision how the site may look and feel once the finishing touches have been applied.

FLOW

DOES THE LAYOUT of the site allow your day to flow smoothly? You want to have an effortless transition with elements of surprise each step of the way as you move from your ceremony (if it's at the same site as your reception) to your cocktail hour to your meal to dancing. The ideal flow occurs at a site that has separate areas for each segment of your celebration. These areas should be in close proximity, to minimize the time you need to proceed from one place to the next, but they should provide enough privacy to keep your guests from gawking at spaces you have yet to occupy.

From the standpoint of your vendors, it is best if each of these areas has multiple access routes, so they can get in and install their stuff without being seen by your guests. Otherwise, your reception band, for example, may need to be completely set up before the first guest sets foot on the property.

While I've been describing the ideal layout of a site in the last two paragraphs, the reality is that not all properties are so perfectly designed. In fact, at many wedding locations, it is necessary to use an area more than once during the wedding day. For instance, a lovely garden patio could be used for both a ceremony and a dinner. During the halftime break, while your guests are sipping cocktails in a nearby courtyard, your vendors can scurry around like decapitated chickens and convert your ceremony site into a superb spot for supping.

The vendors really don't mind doing this chicken dance for you, since that's what you're paying for. It's just that you pay more for a caterer to "turn a room," or for a band to "preset," because extra labor is required on their part.

The bottom line is that a venue that is not configured for an optimal flow may have hidden costs that you experience later when it comes time to hire your vendors. Plus, if you have to put your guests in the same place twice, they may experience the "movie sequel syndrome," where the show isn't quite as exciting the second time around.

SIZE

IS THE SITE appropriately sized for your group? To determine if a venue can accommodate your guests, you need to compare the square footage of their facilities with your space requirements. Because you've been dutifully reading this book, you already know how many guests are expected to attend. To calculate the minimum amount of room you need, just multiply your estimated head count by the following factors for each area of your celebration:

- ceremony area: 10 square feet per person
- cocktail reception: 7 square feet per person
- dining and dancing together (a dinner dance): 20 square feet per person
- dining only: 12 square feet per person
- dance floor and band (in separate area from dining): 8 square feet per person

For example, if you're expecting 100 people at your wedding, you need at least 1,000 square feet of space for your ceremony, 700 square feet for your cocktail hour, and 2,000 square feet if you're having a dinner dance.

During your site visits, many site sales managers will advise you of the "capacity" of their facilities in terms of how many bodies they can hold. However, keep in mind that these people are in the business of selling space, and their capacity figures may not take your guests' comfort into consideration. Always ask for the square footage of the space, or even be prepared to calculate it yourself by bringing a tape measure with you.

Po-tent-ial Issues

IF YOU'RE ENRAPTURED with an outdoor location for any part of your celebration, you need a backup plan in case Mother Nature decides to water her garden on your wedding day. Make sure that the venue you're considering either has an alternate indoor facility available for your use, or allows you to install a tent in the outdoor area.

Even if you're in an area where weather is not an issue, many people feel that tents provide a sensual and sexy ambience, making them the perfect place for a wedding. But like everything else that's sensual and sexy, tents can be very expensive. In particular, if the ground around your preferred pitching place is rough enough to necessitate a subfloor, you can throw your budget right through the clear wall. Typical tent installations start at about $5,000 without subfloors and $20,000 with.

Premises, Premises

WITH MANY SITES, you're buying more than space. Hotels and country clubs are known as "on-premise" facilities because they also have a catering staff on the premises to prepare and serve food and beverages (as opposed to an "off-premise" facility, where you have to bring in an outside caterer). Other venues may be de facto on-premise sites because they have an exclusive working arrangement with a single outside caterer.

In both of these situations, you're not making a decision only about your location. You are simultaneously selecting a caterer. Therefore, if you are seriously considering an on-premise property, I suggest that you first read Week 16 for additional pointers on picking a caterer, especially if the quality of food is critically important to you.

Typically, on-premise locations don't charge a separate fee to rent their space. You can rest assured, however, that menu items are priced in a manner that allows them to recover the operating cost of these facilities. On the other hand, with an off-premise site, you pay a rental fee to the site operator, then separately pay an outside caterer for their services. But don't assume it costs you more to write two checks. In my experience, the only time you have an overall price difference between on- and off-premise is when you have a difference in quality—in other words, you get what you pay for.

HELPFUL HINTS

What to bring on a site inspection:

- *pad of paper and pen*
- *retractable tape measure*
- *digital camera*

Questions to ask:

- *What dates do you have available?*
- *What is the rental fee, if any?*
- *At what time of day is this facility available for my wedding to start? For vendors to load in?*
- *How many hours are allotted for a wedding? What is the fee, if any, for additional hours?*
- *At what time does music have to stop?*
- *Are other weddings or events scheduled that day? If so, when? (Unless you love a particular site more than your fiancé, I advise against selecting a venue that books more than one wedding on the same day.)*
- *Are there specific, designated areas for cocktails, dinner, and dancing, or can I choose where I would like to have these activities?*
- *Do you have a preferred vendor list? If so, am I required to use the vendors on your list?*
- *What is the square footage of each available area? Do you have floor plans for these areas?*
- *What are the typical access routes to each area for guests? If there are stairways involved, are there other ways to get elderly people to each area?*
- *What are the typical access routes to each area for vendors?*
- *Are there staging areas for the vendors to set up?*
- *What parking facilities are available for guests? For vendors?*
- *Are the parking areas lit at night? Is there lighting between the reception area and the parking lots?*
- *Where are the restrooms? If portable toilets are necessary, where can they be positioned?*
- *When was this property built? When was it last renovated? Are there any current plans for construction work on the property? If so, when?*
- *For indoor facilities, are fire sprinklers installed? Heating and air-conditioning?*

- *Where are electrical outlets located for musicians to use? How are the acoustics in this area?*
- *Where are the lighting controls? Are there options for dimming the lights?*
- *For on-premise facilities, are your banquet laborers union or nonunion? If union, when is their contract up for renewal?*
- *For off-premise facilities, is there a kitchen for the caterer to use? A water supply?*
- *Are tables, chairs or other items included with the site rental fee?*

For Brides on a Budget

Public venues, such as parks and community halls, often rent for considerably less than private properties. If you're suffering from severe sticker shock after seeing the price tag on your favorite site, consider a government-run facility instead. While you may have a few more bureaucratic forms to fill out, it can be well worth it.

After you have visited all the venues on your list, carefully weigh the pros and cons of each, then make your decision. Of course, if you decided in the last chapter to have your ceremony in a place of worship, then you must pick a reception site that's available on the same date as your church and at a compatible time. Once you've made your selection(s), you have reached a major milestone in the planning process. You not only have a location for your festivities, you now have set your wedding date!

Choose Your Cast of Characters

NOW THAT YOU'VE decided on a date and place for your celebration, it's time for you and your fiancé to contemplate whom you want to have standing beside you at the altar. Numerous customs have been passed down regarding the composition of the wedding party, most of which you can pass up. Whether you're contemplating a conventional wedding or not, you need to consider two fundamental questions: how many attendants to select and whom to ask.

First, I cover the traditional responsibilities for wedding party members. You may not need or want your attendants to perform all of these tasks, but this list may help you decide who might be best suited for particular positions within your wedding party.

Maid of Honor

- Helps the bride select bridesmaids' attire and the wedding dress
- Helps address invitations and place cards
- Attends the rehearsal
- Helps the bride get into her gown
- Makes sure that all bridesmaids, flower girl, and ring bearer are at the rehearsal and ceremony on time
- Arranges the bride's veil and train before the processional and recessional
- Walks in the processional and recessional
- Holds the bride's bouquet during the ceremony
- Witnesses the signing of the marriage certificate
- Takes care of the bride's gown and accessories after the reception

Bridesmaids

- Take care of their own dress and accessories fittings
- Assist the bride with errands and various prewedding tasks

- Attend the rehearsal
- Walk in the processional and recessional
- Dance with groomsmen and other guests
- Help gather guests for the first dance and cake cutting
- Help look after the couple's elderly relatives or friends

Best Man

- Goes to fitting for tux and picks it up before wedding
- Organizes any prewedding party for the groom
- Attends the rehearsal
- Gets the groom dressed and to the ceremony on time
- Makes sure the groom has the marriage license with him
- Makes sure all groomsmen and ushers are correctly dressed and in place on time
- Delivers any payments to officiant and ceremony musicians
- Holds the bride's and groom's wedding rings during the ceremony until the vows are spoken
- Walks in the processional and recessional
- Witnesses the signing of the marriage certificate
- Welcomes guests at the reception
- Offers first toast to bride and groom at the reception
- Dances with the bride, maid of honor, mothers, and guests
- Helps the groom get ready for the honeymoon
- Gathers up and takes care of the groom's wedding clothes after he changes
- Collects and returns the groom's tux (and his own)
- Helps maid of honor bring gifts to the couple's residence
- Has a car ready for the bride and groom to leave the reception or perhaps drives them to their next destination

Groomsmen/Ushers

- Go to fittings for tuxes and pick them up before wedding
- Contribute to the gift for the groom
- Attend the rehearsal
- Make sure that designated people receive special flowers or corsages
- Greet guests as they arrive
- Seat guests prior to ceremony
- Remember the order for seating of the couple's family members

- Follow any lists of guests who are to be seated in a specific pew
- Hand guests programs when they are seated
- Put the aisle runner in place after guests are seated, before the processional begins
- Stand at altar alongside groom (groomsmen only)
- Direct guests to the reception site
- Look after elderly guests
- Dance with bridesmaids and other guests at the reception
- Return tux after wedding

Quantities

ONE RULE OF thumb may be helpful as a starting point for determining how many attendants to select: There should be one groomsman to every 50 guests at the ceremony. So if you're expecting 150 people to witness your nuptials, plan on employing at least 3 groomsmen to get your guests seated on time. In most cases, the job of ushering rests with the groomsmen, so your groom might consider having at least 3 guys in his entourage. But if you don't feel comfortable with that many bodies at the altar, you can assign the ushering duties to other friends.

Traditionally, the number of bridesmaids was supposed to equal the number of groomsmen. But unless you're inviting your high school algebra teacher to the wedding, don't feel obligated by this antiquated arithmetic. According to formulas of modern math, if you choose to have more bridesmaids than groomsmen, one or more guys in your wedding party will have to escort two lovely ladies back down the aisle at the end of the ceremony (how tragic is that?). Of course, the converse of this theorem is also true: A surplus of groomsmen over bridesmaids means that at least one of your girlfriends will have to be escorted by two gentlemen.

Inviting a large number of attendants to join your wedding party creates a complex mathematical problem that should be avoided. I recommend having no more than 6 bridesmaids and 6 groomsmen, and a maximum of 2 flower girls. Beyond that, the wedding day logistics become unwieldy, and the altar starts to resemble a conga line at your junior prom.

You may have always dreamed of having a multitude of attendants at your wedding, stretching the length of the world's largest cathedral. But did you ever stop to consider how you would get all your bridesmaids to dutifully dress up, line up, and parade down the aisle in front of you?

Have you thought about the cost of that limousine fleet and all the bouquets you'll need? If you're still not convinced that smaller may be better, let's temporarily put the glass slipper on the other foot, Cinderella. Ask yourself how special you would feel if a girlfriend recruited you to enlist in a 21-woman bridal brigade for her wedding. Don't expect your bridesmaids to feel any differently.

The last set of numbers I want to cover are the appropriate ages for younger members of your wedding party. Flower girls and ring bearers should ideally be between 3½ and 7 years old. Younger children may not make it to the end of the aisle. Once they reach age 8, they start to lose that adorable cuteness that makes them so perfect for the job. Eight-year-old girls get promoted to the rank of junior bridesmaid, a title they can hold until their eighteenth birthday, when they're finally allowed to lose the "junior" label. On the other hand, boys are usually "retired" from the wedding business from age 8 until they're old enough to become a groomsman when one of their good friends gets engaged.

Qualities

THE TOUGHER QUESTION is whom to invite into your wedding party.

Many outdated traditions concerning the choice of attendants are vanishing, largely because it's more important for today's couples to pick the people who mean the most to them. No longer is it necessary for you to select your sister as your maid/matron of honor, and likewise the best man does not have to be the groom's brother. (I'm not suggesting that your sister wouldn't be a good choice; just don't feel obligated to ask her.) In fact, your bridesmaids don't even need to be women. A great male friend of the bride can be an honor attendant. So can a dear female friend of the groom.

If the old etiquette rules no longer apply, how do you decide whom to select? As your bridal human resources manager, I believe that ideal candidates for your wedding party should demonstrate some important "abilities":

- **Dependability** Can you count on the best man to hold on to the bride's ring until it's time to exchange your vows, then stay sober long enough to make an eloquent toast at the reception?
- **Stability** Will your bridesmaids be there to support you when you need it most and have the sense to recognize that catfights and

prima donna tantrums are not constructive activities on your wedding day?

- **Affability** Do your groomsmen have outgoing, pleasant personalities that make them well suited to greet your guests and escort them to their seats?
- **Availability** If your bridesmaids live close by, do they have time to help you with your lengthy to-do list? If not, can they at least get together with you once before the wedding for a dress fitting, and quickly respond by phone or e-mail when you need to discuss something with them?
- **Affordability** While a friend or relative may be honored to be a part of your wedding, are his or her financial circumstances strong enough to handle the expenses of being an attendant?

Boiling it all down to the basics, select pleasant, reliable people you have been close to for many years (and who you will remain close to throughout your married life). Weigh all these factors and obligations carefully before making your final decisions. Once you extend an invitation to someone to be a part of your party, it's difficult to uninvite him or her.

Finally, remember that your attendants are agreeing to spend their hard-earned money and donate their valuable time to your wedding. Be sure to give them the consideration they deserve by showing them a good time and letting them know how much you appreciate their participation.

Block Rooms and Air Transportation for Out-of-Town Guests

WHETHER YOU'RE TYING the knot in Tahiti, or celebrating more conventionally in your hometown, chances are that at least some of your guests will be traveling a considerable distance to join in the festivities. With today's on-the-go lifestyles, the challenge of bringing together your faraway friends and family is greater than ever before. To make it easier for out-of-towners to get to your gathering, it's a thoughtful gesture to facilitate their travel arrangements by arranging group air and hotel accommodations for them.

You may be wondering why I'm covering this subject so early in the planning process. Your objective is to soon send out a save-the-date card to your guests. Along with that card, you want to inform your guests about airline and hotel options, so they can save money by booking early.

First take another look at the "Likely to Attend" column on your guest list. Estimate how many people will likely be flying in and how many will probably need hotel rooms. (You can add columns to your spreadsheet called "Likely to Fly" and "Likely to Need Hotel," if you wish.) From my experience, take the numbers you just calculated and cut them by 50 percent. About half of your guests will make arrangements without your help. They may stay with friends or relatives, use frequent-traveler points to secure their flights and hotels, or just do their own thing. The other half of your group will dutifully reserve whatever you arrange for them.

Once you have estimated the number of guests wanting group travel arrangements, you can contact a travel agent or your wedding planner to secure the air and room blocks for you—or you can do the bookings yourself. Depending on your particular situation, there are also a number of travel-related Web sites that may be able to help (I identify them as I go along).

When Money Is No Object

It is never considered necessary to pay for the travel costs of your guests under any definition of proper etiquette. However, if you have the means to do so, it is certainly a wonderful gesture to pick up the tab for people who are near and dear—family members, your wedding party, and so on.

Also, couples who have a significant stash of frequent-flyer miles might consider redeeming them for guests who otherwise would be unable to afford the flight themselves. Just make sure you save enough miles for the honeymoon!

Group Air Travel

IF YOU HAVE a group of 10 or more, you should contact the various airlines directly for group rates. In most cases, they offer a fare discount of about 5 percent.

To determine which airlines to contact, first check the Web site of the airport closest to your wedding location. It should list all the airlines that service that airport. Follow up with a phone call to the airport to find out which airline offers the most flights (or uses the most gates). This is probably your best choice from a convenience standpoint.

Specific information about group air programs offered by major carriers is provided in the table below.

Airline	Dept./Program Name	Contact Info.	Special Features
American Airlines	Group Travel Wedding Services Desk	1-800-545-8193	partnership with Avis for discounted rental cars
Delta Airlines	Group Sales	Domestic: 1-800-532-4777 International: 1-800-337-4777	
Hawaiian Airlines	Wedding Wings	www.hawaiianair .com/groups/ wed_wings.asp	a free one-way first-class upgrade for every 10 bookings secured
Northwest Airlines	Group Travel	1-800-645-9696	
Southwest Airlines	Group Program	1-800-433-5368	

United Airlines	GroupPlus	www.united.com	partnership with Avis for discounted rental cars
US Airways	Group and Meeting Travel Services	1-877-US-GROUPS (877-874-7687) or www.usairways.com/travel/group/weddings/index.htm	additional 5% discount off most published fares if tickets are purchased at least 60 days in advance

If your group is fewer than 10 people, there are Web sites handling smaller group travel that may be able to get you some discounts. Check out www.groople.com or www.travelmanager.com.

Hotel Room Blocks

IT'S IMPORTANT TO understand that the price of a hotel room hinges on whether your wedding is at a peak or off-peak time for the hotel. In cities, weekends are usually off-peak (hotels are busier during the week with business travelers), so the rates can be relatively lower. But in resort areas and tourist destinations, the opposite is true. Weekend rates can be much higher, and popular destinations often require a two-night minimum stay.

If you're a member of the American Automobile Association (AAA) and your wedding location is somewhere in the United States, go to their nearest office and get a free tour book, so you can see how hotels in the area are rated. While the AAA diamond system is not gospel, it is one of the most widely recognized ratings in existence.

Next, look at rates online for hotels in the area. A great site is www.tripadvisor.com, which provides rankings of hotels based on guest comments and travel guide reviews. It also has a feature allowing you instantly to compare rates offered by major online travel sites, including Expedia, Hotels.com, and Orbitz. From this Internet research, you should be able to identify hotels of potential interest.

Once you have a list of hotels to contact, call and ask for a group sales manager. If the hotel is part of a national chain, call the local number, not the national reservations toll-free number.

Many hotels block rooms and give you a group rate only if you want to block ten or more rooms on your wedding night. (Again, Web sites like groople.com and travelmanager.com may be able to help if you need fewer rooms.) Assuming that the hotel can accommodate your group size, ask the sales manager for the "best rate" the hotel can offer. If the best rate is worse than something you saw online, bring that to his or her attention and ask if he or she can do better. Assuming the new price beats the Web offerings, also ask if there is a "comp policy," where the hotel provides a free room if a certain number of rooms are secured. At many hotels, you get one complimentary room for every fifty rooms picked up by your guests.

You need to sign a contract to ensure that the hotel will hold the rooms you want for a particular rate. However, you do not want the contract to contain any cancellation fees or attrition penalties, where you will be held financially responsible if some of the rooms you blocked aren't picked up by your guests. Instead, agree to a cut-off date for the room block. This means the rooms will be held until a specific date (anywhere from 2 months to 3 weeks prior to the wedding, depending on the hotel), at which point any unreserved rooms will be released for sale to other people.

Also, you should not have to pay an up-front deposit for the room block. Instead, a reservation procedure should be set up where your guests call individually to reserve the rooms, securing them with their own credit cards.

Remember that you are trying to do your guests a favor here. You don't need to bankrupt yourself in the process. If the hotels you have contacted insist upon contracts with cancellation penalties or deposits, just say no. You can still provide information about the hotel on your save-the-date card, and your guests can individually call or go online to book their own rooms.

Hotel Site Inspection

IF YOU FIND some hotels that offer attractive pricing and terms for a block of rooms, your next step—before signing any contracts—is to visit these hotels, if possible. You want to look for the following:

- Comfortable, clean bedrooms
- Clean hallways, including prompt removal of room service trays from halls
- Beds and furniture in good condition
- Modern bathroom fixtures
  - adequate lighting and mirrors
  - blow dryers
- Adequate closet space and hangers

- Irons and ironing boards (provided by the housekeeping department)
- Safety features
  - smoke detectors in the room
  - fire exit information clearly posted

Here are some questions to ask as the hotel sales manager shows you around the property:

- Do you provide, or can you arrange for, transportation to and from the airport?
- Are any meals included as part of the stay?
- Do you have suites available in addition to your standard rooms? If so, what rate can you offer for suites?
- Do you provide roll-away beds to accommodate children?
- If we bring small gift baskets for our guests, will you deliver them to their rooms?
- Is there a charge for
  - parking?
  - local telephone calls?
  - use of the health club or resort facilities?
- What are the normal check-in and check-out times? Is it possible to request early check-ins or late check-outs?
- Are there any plans for renovation work at this hotel before the wedding date? If so, when?
- Are any union contracts up for renewal before the wedding date? If so, when?
- Where are the nearest restaurants? Banks or ATMs? Pharmacies?

If you find hotels with a range of different price categories (or AAA diamond ratings) in your area, you may wish to block rooms at two different hotels—one "luxury" and one "economy"—in order to give your guests a choice. But I wouldn't select any more than two hotels. It gets too complicated and confusing for your guests, and they probably won't have as much fun being spread out over several different locations.

Finally, take this opportunity to book a hotel room for the two of you on your wedding night. Obviously, it need not be in the same hotel where your out-of-town guests are staying. Pick something luxurious, secluded, and, of course, very romantic.

Design and Purchase Save-the-Date Cards

IT'S FINALLY TIME to spread the word beyond your close inner circle. With today's busy lifestyles, the save-the-date card has become an invaluable way to let guests know when your wedding will take place, so they can schedule you on their calendars. Save-the-dates give your guests the opportunity to inform their employers when they need the day(s) off and to arrange for child care if necessary. Plus, if your wedding is happening at a hot spot, it's essential for your guests to book their travel arrangements well in advance. Besides, the earlier people know about your wedding, the fewer excuses they have for not attending!

For many of your invitees, the save-the-date card is the first information they receive about your wedding, so you want to make a great initial impression on them. You've spent some quality time developing a design concept, and now you should begin to share it with your guests in a way that makes them look forward to your big day with anticipation and excitement.

Selecting an Appropriate Design

YOUR SAVE-THE-DATE CARD should reflect your wedding visions and the overall feeling you want to convey. Its appearance—paper, colors, fonts, and style of printing—should be consistent with your actual invitation as well as the remainder of your printed materials. That doesn't mean all of your paper products need to look identical. Instead, it's like making a fashion statement. All of the accessories in your wardrobe should coordinate and fit together nicely.

To start searching for a suitable save-the-date card, first visit the stationery shops in your area that sell wedding invitations. Bring a pad of paper with you and make notes about any samples that appeal to you.

Share your wedding design concepts with the salespeople. They can help you focus in on albums that are most likely to interest you.

Don't restrict your search to only the wedding books. The perfect save-the-date card might be hiding in an album of party invitations, or even bar and bat mitvah invites. In fact, some invitation manufacturers now have finally recognized the importance of save-the-date cards and have entire albums devoted to them.

HELPFUL HINTS

There are four major methods used in printing. **Engraving** *is the most traditional printing method, first introduced in the 1600s. The printing process involves etching the lettering into a metal die, inking the etched depressions, and then pressing the paper against the die. The result is that the letters are raised on the printed side of the paper. Engraving is used primarily on traditional, formal invitations. It provides sharp, intricate lettering that has a three-dimensional quality, but it is a costly process and often requires a long turnaround time—occasionally up to two months.*

Another classic printing method, **letterpress,** *was on the verge of extinction before recently enjoying a renaissance in popularity among wedding stationers. Letterpress can be considered the opposite of engraving—the lettering on the printing plate is raised, which creates indentations in the paper during the printing process. Letterpressing is especially suited for luxurious handmade papers.*

Thermography *is similar to engraving, in that it produces raised lettering on the printed side of the paper. To create this lettering, the paper is first printed with standard ink, then the paper is dusted with a resinous powder and passed through a heating unit. The thermographic lettering is not quite as fine as what you get with engraving, but it is popular because the raised lettering gives the invitation an elegant look at a substantially lower cost than engraving or letterpress.*

Lithography, *or offset printing, is less expensive than thermography and faster to print. Lithography is basically a photographic printing method, where negatives are transferred to a thin metal plate that is wrapped around the cylinder of a sheet-fed press. A virtually unlimited variety of typefaces and colors can be selected.*

With the availability of special software and font packages for personal computers, as well as economically priced color printers, couples can now create their own wedding invitations and even print matching addresses on the envelopes. It is most practical to consider computer-generated invitations when the number of invited guests is small. With larger weddings, offset printing is probably more economical, more versatile, and higher in overall quality.

If you find a design in a standard invitation album that fits like your favorite pair of gloves, congratulations! You're either very lucky or very easy to please. But if the regular cards in the invitation books aren't your style, you probably want to have your save-the-date card custom designed.

Many couples find papers, fonts, and ink colors that work well for their wedding vision, but the little leaves, simple swirls, and mundane monograms shown in the sample books don't fit their design concept. Some invitation suppliers allow you to submit your own digital artwork, so before you run out the door of the stationery store, ask the salesperson whether this is a possibility with any of the invitations you find somewhat appealing. If so, ask what image file format(s) they prefer.

Your dream drawing might just be waiting for you in an online clip art collection. Check out www.clipart.com, which has an extensive library of images in multiple file formats. It also provides a keyword search feature to help you find the kind of artwork you're seeking. The site's images are "royalty free," but you pay by becoming a member of the clip art club. A one-week membership costs $14.95.

If the online clip art doesn't cut it, you can hire a graphic designer to create custom artwork. Ask friends for referrals or look in your Yellow Pages under "Graphic Design." Just remember, this is not going to be the most economical way to go.

Maybe you fell in love with letterpress printing during your visit to the stationery stores. Many of the boutique letterpress studios have in-house designers on their staffs. Certain studios will work with you directly (not through a retailer) via e-mail and phone, so you don't need to be living next door to them. Here are some top letterpress companies that can custom-design your save-the-date, as well as your complete stationery ensemble:

- 9spotmonk Design, Hoboken, New Jersey, www.9spotmonk.com
- Bella Figura, Syracuse, New York, www.bellafigura.com
- Creative Intelligence, Los Angeles, www.creative-intelligence.com
- A Day in May Design, San Francisco, www.adayinmay.com
- Elizabeth Hubbell Letterpress Studio, Berkeley, California, www.elizabethhubbellstudio.com
- Pantry Press, Toronto, www.pantrypress.net

- Peculiar Pair Press, Oakland and San Francisco, www.peculiarpair press.com
- Purgatory Pie Press, New York, www.purgatorypiepress.com
- Twig & Fig, Berkeley, California, www.twigandfig.com

While you're trying to get your save-the-date designed, keep in mind that this card should be mailed 6 months to a year before your wedding date. You may need to strike a balance between your design issues and timing constraints. Graphic designers and printing companies often have significant lead times, and you need to evaluate these lead times in choosing how to create your save-the-date. Yes, you want a card that's consistent with your wedding vision, but it defeats the purpose of a save-the-date card if you can't get it to your guests in a timely manner.

So if a custom-designed card is going to take too long to produce, you may have to pick a speedier alternative. One option is to save your custom artwork for the invitation and use similar papers, colors, and fonts on your save-the-date.

For Brides on a Budget

If you can't afford pricey designer prints for your entire stationery wardrobe, consider making your own save-the-date cards and saving your funds for the invitation. Your local stationery store may carry "imprintable" cards that you can print at home. These cards come in a wide variety of sizes, shapes, and colors, so you can pick something that best fits your wedding vision. If your local stores have nothing to your liking, look online at www.mygatsby.com or www.paper-source.com and check out their offerings.

A Word on Wording

SAVE-THE-DATE CARDS ARE a modern-day phenomenon. Unlike wedding invitations, they're not encumbered by centuries of etiquette regarding proper wording. There are no real rules, and I only have two suggested guidelines to follow: (1) The save-the-date should be in good taste. (2) Tell your guests only what they need to know now. If you reveal every detail about your wedding in the save-the-date, there's no drama left for the invitation.

Here's my short list of what needs to be included on a save-the-date card:

- the bride and groom's names
- some sort of proclamation that you're getting married
- the wedding date and a request to save it

On a separate insert, include the following:

- Hotel room and airline information; if you're having a foreign destination wedding, also indicate passport and visa requirements.
- Anything else that may intrigue and inspire your guests to attend. (For a Las Vegas wedding, for instance, you might want to list major shows playing on the Strip, so your guests can book tickets ahead of time.)

Many people also indicate the city where the wedding is taking place on the save-the-date card, but this is usually self-evident from the hotel information. Another popular line is "Invitation and Additional Information to Follow." To me, this is no more necessary than the voice mail greeting that tells callers to leave their name and number after the beep. Don't we already know what to do when the beep sounds?

Save other details, like the wedding location, driving directions, weather conditions, and appropriate attire, for your invitation. Don't disclose everything now. You want to build the anticipation for your wedding. Besides, the earlier you send this kind of information to your guests, the more likely some of them will lose it. Also, if you've created a Web site for your wedding, don't post these details there either, for the same reasons.

ONE COUPLE'S STORY

*M*arissa and Steve live alongside the beautiful beaches of Florida, but they decided to plan a destination wedding at the spectacular Annadel Winery and Gardens in California's Sonoma Valley. The ruins of the original stone winery, built in the 1800s, provided a focal point at this facility, evoking a feeling of being in the French countryside. Inspired by this ambience, I worked with Marissa to create an Old World theme for her wedding.

To give her save-the-date card a look and feel of antiquity, Marissa selected a thick handmade paper with irregular deckled edges from Twin-rocker, a supplier and printer based in Indiana. Similar papers in a variety of sizes and shapes were also used for the invitation, response cards, escort cards, and ceremony program covers. The entire stationery ensemble was printed on Twinrocker's letterpress, using a calligraphic script for each piece. To save time and cost, no artwork was used on her save-the-date card. Later, the owner of Annadel Winery and Gardens supplied a historical photo of the winery building, which was digitally enhanced, then incorporated into the other printed materials.

Along with their save-the-date card, Marissa and Steve provided details about hotel room blocks that had been secured for their guests, as well as air travel information, on a separate enclosure. To further entice their guests to travel to the Sonoma wine country, they also supplied the skinny on area wineries and attractions.

Finally, how many save-the-date cards should you order? Look at your guest list spreadsheet and count the number of *rows* of Yeses. Remember, you're not sending one card to every guest, since many of your invitees are probably couples or families. Once you have determined this quantity, add another 10 percent to allow for keepsakes and problems with addressing envelopes (human error with calligraphers or printer jams with machines). Many invitation suppliers accept quantities only in increments of 25, so you may need to round up to the next allowable amount.

Choose Your Wedding Gown

WHETHER YOU'VE DREAMED about your wedding gown since childhood or didn't give it a thought until your beau popped the question, you want to feel perfect in your gown so you'll always remember the wonderful experience of being a bride. Your gown should embrace your individuality and make you feel fabulous. Most important, you must be completely comfortable in the gown so that you can move as effortlessly and flawlessly as your wedding day itself.

Gown Types and Tips

TODAY, THE FASHION police don't patrol bridal parties with the unbridled frenzy they exhibited in days gone by. Second- or third-time brides are now allowed to wear white if they wish, and you don't need to wait until 5 P.M. to walk down the aisle in a cathedral train and veil. While yesterday's rules of the robe may have largely vanished, your surroundings can still affect your selection of apparel. For instance, if you're getting married at an Aspen ski resort in January, you might feel a little funny (and chilly) wearing a strapless ball gown. So before you begin to shop, you need to understand some of the basics of bridal outfitting.

It's most important to understand terminology involving the gown's overall shape or "silhouette," because certain body types go better with certain silhouettes. In other words, your physique is a major factor in selecting an appropriate gown, and you can simplify your search for the perfect one by focusing on the most suitable silhouettes. The table below identifies the major silhouette types and compatible body structures.

Type of Silhouette	Description	Best Body Matches
Ball Gown	A lavish full skirt accented by a natural waistline and fitted bodice.	• Tall • Full figured • Large thighs and legs
Empire	The waistline is about 1" above the natural waistline, with a slim flowing skirt.	• Slim but not curvaceous
Mermaid	Form-fitting like the sheath but flares out below the knees.	• Slender and curvaceous
Princess (or A-Line)	A flared skirt that creates an A shape. The top of the gown gracefully blends into the skirt.	• Hourglass figure • Short torso • Pear shape • Works for all body types
Sheath	Tube-shaped gown following the contours of the body.	• Petite • Thin

The other aspect of gown design that should be appropriately matched with your figure is the neckline. Below, I describe the basic types of necklines and identify harmonious anatomical features.

Neckline Type	Description	Best Fit
Bateau	Neckline gently follows the curve of the collarbone almost to the top of the shoulder in front and back.	• Small chest
Halter	An abbreviated top that fastens behind the neck or across the back to hold up the bodice.	• Broad shoulders
Jewel	Fabric circles the natural neckline.	• Small chest
Off-the-Shoulder	Neckline starts below the shoulders to highlight your collarbone and shoulders, with sleeves covering part of the upper arm.	• Full chest • Pear shape
Portrait	Open neckline with a high back characterized by a wide, soft scoop from the tip of one shoulder to the tip of the other.	• Fuller arms • Prominent collarbone
Sabrina	High, straight neckline that begins 2" inside the shoulder line.	• Small chest
Scoop	Low, curved sweep, extending to the shoulders; may be cut deep in front, back, or both.	• All body types
Strapless	Fabric circles the torso directly above the bustline; needs boning for support.	• Prominent shoulders and collarbone
Sweetheart	Shaped like the top of a heart; the back is higher and straight across.	• Full chest
V-Neck	Neckline comes to a point in the shape of a V, giving the neck a longer, slimmer look.	• The moderately endowed

There are still more options and terms for you to consider as you search for the perfect gown. Here are some additional bridal buzzwords that you may need to know in order to shop intelligently for your gown.

Fabrics
The fabric choice affects the shape of the gown and how it drapes. Here are fabrics for less structured gowns.

- **Charmeuse**   A lightweight, smooth, semilustrous satin fabric.
- **Chiffon**   A sheer fabric of a simple weave made of silk, rayon, or synthetics; must be lined.

- **Crepe**   A fabric made of synthetic or natural fibers that are twisted to give a slightly crinkled texture.
- **Georgette**   Heavier than chiffon, a silk or synthetic crepe with a dull texture.
- **Jersey**   A stronger fabric of wool, silk, or rayon.
- **Shantung**   Plain-woven silk or synthetic fabric with a rough, randomly nubby texture, produced by weaving together uneven fibers.
- **Silk**   The lustrous, fine fiber produced from the cocoon spun by the silkworm.

For a more structured gown, the following types of fabrics are commonly used:

- **Satin**   A densely woven silk or synthetic material with one lustrous side and one matte side. Duchess satin is a lighter-weight, glossy satin-weave fabric and may be silk or rayon. Both are excellent for A-line, ball gown, empire silhouettes.
- Satin-faced **organza**   A sheer, nearly transparent fabric that is heavier and stiffer than chiffon but lighter in appearance and opaqueness than duchess satin. Comes in a selection of weights and finishes.
- **Taffeta**   A crisp, lightweight fabric with a smooth finish, with a small crosswise weave made in silk, cotton, rayon, or synthetics. Taffeta looks better when gathered for fullness.
- **Tulle**   A sheer, meshlike weave with hexagonal holes, made of silk, cotton, nylon, or rayon. Was originally used for petticoats.

Lace
Delicate yet dramatic, lace can provide a look that is both timeless and traditional. Here are the most popular types found in wedding gowns.

- **Alençon**   A delicate needlepoint lace with a pattern of neatly arranged flowers and swags outlined with cord.
- **Chantilly**   A delicate handmade bobbin lace with a hexagonal mesh background and floral designs with a scalloped edge outlined with silk thread.
- **Venise**   A heavy raised needlepoint lace, made of cotton or linen, of floral leaf or geometric motifs, connected with irregularly spaced bridges.

Sleeves
Traditional poufy sleeves have gone poof, and many brides now select sleeveless styles. If you want to cover at least part of your arms, here are your options:

- **Cap**   A short sleeve that covers just the top of the arms.
- **Off-the-shoulder**   The upper parts of the arms are covered while the tops of the shoulders are left exposed.
- **Three-quarters**   Ending midway between the elbow and the wrist, this sleeve style has a classic, ladylike feel.
- **T-shirt**   The length of the sleeves on your favorite T-shirt, covering your triceps and biceps.

Trains

More than a mode of transportation, the train is a trailing attachment to your gown. Its length is directly proportional to the regality of your celebration.

- **Sweep**   The shortest train, barely sweeping the floor.
- **Court**   Falls to the floor, about a foot longer than a sweep train.
- **Chapel**   Extending from the waist, flows about 3 to 4 feet behind the gown.
- **Cathedral** or **monarch**   A cascading train extending 6 to 8 feet behind the gown; generally used for formal weddings.

If you select a train that is not detachable, following your ceremony and posed photos it will need to be bustled—gathered up with loops and ties on the back of your gown—so you aren't doing the janitor's job during the reception.

Colors

Perhaps you've never noticed this, but white actually comes in a variety of tints and shades.

- **Stark white**   The brightest white available, best for people with darker skin.
- **Silk, diamond,** or **natural white**   A shade off of stark white but much more flattering on most people.
- **Ivory, eggshell,** or **candlelight**   Has creamy yellow undertones.
- **Rum** or **champagne**   Has pink undertones.

Locating Gowns and Salons

WITH THESE GENERAL guidelines in mind, start looking for gowns that appeal to you in bridal magazine ads, and flag styles that you like. Rather than tearing out your favorite pages, keep the magazine intact for now. It may be more helpful for a salon to research a gown if they know what issue the ad appeared in. You can also look online for inspiring ideas. Major wed sites have large galleries of gowns that can be viewed by designer, silhouette, neckline, and budget.

Speaking of budget, if you want a designer gown, prices generally start at around $2,000 and often run to the $5,000 to $10,000 range. Whatever you plan to spend on your wardrobe, the amount you set aside should also include an allowance for a headpiece/veil (usually about $250 to $500), shoes ($75 to $400), and miscellaneous accessories like a purse, gloves, lingerie, and so on.

One more point to keep in mind before you start shopping: If you're getting married in a house of worship, check to see if it has any dress codes. Many religious sites frown upon bare shoulders, so if you love the strapless styles, look into a wrap or shawl for the ceremony.

As you spot photos of gowns that grab you, make a list of salons in your area that carry the designer's lines. Ask recently married friends if they've had any experience with the shops you have jotted down and make note of the salons they recommend. Research which salons are most appropriate for your budget by calling or visiting their Web sites. Verify that they carry designers you are interested in and ask if they accept credit cards. Narrow down your list to about three shops to visit.

Shopping for a Gown

IT IS ADVISABLE to make an appointment before getting in your car. In fact, many salons require appointments. If you can spare the time, it's best to schedule your visits for midweek, when you're not competing for the salesperson's attention with dozens of other brides.

On your first trip to the bridal shops, bring along your favorite photos, a notepad, pen, and trusted female friend—but leave your money at home. Wear undergarments similar to what you will be wearing on the day of your wedding, such as a strapless bra and panty hose. Also bring a pair of shoes with the heel height you plan to wear. As you try on gowns, have your friend take detailed notes, including the designer's name, identification numbers, fabric type and color, and significant style features. If permitted by the salon, have her take photos of you as well.

For each gown that you test-drive, put it through a range of motions with your body to see how it feels. You'll be wearing the gown for at least 8 hours on your big day, and during that time you will be sitting, dancing, and perhaps kneeling and tossing a bouquet. Ask if the gown comes with coordinating accessories such as a veil or shawl, and try these on as well. But don't feel pressured to buy your accessories at the same time as the gown. You still have plenty of time to shop around for them.

If the salesperson suggests a particular gown to try on that was not in your photo collection, be open-minded and give it a shot. Most salespeople have looked at a lot more gowns than you ever will and are experienced in matching brides with their perfect gown. Also be aware that many gowns can be special-ordered in alternative forms. For example, if you love what a designer did with the bodice on one gown and the skirt on another, ask if you can have the best of both. Just keep in mind that the more you deviate from the standard design, the more it may cost.

How do you know when you've found the perfect gown? I suggest taking the "two-teared test." If tears well up in both your eyes and your friend's when you first see yourself in a particular gown, you may have a winner. Even after you're sure you've found your dream gown, sleep on it (figuratively speaking) to be sure it's the one. To place an order, most salons require you to fork over a nonrefundable deposit, so take some time to think things through before making a final decision.

If you can't find the gown of your dreams in a salon, consider a bridal couture studio that can custom-design a gown for you. It can create a unique gown conforming both to your wedding visions and your body. However, custom-made gowns can be quite expensive.

When you've settled on a gown you love and can afford, go back to the salon where you found it to have your measurements taken. Many designers have sizing scales that don't match standard off-the-rack sizes in department stores. Every designer has his or her own measurement chart. Ask to see this chart and have the salesperson explain how it works. Your largest measurement is typically used to order the appropriate size, because it is better to have too much fabric in a garment than too little. Often, your gown size can be a bit higher than you are accustomed to seeing when buying "regular" clothing.

HELPFUL HINT

Of course, you promise yourself you will lose twenty-five pounds by the big day. Maybe you will, but probably you won't. Choose a style that looks good on you now, not on your fantasy body. Also, order the gown in your actual size. It can easily be taken in if you are smaller six months from now. It is difficult—often impossible—to let it out.

Before signing on the dotted line, discuss alterations. Inquire about the experience and qualifications of the salon's in-house alterations department and ask to meet the person in charge of alterations. Based on how your measurements compare to the designer's sizing scales, they should have a clear idea of the kinds of alterations that will be necessary. Ask for a written estimate for alterations before you sign a contract for the gown.

Finally, double-check all the information on the contract before signing. Make sure it includes the correct specifications for your gown, the agreed-upon total price, and the promised delivery date, which should be at least 45 days before the wedding. Pay by credit card if possible. Get a copy of the contract for your record, and put it in your staging guide under "Gown."

For Brides on a Budget

There are almost as many ways to save on the cost of a wedding gown as there are styles to choose from. Here are just a few suggestions to consider:

- **Less costly materials**   A gown that you saw in silk might easily be made with polysatin instead, saving you some big bucks. Or you could choose to lose the expensive embellishments like lace and beading, to keep your gown simple and keep yourself out of the poorhouse.
- **Off-the-rack shops**   Many metropolitan areas now have large bridal gown stores that sell gowns on a cash-and-carry basis. While the cost of gowns at these locations can be significantly less than at full-service salons, you need to have a clear idea what you want, and you will probably need to hire a seamstress to take care of any necessary alterations. Also, in most cases, the top-of-the-line designers that make the highest quality garments are not generally carried in these stores.
- **Online shopping**   Many salons have Web sites that allow you to purchase a gown online at a discount. Again, you need to know exactly what you're looking for. If you try to return or exchange a gown you bought on the Web, you may be out of luck, or at the very least you will be subject to a hefty restocking fee. If you're an experienced online auction shopper, you might just find the gown of your dreams on eBay. The usual warnings about online auction transactions certainly apply to wedding gown purchases as well.
- **Sample sales**   Salons periodically sell off gowns that their customers try on, often to make room for new designs. December and May are the two

best months to be on the lookout for sample sales. If you purchase one of these gowns, you can save a bundle, but beware of excessive wear on these samples and be prepared to pay for dry cleaning and alterations, since these gowns are generally sold "as is."

One final thought on your gown shopping alternatives. Bridal salons typically charge more than discount stores or Web sites because, at least in theory, they provide better customer service through experienced salespersons who can guide you to your dream gown. In reality, if you visit a salon that treats you in a condescending manner, or engages in deceptive or high-pressure sales tactics, leave. There are always other options for finding the right gown.

Request Caterer Proposals

THE TYPE OF reception site you have selected affects your choice of a caterer. If you selected a venue such as a banquet facility, hotel, private club, or restaurant, it will have an on-premise catering food and beverage manager you will work with. If, however, the reception site you selected does not come with a food and beverage operation, you need to contract with an off-premise catering company. Many times an off-premise site does not even have a kitchen. Not to worry. The right off-premise catering company will work magic for you!

Before you begin searching for a caterer, think about the kind of meal you wish to serve to your guests. To help with that, I'll give you some background on different service options and ideas to consider.

Depending on the time of day they have selected for the reception, most couples choose to serve either a lunch or dinner to guests, or they opt for a cocktail party format. You may also want to consider a breakfast, brunch, high tea, or desserts-only reception. While I never discourage out-of-the-box thinking, I focus on the more popular options below. However, much of the information about dinners and cocktail parties is equally applicable to breakfasts and afternoon teas.

Mingle Around

THE COCKTAIL RECEPTION allows guests to rejoice in your newly wedded bliss and socialize after the ceremony. Often, a cocktail hour precedes a lunch or dinner. But you can also have a reception with hors d'oeuvres only and no meal served. There may be a number of reasons why you would choose a cocktail party over a seated meal.

- You can't bear the thought of being tied to one table all night.
- You have limited space. For cocktail parties, you need to provide seating for only about one-third of your guests.
- You have limited finances.

- You don't want to be traditional.
- This is your third marriage, and you're not trying to impress anyone.

The entire length of the food service for a cocktail party should be about 3 hours. Shorter than 3 hours feels rushed; anything longer gets uncomfortable for your guests. For the first 2 hours, serve a combination of hot and cold hors d'oeuvres. Allow for 12 items per person, as the average person eats 8 hors d'oeuvres the first hour and 4 during the second hour of a reception. During the third hour, you probably want to serve desserts—perhaps a "sweet endings" table with a cappuccino or espresso bar, as well as wedding cake with champagne.

In addition to passing out hors d'oeuvres, a cocktail party is more fun if you have "stations"—tables where guests can go to pick up food. One extremely popular type of station is called an action station, where a chef prepares a particular type of food to order, then serves it to guests.

Have a Seat

MANY COUPLES CHOOSE to serve a sit-down meal because it is a more gracious, elegant way to break bread with their guests. Additionally, some of the traditional rituals of a reception—such as the best man's toast, or a blessing from your officiant—are easier to implement if you have a captive audience sitting at attention.

The seated meal is usually preceded by a "cocktail hour," which can actually range in duration from 45 minutes to 1½ hours. I find the ideal length to be about 1 hour and 15 minutes. However, if you and your fiancé do not plan to see each other before the wedding, you might consider a longer cocktail time so you can get your requisite newlywed photos taken without missing the entire reception. Estimate 3 to 6 hors d'oeuvres per person when the cocktail reception precedes a meal. To provide a variety of options, you could have two hot and two cold passed hors d'oeuvres and two food stations.

Once the cocktail hour is completed, guests are graciously invited by the catering staff to move into the dining area. There, you have two basic choices: Your guests can either serve themselves at buffet tables, or the caterer's waitstaff can serve them at their seats.

Self-Serve

FORTUNATELY, THE TRADITIONAL long rectangular buffet tables, exhibiting all the ambience of an army mess hall, have been dishonorably discharged from service. Today's presentations feature food stations or more contemporary buffet stations. A food station serves one type of food, and the menus are designed so that foods can be eaten on small plates with forks only. Various types of food stations can be positioned around the room, each with its own linens, decor, or theme. If you like a variety of ethnic cuisines, food stations showcase this best. Reception station portions generally amount to 3 or 4 ounces per serving. For the entire reception, at least 3 to 5 stations are necessary to comprise a meal in lieu of a served meal.

Buffet stations have more than one type of food served at the table. Instead of tediously stretching for miles, interesting buffet table configurations can be designed by your caterer and tastefully decorated by your florist. While many couples think buffets are a cost-saving alternative, they can actually be more expensive than a served meal because portion sizes cannot be controlled, and the food always needs to be replenished to look appealing. It takes time for guests to go through a line and serve themselves, so a double-sided buffet can accommodate more guests. Mirroring the room with buffet tables on each side is necessary for more than 100 guests. This configuration requires more room setup space.

Full-Serve

THE MOST TRADITIONAL wedding meal is the served three-course menu, with a first course, entrée, and dessert. However, the trend is to now start with an *amuse bouche*, which is a bite-sized treat that excites the tongue and delights the eye before the meal is served. The next course can be salad, soup (which is becoming more popular than salad), or perhaps fish. For the entrée, beef and lamb are always popular choices, but you may wish to consider other alternatives based on your personal palate preferences. You can offer your guests a choice of entrée. However, most caterers want to know how many of each kind of entrée to order about two weeks before the wedding. Therefore, you need to ask guests to select their entrée choices in advance on your invitation response card. (See Week 26 for more information on response cards.) For the sky's the limit wedding couple, an "intermezzo course," such as an apple sorbet, is a must! Tiny fruit sorbets, presented in carved ice bowls and often lit from within, make for a very dramatic presentation.

There are a variety of service styles to consider, which affect the price you pay, because they involve differing amounts of labor. Here is a brief rundown of the ways your waiters can do their thing:

- The most common food service in the United States is **American** or **plated**. Found commonly when dining out, the food is plated in the kitchen and placed before the guests. This is the easiest and least expensive way to serve your guests.
- **Butler** service has the appearance of being elegant and expensive, but in reality it controls the food budget. Guests help themselves to individual food items from a platter offered by a server who is circulating the room.
- In **English** service—also known as "family-style," "Chinese," or "what mom did at home growing up"—food is brought to the table on large serving platters or bowls for guest to serve themselves.
- **French** service is labor-intensive, as food is heated and garnished on a cart near the dining table using elegant serving pieces. The food is then plated and served to guests by the waiter.
- With **Russian** service, the food is fully prepared and precut in the kitchen. The server places the proper plate in front of each guest. After the plates are placed, the server returns with a platter of food, and with lots of flair and showmanship, transfers the food from the platter to the guests' plates with a spoon and fork.

What's Hot, What's Cool

IF YOU WANT to incorporate some of the latest trends in food service into your wedding, here are some tips for turning your reception into a festive feast.

SMALLER HORS D'OEUVRES

- One bite, pop them in your mouth, guaranteed not to crumble or dribble
- Food items served in miniature mugs or votive holders
- Silver or edible spoons for presenting hors d'oeuvres
- Food skewered on forks displayed upright as hors d'oeuvre lollipops
- Individual servings in glasses, small bowls, unusual containers

- Soup sips served in a footed shot glass, either butler-passed or at a station

ENVIRONMENTAL CONSCIOUSNESS AND CULINARY RESPONSIBILITY

- artisanal cheeses made in small batches, usually by hand, using traditional methods
- farmstead foods
- organic vegetables
- sustainable fish whose population can support their catch in a safe and legal manner

STRIKING ARCHITECTURAL DISPLAYS OF ICE

- a raw bar of oysters, shrimp, and crab
- beautifully carved ice sculptures, such as a champagne bucket or a monogram of the couple's initials
- a complete bar made of ice with mixers, vodka, and other liquors

INTERNATIONAL NIBBLES

- Today's couples are not only influenced by their own heritage, but they're also adopting other cuisines they love: Spanish, Italian, Indian, Thai, Mexican, Japanese, Chinese, Cajun, Peruvian, Brazilian.
- Fusion cuisine—a blend of ethnic influences, usually two or three cultures combined, such as Asian-Latin. For example, at a recent wedding we had a Wonton Taco Station with a choice of chicken, beef, or soy-glazed vegetables. Each delicate wonton taco shell was filled by a chef and presented on shaved cabbage to the guests.
- If there is a sit-down meal, the ethnic experimentation is usually limited to the hors d'oeuvres, and the entrée is usually a more conventional choice.

Finding a Caterer

BECAUSE A BIG chunk of your total budget will be spent on food, consider your own expectations of the most expensive meal you are about to serve. Is the food simply a matter of function, or do you place a high priority on a dazzling presentation? A skilled caterer is always willing to custom-design a menu to your liking. Gone are the days of cookie-cutter catering, where the bride and groom were required to select package one, two, or three.

If you've selected an on-premise facility for your reception, your decision on a caterer has already been made, and you can skip ahead to the section called "Talking Turkey with the Chef." Otherwise, your reception site may provide you with a list of preferred caterers. This list should include caterers for a range of budgets, not just on the high end. Often, you are required to select a caterer from the venue's list, or you might have a buy-out option, which means if you pay the site a designated fee, you are allowed to bring in your own licensed caterer.

If your venue does not provide helpful catering leads, try the Leading Caterers of America. It is an excellent source to connect with off-premise caterers through the Internet. Go to www.leadingcaterers.com and click on "Find a Caterer." Numerous tips and articles on catering are also posted on this site.

The International Caterers Association is a nonprofit organization dedicated to education in the catering industry. Check out its Web site, www.icacater.org, then e-mail headquarters to obtain information on members near you. Their Web site also features some innovative ideas in food service.

SELECTING A CATERER

RESEARCH ALL THE catering company referrals on the Web first, then narrow down your selections to three caterers that you would actually like to speak with on the phone and eventually meet in person. In your initial phone call, be ready to provide the following information: your wedding date, reception location, time of day, number of guests, and budget.

When you first contact a caterer, ask if he or she has the following credentials:

- a business license
- business insurance
- product liability insurance (protects against claims such as food poisoning)
- worker's compensation insurance

Also ask if the caterer has a liquor license to buy and serve alcohol. If so, it may be most efficient to have this caterer provide both the beverage and food service for your wedding. (Read the next chapter about beverages before making a final decision about this caterer.)

If you decide to proceed with a meeting, ask to speak with the catering sales manager and chef you will be working with on your wedding. You want to look for a number of things:

- Ask to see photos of successful weddings at your reception site as well as food photos. If the caterer has not worked the venue before, make sure the caterer is approved to work there and willing to do a site inspection.
- Note the cleanliness of the caterer's kitchen.
- Always ask for and check references.
- See if a certificate of inspection is placed in the kitchen.

TALKING TURKEY WITH THE CHEF

PREPARE A WRITTEN list of foods you love, foods you do not care for, food allergies, and any religious or dietary concerns you and your guests have. Bring this list to your meeting. Although your menu selection should incorporate your personal tastes, here are things to think about when planning your wedding menu:

- Your food should reflect the degree of formality you want in your wedding, so your selections may vary depending on whether you want country casual, urban chic, or a traditional glittering gala.
- Consider the demographics of your wedding guests when making a menu selection—the average age of your guests, their ethnicity, religion, and where they are from all affect their culinary palates. For example, if you're getting married at a beach resort in California, you should still consider a red meat and potato as an entrée choice if most of your guests are coming from Iowa.
- Avoid hard-to-produce foods, such as soufflés and rare roast beef. Difficult food preparations increase labor costs. The chef should be able to advise you of such situations.
- Select foods that are in season at the time of your wedding. These foods have the added benefit of being less expensive than something that needs to be imported.
- Consider the total balance of the menu for flavors, colors, textures, and shapes. Unless you're having an all-white wedding (which I don't recommend), you probably don't want to serve a white fish with mashed potatoes and cauliflower. Or if you're serving a mini–beef carpaccio crostini for an hors d'oeuvre, you may not want to serve filet of beef as an entrée.
- Ask the chef about his or her personal style, interest, and food strengths and weaknesses. What foods does he or she love to prepare? Want to avoid?

If you feel that a particular caterer is a good match, request a written proposal with a custom-designed menu. Give the caterer the estimated number of guests attending the wedding, based on the "Likely to Attend" column in your guest list spreadsheet. Ask for a separate menu for children 3 to 10 years of age. This will be less costly than an adult meal. All children over 10 typically eat like human vacuum cleaners, so caterers consider them adults for pricing purposes. Eventually, you also need to determine the number of vendor meals to be prepared, but you can provide this estimate later. It will impact your final price but should not affect your choice of a caterer.

Making a Decision

ONCE YOU HAVE received all the proposals you requested, put them in your staging guide under "Caterer." Read all paperwork carefully and do a cost analysis comparing one caterer to the next. You should have no more than three proposals to compare. Here are some things to look for in a proposal and eventually in a catering contract:

- Does the menu appear to be custom designed or a standard banquet menu?
- Does the proposal indicate your correct names, wedding date, setup and break-down times, estimated number of guests, and location of the reception site?
- Are the menu items to your specification? Are there additional fees for ice bars, raw bars, or action stations?
- Is there a separate menu and price for children's meals?
- Is the unit price of each vendor meal indicated (even though you don't yet know the actual number of vendor meals needed)?
- Are standard items included, such as fresh-baked breads, regular and decaffeinated coffee, and herbal tea?
- Is the proposed staffing indicated and does it appear to be sufficient? Typically, you want the following amounts of service personnel:
  - for a plated meal service, 1 server per every 8–10 guests for fine dining, or 1 server per every 16–20 guests for more casual dining
  - 1 chef per action station
  - 1 waiter per every 50 guests for unstaffed buffet tables
- Is the attire specified for the waitstaff? What will they wear—bistro attire, tuxedos, jeans?
- What is the total number of captains, chefs, floor managers, setup crew, and waiters? How many hours are proposed for each?

- Is there a cake-cutting fee? If yes, try to get this fee waived.
- Does the proposal include rental fees for kitchen equipment and rentals for service and kitchen preparation?
- Does the proposal include rental fees for guest tables, chairs, linens, china, flatware, and stemware? If so, make sure that the caterer will allow you to pick out your preferred styles of rental items. (I cover this topic in Week 31.)
- Are the amounts indicated for tax and gratuity/service charges reasonable? Tax and gratuities typically comprise about 20–25 percent of your food bill.

Frequently, a caterer's suggested menu is not perfectly matched to your personal preferences on the first proposal. Don't be afraid to go back to the caterer and request changes to meet your needs. Sometimes, the price of the proposal exceeds the amount you have budgeted. Work with the caterer to identify ways to cut costs without sacrificing those aspects of the food service that are most important to you.

If you're having trouble deciding which caterer to choose, you may wonder whether a tasting can be arranged. According to Bill Hansen, president of the Leading Caterers of America and author of the book *Off-Premise Catering Management,* "Whenever off-premise caterers gather to discuss common needs and problems, the topic of food tastings is one that generates much discussion. Some off-premise caterers allow their prospective clients to taste the food, while others strictly refuse to do so." It is a rare caterer that gives away a free meal. It is very expensive and time-consuming for a caterer to do a tasting. So if you are interested in a tasting, first offer to pay for it. If the caterer does not do tastings as a policy matter, ask if there is an upcoming public event that you may be able to attend and perhaps obtain an extra sampling of something that is being prepared by the caterer.

As part of your signed contract a caterer should offer a trial meal, which is different from a tasting. A trial meal is usually scheduled 2 to 3 months before the wedding and is the actual menu you have selected to serve at your wedding. I discuss the trial meal in Week 39.

Raise the Bar with Beverages

REGARDLESS OF YOUR personal preferences, delectable libations can help foster a festive wedding celebration. Whether you're an East-West fusion couple sipping on saketinis or urban chic newlyweds quaffing Courvoisierpolitans, you want to feature fabulous beverages at your reception.

Nowhere in the rules of etiquette does it say that you *must* serve alcohol. Consider the needs of all your guests and provide beverages that would be appreciated by all. If alcohol is an issue for religious, personal, or health reasons, consider a morning wedding followed by a brunch reception, where alcohol won't be missed.

Whatever you decide to serve, make sure that you host the beverages. A "hosted bar" means that the beverages are being paid for by the host—the couple, the parents, or whoever is picking up the tab for the reception. On the other hand, with a "no-host bar," guests pay individually for drinks they consume. Never under any circumstances ask your guests to buy their own drinks; you wouldn't ask them to pay for their own meal. Since you are hosting, your servers should never put out their hands—or a jar—for tips.

Service with Style

WHEN GUESTS FIRST arrive at a reception, they are primed to party, so the location of the bar is often uppermost on their minds. Rather than having a thirsty throng clamoring for the bartender's attention, you can arrange for a special beverage service that better satisfies the initial demand for liquid refreshment. As your guests enter your cocktail reception area, servers can greet them at the door with trays of beverages. This is a wonderful opportunity to introduce a favorite specialty drink, or you can offer champagne, wine, or sparkling water. (To be politically correct, "Champagne" should be used only to describe sparkling wines produced in the Champagne grape-growing region near Paris. If it's not produced in this region, you're supposed to call it "sparkling wine." But in the interest of simplicity and clarity, I side with the vast majority, who just call all sparkling wines champagne with a small *c*.) Figure on staffing 1 server for every 50 guests for this initial offering.

Of course, not every guest will accept the selection at the door, so you want your regular bar service to be up and running as well. Typically, you want 1 bartender and 1 backup (an assistant) per 75 guests (although you may have fewer people behind the bar at first while the waitstaff is out tray-passing beverages to arriving guests). Position your bars away from the doors and on opposite sides of the room if you need more than one bar. Standard 6-foot and 8-foot rectangular tables can be used for beverage stations and back bars, but other shapes can be much more interesting. If space permits, have a fabulous and very dramatic "bar-in-the-round" by using four curved 7-foot, "serpentine" tables to complete a circle.

If you're having a seated meal, you generally want to offer a poured wine service at the tables. If a guest prefers scotch to chardonnay, the waitstaff should be able to accommodate the situation by bringing the requested drink from the bar. Overall, though, the vast majority of guests will opt for the offered wines.

On and Off

IF YOUR WEDDING reception is at an on-premise facility, the catering staff at the reception site provides your beverage service. If your reception venue is an off-premise site, your caterer may or may not be able to serve alcoholic beverages, depending on its licensing and the liquor laws in your area. You may be faced with any one of three possible scenarios for serving alcoholic beverages at your wedding reception:

• Your caterer does not have a license to buy or serve alcoholic beverages. You must secure the services of a beverage catering company that is specifically licensed to serve alcohol.
• Your caterer has a license both to purchase and serve alcoholic beverages at off-premise locations. You can get competitive price quotes from your caterer as well as beverage catering companies.
• Your caterer is permitted to serve alcoholic beverages but does not have a license to buy or sell them. You can either hire a beverage caterer or purchase your own beverages and deliver them to the caterer. Make sure your caterer has appropriate liability insurance to cover alcoholic beverage service.

Grading the Grog

NOT ALL ALCOHOL is created equal, and whether you're at an on-premise or off-premise location, you usually have a choice of different grades of beverage service. Typically, there are three levels of libations and corresponding prices. The terminology may vary from one location or beverage company to the next, so ask for an explanation and specific examples of liquor choices before making your grade selection.

- **Standard, house, well,** or **moderate** are generic brands of liquor that are economically priced. The standard bar includes scotch, gin, vodka, bourbon, rum, and Canadian whiskey. The standard bar also includes ordinary red and white wines, as well as domestic beers, soft drinks, mixers, and garnishes.
- **Call brands** are medium-priced spirits that guests request by a specific name according to personal preference, as in, "I'll have an Absolut and tonic." The call bar includes every kind of liquor a house bar provides plus one brand each of blended whiskey, rye, brandy, champagne, and imported beers. It may also include at least one or two specialty drinks such as margaritas or daiquiris.
- **Top shelf, premium,** or **super premium** are the most expensive top-of-the-line brands of alcohol that you can serve as long as you are willing to pay the additional costs. These bars typically include such exquisite offerings as single-malt scotches, vintage cognacs, and exceptional liqueurs.

Instead of offering a full bar, you may select a **California bar** (also known as a **soft bar**), which consists of beer, wine, champagne, soft drinks, and juices. In fact, some facilities may not even allow you to serve hard liquor. In either case, choose wisely. Depending on the price of the wines and champagnes selected, a California bar may be no less expensive than a full bar.

Pricing Possibilities

SPEAKING OF MONEY, there are several ways to pay for your beverages. An on-premise facility may give you up to three different options:

- **By the drink**   Liquor or any type of beverage is served and charged by the number of drinks. This is also known as "on consumption."

The bartender keeps track of the number of drinks sold, and the host pays for each beverage served. This option works best if you have invited a light-drinking crowd to your wedding. On average, for a "cocktail hour" preceding a meal, guests consume about 2 drinks per person. For a four-hour cocktail party with hors d'oeuvres and stations only, figure on 4 to 5 drinks per person.

- **By the bottle** Liquor is served and charged by the full bottle. The host pays only for the bottles opened, whether they were poured from or not. The per-bottle method is typically used when poured wine, beer, or champagne is being served. Or perhaps you have a specialty vodka martini bar, where you pay for all the vodka bottles opened. You certainly don't want the bartender or server to open unnecessary bottles. Depending on state liquor codes, the host may have the right to take bottles opened but not completely used. The bottles can be recorked and given to the host upon departure.

- **By the person** The host pays a fixed price for the total number of hours for the reception, or for each hour, whether the guests choose alcoholic beverages or soft drinks. The per-person charge is based on the total number of hours the reception lasts. The longer the reception, the higher the per-person price. This is a good way to go if your guests are big imbibers.

If your reception is at an off-premise site, licensed caterers almost always quote their prices on a by-the-person basis.

BYOB

IF YOU HAVE some particular preferences that do not appear on the beverage menus you're shown, it may be possible for you to buy your own beverages and have them delivered to your reception. However, carefully consider the costs and accompanying hassles before you decide to venture down this road. Below, I present some guidelines to follow and pitfalls to avoid for a variety of situations that you may find yourself in.

CORKAGE FEES

WITH AN ON-PREMISE site, you might have the option to bring in your own wine and champagne for a corkage fee, which is charged on a per-bottle basis. While in theory the corkage fee covers the estimated cost to handle and serve the product, in reality it amounts to a privilege tax assessed for bringing personal liquor into a licensed establishment. The charge usually includes the cost of labor, glassware, and ice for chilling. Corkage fees can range from $5 to $25 per bottle and may be negotiable. It is not always the least expensive way to go (do the math), unless the wine or champagne has been gifted to you, or you happen to own a winery.

BAGGING THE BOOZE

WITH OFF-PREMISE locations, you typically have more freedom to bring in your own libations. However, when buying your beverages, order more than enough, to avoid potential embarrassment. You don't want the best man running off in search of a liquor store in the middle of your reception. When determining appropriate quantities to purchase, consider the drinking habits of your guests, length of your wedding, time of day, and temperature if it is an outdoor wedding reception.

Bill Hansen, president of Leading Caterers of America and author of *Off-Premise Catering Management*, offers the following general recommendations, based on a 4-hour bar service for 100 guests:

Item	Quantity	Unit of Measure
Liquors:		
Scotch	6	Liters
Vodka	6	Liters
Rum	4	Liters
Gin	3	Liters
Blend	3	Liters
Bourbon	3	Liters
Vermouth, sweet	1	Bottle
Vermouth, dry	1	Bottle
Beer, case	2	Cases
Lite beer, case	2	Cases
White wine	24	Bottles
Red wine	8	Bottles
Soft Drinks:		
Cola	14	Liters
Diet cola	11	Liters
7Up	7	Liters
Lemon-lime	7	Liters
Ginger ale	7	Liters
Club soda	9	Liters
Tonic	9	Liters

Item	Quantity	Unit of Measure
Sparkling water	9	Liters
Orange, grapefruit, and cranberry juice	7	Quarts
Garnishes:		
Limes	9	
Lemons	2	
Olive skewers	10	

The table above does not include champagne or dinner wines. For wines served at a sit-down dinner, plan on providing ½ bottle of wine per guest. Champagne quantities can vary considerably, depending on the extent you wish to serve it at your reception. For a single toast, allow 1 bottle of champagne for every 6 adults.

To minimize the hassles of buying your own beverages, try to find a liquor store that will chill your white wines and champagne in advance and then deliver them directly to your reception site on your wedding day. Let the liquor store's employees—not your groomsmen—get sweaty schlepping boxes of booze.

Whether you are purchasing beverages through your caterer or on your own through a beverage outlet, ask if you can return any unopened and undamaged bottles of liquor or wine for a full refund. If this is permissible, inform the caterer that bottles should not be preopened but only as needed. Also, in order to avoid damage to labels on bottles that need chilling, they should not be placed directly on ice but instead kept in a refrigerator if possible.

You certainly don't want to deal with the leftovers on your wedding night, so ask a family member or groomsman to handle this for you. If you want to save any partially opened bottles for future consumption, check your local liquor laws to be sure that these bottles can be legally transported.

Not Your Father's Highball

IF YOU WOULD like to serve some trendy libations at your reception, here are some ideas to consider.

A signature specialty drink is a great way to kick off the reception, and there are myriad possibilities to choose from. But it is best to limit your specialty drink selections to no more than two or three, or they won't be so "special" after all. Design the specialty drink menu to complement the design concept of your wedding. For instance, if cranberry is the color of your day, then perhaps a Red Hot in Rio cocktail made with Rémy Red, Absolut Vanilla, pineapple juice, and pomegranate juice is the drink of choice.

Microbrew beer bars appear to be a winner among the hip drinking crowd. You might also consider serving beers from around the world or those that represent your ethnic heritage. Serve them in Pilsner glasses for a touch of class.

Typically the wines selected for your bar will be different from your dinner wines. Save the best for last. Dinner wines are usually better-quality wines since they are paired correctly with your menu selection. From a New Zealand sauvignon blanc for sea bass to a French Bordeaux for filet of beef, there are a multitude of wines to choose from. Pair your dinner wines after you have made your menu selections. Your catering manager or a local wine shop should be able to assist you with appropriate recommendations.

You may wish to provide after-dinner drinks for your guests from cognac in brandy snifters to Amaretto in cordial glasses. There are a number of ways to spice up your presentation of these beverages: The waitstaff can tray-pass, the classic cordial cart can be wheeled to tables, or a specialty cordial/aperitif bar can open in the club lounge during dancing. Choices include

- cognacs
- cordials
- Amaretto
- Benedictine
- Drambuie
- Galliano
- Grand Marnier
- Sambuca
- Tia Maria

After-dinner specialty stations can also include cappuccino, espresso, and Cuban coffee. A hot cocoa bar is a fun interactive bar for guests to "accent" and create their own style of cocoa with

- Kahlua whipped cream
- shaved Mexican chocolate
- minimarshmallows
- peppermint sticks

When we think of weddings, most of us think champagne. But you certainly don't have to have a champagne fountain flowing all evening to be festive. Consider reserving the bubbly for the best-man and father-of-the-bride toasts. Better yet, butler-pass it as guests gather around you for your toast at the cake-cutting ceremony. If you're having a morning wedding, forgo the full bar and serve mimosas (champagne and orange juice) or bellinis (champagne and peach juice).

Sensible Alcohol Service

I DON'T MEAN to be a party pooper, but as part of our society's increased awareness of the devastating toll that alcohol abuse takes on innocent victims, most states have passed "social host" liquor liability laws. If an intoxicated guest at your wedding injures himself or herself or a third party, the beverage servers and the party host (that's you!) could be named in lawsuits and be liable for a portion of the damages.

There are a number of steps for serving alcoholic beverages responsibly at your wedding and therefore reducing the chances of any legal problems:

- Speak to the owner of the catering company or director of catering to ensure that all waitstaff serving alcohol are briefed on sensible alcohol-serving procedures.
- Do not serve alcohol to minors or to anyone who appears intoxicated.
- Do not pour shooters, slammers, or double-shot drinks.
- Do not give bottles of wine, champagne, or liquor to guests. Pour dinner wines rather than leaving them on the table—this makes for a much more gracious service anyway.
- Close the bar 30 minutes before the wedding is over and serve milk shooters with chocolate chip cookies, or gourmet teas and cappuccino.
- Intoxicated guests should be asked to leave the premises by the catering manager with the support of the wedding host, with supervised transportation arranged.

Make an Appointment with and Choose a Photographer

PRICELESS MOMENTS FROM your wedding will remain with you forever in photographs. In order to capture these perfect images, one of the most important vendor selections you have to make is your photographer. Before you start looking for a photographer for your big day, it is helpful to understand some basic issues about wedding photography, so you can make an informed decision.

Styles of Photography

THERE ARE TWO fundamental styles that wedding photographers employ:

- **Posed** (aka **traditional photography**) The images of the day are orchestrated by the photographer, as subjects are directed to a particular positioning. This style of photography includes formal photos of the bride and groom alone, then together, then with various groups of people such as attendants and parents. It also includes "still life" images of reception room decor, as well as photos of orchestrated events, such as the bride and groom cutting the cake. To put a more modern spin on traditional photography, many photographers place their subjects in settings with interesting backgrounds or lighting. Photos of objects like wedding cakes or floral arrangements are typically taken from unusual angles or vantage points to give them a unique look. Photographers who specialize in posed photos typically take about 500 shots during the course of a wedding.
- **Photojournalism** (aka **documentary photography**) A photojournalist records the wedding day as it unfolds, without directing, coaching, or

prompting any of the participants. While photojournalism may seem passive, it requires that the photographer be constantly alert and prepared, in order to capture the natural, candid images of the day. In the words of Denis Reggie, the nationally renowned photographer who pioneered the style, "The hallmark of the concept is both perspective and attitude, based on a mandate to be truly reactive rather than proactive, and a dedication to record events as historian rather than director." To effectively record the day, photojournalists generally take more photos than traditional photographers—around 1,000 shots during a typical wedding.

For variety, most couples want a mixture of both styles in their wedding album, although they usually prefer one particular style over another. Most photographers specialize in one particular style. When searching for your photographer, match your preference with his or her specialty.

Black and White Versus Color

COUPLES OFTEN DEBATE whether they want color or black-and-white photos of their wedding. Here are some advantages of each:

- **Black and white** For documenting emotional moments of your big day, like the ceremonial kiss or the first dance, black-and-white photography is often preferable. The mood is brought into better focus with black-and-white imagery because there are fewer colors for the brain to process, which draws attention to the subject more effectively.
- **Color** For today's couples, the traditional white wedding has been transformed into a dazzling display of color. All of the vibrant elements of design that you creatively select—flowers, table linens, food presentation, cake—can be captured better in color. Even in dim lighting such as a candlelit setting, color photography can effectively exhibit a warm, romantic feeling.

So which option should you choose for your wedding? Both. To give you a creative variety of images, your photographer should take advantage of the best features of each medium. According to Denis Reggie, a typical ratio for most weddings is about 80 percent color and 20 percent black and white. If your photographer shoots with a digital camera, the decision on how many of each can be postponed until after the wedding. It is a simple matter to convert digital color images into black and white.

The Digital Divide

FILM CAMERAS MAY soon be relegated to museums (alongside record players). But at this time, they are still being used by many professional photographers. In fact, digital photography remains the subject of some debate within the photographic profession. Fans of film insist that it produces a superior quality image, while digital devotees praise the ease of use and flexibility of their high-tech devices.

How does this controversy affect you, the consumer? Very little. The digital cameras used by professional photographers are far more sophisticated than the varieties sold in your local electronics store. Even if film still delivers a higher quality print than digital, we amateurs can't tell the difference (and neither can many professionals). The bottom line is that your choice of a photographer should depend primarily on whether you like his or her work, not what kind of camera is used.

That being said, recent advancements in the area of online viewing and purchasing of wedding photos may tip the balance further to the digital side of the spectrum. Here's how it works: After the wedding, the photographer sets up a secure Web page where the digital wedding images are uploaded. The bride and groom can then go online to select shots to include in their album. Meanwhile, family members and friends can also view these images on their own computers, and they can even order prints of their favorite photos, which are shipped directly to them. With the simplicity and convenience of this method (and the prospect of additional sales for photographers), the popularity of digital photography should continue to increase.

Album Types

A DECADE AGO, wedding albums all looked similar. Most were a collection of sequential images, all similarly laid out with one image per page. While traditional albums certainly still exist, there are many more choices for today's couples. Here is a brief rundown of currently popular options:

- **Library bound**   The classic wedding album. Photographs are individually matted, mounted, then bound as a book with a personally crafted leather cover. This is an expensive but elegant and long-lasting album. The major manufacturers of these albums are Leather Craftsman, Capri, and Zookbinders.

- **Z-page**   Photographs are slid into a page, which forms the border or mat. Each page has steel pins on one edge for snapping into a slotted binding. Most covers are made of simulated leather, the most popular being a product from Art Leather called aristohyde. It is a more economical album than the library-bound style, and it allows pictures to be changed later, but it does not have the luxurious feel of a leather album.

- **Magazine** or **coffee table albums**   These contemporary albums were inspired by graphic design techniques from the publishing industry and made possible with the advent of digital imaging. Instead of using mats, electronic images are laid out and printed directly on photographic paper, which then forms the album page. Each page is essentially an artist's canvas, and the space can be filled with images in any orientation and size. In order for film photographers to provide this style of album, it is necessary for their images to be professionally scanned into a digital format.

- **Custom-matted albums**   This approach combines traditional and contemporary styling. Prints can be laid out on a page in an unlimited variety of artistic arrangements. Using computer-controlled machinery, the album manufacturer then custom-cuts mats to fit the photo layout. Two producers from down under, Jorgensen and Queensberry, are widely used.

Finding Photographers

TO FIND A photographer who's right for you, look in regional and national bridal magazines, not so much for photography ads but for feature stories of real weddings. If you like the accompanying photos, make a note of the photographers—their names always appear in the credits. All magazines employ experienced photo editors who receive hundreds of submissions from photographers. These editors select the best work to showcase in their magazines.

For additional qualified leads, contact the Professional Photographers of America (PPA), a not-for-profit association with 14,000 member photographers. Look for PPA members who have submitted their portfolios and passed rigorous exams for certification. You can call PPA toll-free at 800-786-6277, or visit www.ppa.com.

Once you have a list of prospects, I suggest researching five to ten photographers online initially. After reviewing their work and credentials, call to ask whether the photographer is available for your wedding date. Make an appointment to meet and view the work of at least three photographers, but no more than five.

SELECTING A PHOTOGRAPHER

WHEN VISITING PROSPECTIVE photographers, look at current albums that show wedding coverage from beginning to end. Does the album tell a story? Are the images sharp and clear? Can you notice the fine details on the wedding gown and cake? Or does the photographer simply pass it off as soft-focus when it's really out of focus? Check out the style of gowns and men's clothing. Nothing gives away a dated album more than wedding attire.

To get the best insight into the photographer's relative expertise with photojournalism versus posed photos, ask to see a completed book of proofs. This is the collection of images that the photographer sends to the couple so that they can select photos for their album. If the proofs are posted online, ask to view them there. If the photographer says he or she is a photojournalist, but you see mostly posed pictures, it's a red flag.

Ask if the photographer has worked at your ceremony and reception site before. If not, ask what he or she typically does to prepare for a site that he or she has not previously worked at. Also, if you're getting married in a house of worship, there may be strict written guidelines that the photographer must follow. Take these rules seriously and don't mess with the church lady.

Here are a few more questions to ask during the interview process:

- How did you get started in photography?
- What formal training and education do you have?
- How long have you been photographing weddings?
- How do you typically dress for a wedding?
- What equipment do you use? What type of backup equipment do you have?
- Do you work alone, or do you have any assistants? Do your assistants take photographs also, or do they just carry and position your equipment? If they photograph, what are their credentials and training?
- How many photos do you typically take at a wedding?
- If a guest wants to take a shot of the same posed photo you are shooting, is that acceptable?
- What kinds of albums do you offer? Can we see samples of each?

- How long does it usually take after the wedding before proofs are ready? Once images are selected for an album, how long does it take to produce the album?
- What is your policy regarding copyrights and our personal use of your images? (For film photographers: What is your policy regarding negatives?)
- What backup arrangements do you have in case you have a crisis on the day of the wedding and can't show up?

Finally, ask for references and talk to other brides and grooms to find out how the photographer treated the wedding party and guests throughout the wedding.

ONE COUPLE'S STORY

Eileen and Tony from Connecticut decided to trim their expenses by selecting a photographer who worked for a local newspaper. Although he was a good photojournalist for the newspaper, weddings were outside his area of expertise. He was inexperienced at positioning people for group photos and was unprepared to photograph key moments during the reception, like the best man's toast, the first dance, and the cake cutting. As a result, Eileen and Tony ended up with few good photos.

You have only one chance to get it right on your big day, so be sure to hire a professional photographer who is experienced with weddings.

Contract Terms

ONCE YOU HAVE identified your preferred photographer, you need to sign a contract to secure his or her services. The contract should contain the following information:

- Arrival time, length of shooting time, fees, and overtime charges
- Name of the professional whose work the bride has seen and who will photograph the wedding
  - number of assistants
  - attire to be worn
- Number and kind(s) of cameras to be used
  - equipment on site

- in the event of equipment failure, a guarantee that a backup camera will be on hand
- name of an acceptable substitute in case of emergency
- Approximate number of pictures to be taken
  - if film, approximate number of rolls of color and black and white to be shot
- Number of proofs you'll receive, and complete package details
- Date your proofs will be ready and how long you can keep them
- Album(s) to be provided
  - number of leafs or sides
  - delivery times
- Rights of ownership and reproduction
  - if film, length of time photographer keeps negatives
- Policy on ordering of reprints and unit prices for extra albums, prints, etc.
- Price
  - detailed cost of specific coverage
  - cost of album(s)
  - overtime fee, if applicable
  - whether sales tax is added to the entire order
  - deposit and payment schedule

The typical price for a professional photographer ranges from $3,000 to $15,000. The price you pay depends on the experience of the photographer, the length of time he or she is at your wedding, and the number and style of albums you want.

For Brides on a Budget

For many weddings, the cost of photo albums represents a substantial portion of the photographer's total price. Instead of purchasing large albums for both yourselves and your parents, consider smaller "parent albums." Or purchase just a few prints for your parents, which can be framed and hung on a wall.

If money is really tight, you can just purchase digital images from your photographer on a CD, then make your own album. You can construct and order your own albums online at www.mypublisher.com. Alternatively, you can hold onto the CD until you have replenished your piggy bank, then get your album professionally printed.

Wedding photography is both an art and a science, requiring someone with the proper skills and equipment, as well as the disposition to remain calm, cheerful, and creative under pressure. In making a final decision on a photographer, carefully consider how much you love the person's work as well as the price quoted. Most important, select someone you trust and feel comfortable with. You should genuinely enjoy the company of your chosen photographer because he or she will be with you all day long and, of course, you want to be smiling for the camera.

Research and Select a Videographer

THE ART AND science of wedding memory preservation has taken a giant leap forward in recent years, due in large part to major technological advances in the field of videography. Long gone are the gigantic cameras with glaring headlamps and recorded tapes resembling a home movie from your father's camcorder. Today, using digital video cameras and computer-based editing techniques, the professional videographer can create a wonderfully entertaining, personalized, Hollywood-quality movie. As the stars of the show, your script simply reads, "Enjoy your wedding celebration!"

Videography Styles

LIKE PHOTOGRAPHY, THERE are two basic styles that videographers use. Unlike photography, the two videography styles are related not to how the wedding day is shot, but rather the way the video is subsequently edited.

- A **documentary style** video presents the wedding-day activities in the sequence they occurred and requires minimal to moderate editing. Typically, the shots in a documentary video include the couple getting ready for the wedding, the ceremony and reception, and interviews of people close to the couple. The finished piece runs about 2 hours in length, with a 10- or 15-minute summary, also known as a recap, at the beginning or end.
- **Cinematic style** videography utilizes artistic and thoughtful editing to portray a moving story of the wedding day through images and sounds. The most beautiful images are selected, and effects such as slow motion, black and white, sepia tones, and dissolves are added to enhance the mood. Video clips may be taken out of order and emphasized to focus on the emotion of the day. Two cameras are usually used to show the wedding festivities from different vantage points,

which adds drama and excitement to the edited piece. The finished product typically runs 30 minutes to 1 hour, and it looks and feels like a movie.

In comparing these two styles, it is interesting to note an apparent paradox: The shorter the finished video, the more editing required to produce it. While a documentary video is lengthier, it is cheaper because it requires less of the videographer's time after the wedding day. On the other hand, cinematic-style videos can require anywhere from 30 to more than 100 hours of editing time. Therefore, this type of video takes longer to produce, and consequently it is more expensive.

The real bottom line is that a cinematic video is much more enjoyable to watch. You will probably want to invite friends and relatives over, break out the popcorn, then sit back and be entertained by the way the videographer has artfully captured your special day. And you will want to watch the video over and over again in the years to come.

Technical Stuff

BEFORE YOU BEGIN checking out videographers to hire for your wedding, it is important to have a basic understanding of the equipment that is now being used to create top-quality videos. Make sure that the videographers you consider are keeping up with the times.

CAMERAS

ALL PROFESSIONAL-GRADE VIDEO cameras are now digital, and made by Canon, JVC, Sony, or Panasonic. Central to the operation of the camera are three electronic chips, which turn the subject matter into digitally recorded video images. In contrast, most camcorders sold to the general public have only one chip, and the resulting quality is much lower.

Another important feature of a professional video camera is its lux rating. Lux is a measure of how much light the camera needs to operate properly. A lower rating is better, because it means less light is required. A professional-quality camera should have a rating of less than 5 lux, preferably in the range of 1 to 2 lux.

MICROPHONES

RECENT ADVANCEMENTS IN microphones have made it possible for the sounds of your ceremony to be clearly, yet unobtrusively, recorded. Tiny wireless UHF (ultrahigh frequency) microphones smaller than an earring can be discreetly clipped to your groom, your officiant, and the podium where your readers are situated. The best wireless systems have diversity transmitters and receivers, a technology that ensures you get clear, uninterrupted sound.

The video camera itself comes with a built-in microphone, but most videographers choose to replace it with a shotgun microphone to improve audio reception. Standard handheld microphones are typically used for recording musicians and interviewing your guests. Finally, be aware that microphones are extremely sensitive to air movement, so if you're having an outdoor wedding, make sure your videographer uses windscreens to reduce the wind noise.

EDITING

TODAY, ALL PROFESSIONAL videographers digitally edit their recordings using computer software programs, instead of the old, cumbersome, tape-based editing equipment. This computerized method of editing is also referred to as "nonlinear editing."

More than any other digital development, nonlinear editing has enabled the cinematic style of video to flourish. Editing software allows professional videographers to push the envelope in creating beautiful, entertaining movies. In so doing, they are spending more time on the editing process. As a result, while the quality of the finished product has significantly increased, so has the price. As the saying goes, you get what you pay for.

THE FINISHED PRODUCT

AS THE FINAL part of a completely digital production process, the DVD has replaced VHS as the end product for your wedding video. Since your video images have been captured and edited with digital equipment, they can be directly transferred onto a DVD with minimal loss of quality.

DVDs also offer greater convenience, because you can jump forward or backward on a DVD instantly at the touch of a button. To take advantage of this feature, most professional videographers create a customized selection of chapters for your video. When you load the DVD into a player, a creatively designed menu pops up, showing the various chapters, allowing you to cut right to a key moment, such as the exchange of vows or the cake cutting.

THE NEXT DEVELOPMENT

THE NEWEST TECHNOLOGICAL trend in videography is high-definition (HD) video, which delivers even clearer, more lifelike images. To take advantage of this development, manufacturers of professional video cameras are now selling HD cameras, but their lux ratings are not as good as regular digital cameras. You can buy HD televisions and HD-DVD players as well, but since the technology is new, they are still very expensive and not widely used. However, prices of high-tech devices typically start falling as they gain wider acceptance into the marketplace. So by the time you're reading this, you may already own an HD video system. If that is the case, you may want to look for a videographer who can shoot your wedding in HD format.

HELPFUL HINTS

In addition to having your videographer cover the wedding day, you may want to consider a custom-produced "Love Story Video" (also called a "Reflections Video" or "Concept Video"). This short video tells the story of how you both met and fell in love, and it is usually created in advance of the wedding so you can play it for your guests on your wedding day (during the cocktail reception is usually the best time).

Another popular selection of video entertainment on your wedding day is the "instant replay." After shooting the ceremony, your videographer plays it back on a television monitor at the reception for your guests' enjoyment. It is especially appreciated by those guests who were unable to get to the church on time.

Finding a Videographer

MANY PROFESSIONAL VIDEOGRAPHERS belong to the Wedding and Event Videographers Association (WEVA). Go to their Web site, www.weva.com, and click on "Find a Videographer" for a form you can fill out for referrals in your area. The Professional Videographer Association of America also has a Web site, www.pva.com, that provides listings and links to regional chapters across the country.

Also, check with your ceremony and reception sites to see if they have any referrals on videographers; it may be to your advantage if the videographer has worked at the location before and is familiar with its layout. Ask your photographer for referrals as well. Since your photographer and videographer often want to capture the same images and moments of your wedding with their cameras, it is important that they respect each other and enjoy working together.

MEETING AND SELECTING VIDEOGRAPHERS

AFTER YOU HAVE compiled a list of prospects, check their Web sites for more information. (If you have high-speed Internet access, many videographers have sample streaming video clips you can view online.) Then call to see whether they are available on your wedding date. Set up appointments with your top two or three choices and ask to meet with the person who will actually be shooting the wedding.

Before you go to your appointments, think about the amount of video coverage you would like, so you can obtain comparable price quotes. Do you want the videographer present with two cameras for the entire day through the cake cutting (that is usually about 8 hours), or can you afford only one camera for a shorter duration? Do you want additional coverage, such as the rehearsal dinner, or special services like the Love Story or instant replay? Depending on the specific services you want, the fee for a professional videographer typically ranges between $1,500 and $15,000.

When you meet with a prospective videographer, ask if you can borrow a copy of an entire wedding DVD (not just a brief demo), preferably made by the same people who would be shooting and editing your wedding. That way, you can get an accurate understanding of the videographer's capabilities and style, and the quality of work you would actually receive.

Also inquire about the videographer's editing personnel. While some videographers send their work out to be edited, it is best to hire a company that does its own editing on premises, because it will have a better understanding of your needs, as well as the means to correct any problems right away.

In evaluating a video, Chuck and Jewel Savadelis, owners of Savadelis Films in Sunnyvale, California, recommend that you consider the following top ten questions:

1. Is the focus sharp?
2. Is the exposure level appropriate (not too dark or too light)?

3. Is the color consistent?
4. Is the camera steady?
5. Is the sound clear?
6. Is the picture composed from a good vantage point and beautiful to look at?
7. Are the images arranged to tell an interesting story rather than appearing to be randomly placed in a moving slide show?
8. Does the tone of the music match the feeling of the images?
9. Are the images cut to the beat of the music?
10. Are special effects tastefully used, and do they contribute to the story?

After you have met with each prospective videographer, looked carefully at their work, and obtained price quotes, you're ready to make a final decision. The videographer you choose should prepare a written contract that lists in detail the specific coverages and products you want. When you sign the contract, you need to give the videographer a deposit (usually 50 percent).

Securing the services of a videographer is the best way to capture the sights, sounds, motion—and most important, the emotion—of your wedding. If a picture is worth a thousand words, then a professional quality video of your special day is surely worth a million.

Find a Florist

FINDING THE PERFECT florist to translate your visions into reality should be fun. Look for floral designers who understand your concepts and who can thread your vision throughout every element of design, from ceremony through the last dance.

More than any other vendor you hire, your florist is instrumental in ensuring that everything you have envisioned for your perfect day comes to fruition. There is no better way to stamp your personalities on your wedding than through details of decor that give your big day a distinctive look.

If you haven't already done so, thumb through your favorite bridal magazines for floral ideas. Clip photos you like and group them together by category: bouquets, boutonnieres, ceremony decor, cake decor, table settings, and so on. Place the photos in your staging guide under "Flowers."

How to Use Flowers at the Ceremony and Reception

FLORAL DESIGNERS TAKE their lead from trendy fashion designers. Hot-hued colors are replacing all-white bouquets. No longer are you required to be married to just one or two "wedding colors." In fact, if you selected only chocolate and pink for your entire wedding, the decor would be completely predictable by the time guests arrived at the reception dinner. Instead, keep your guests guessing. Select one color scheme for your ceremony, a different look for your cocktails, and yet another for your reception. Think of your wedding like decorating your home. You wouldn't use the same two colors throughout the entire house, would you?

Like fashion, colors come and go. However, the tradition of having personal flowers is here to stay. Personal flowers are those that are carried or worn by you, your attendants, immediate family members, readers, or anyone else you wish to honor at your wedding.

BOUQUETS

JUST LIKE A clothing accessory, the bridal bouquet should convey importance and make a statement that complements the overall look of the wedding. From cascading variegated lavender to rhinestone-studded broache bouquets, posh trends give way to the tradition to have, hold, and toss. Generally, the bridal bouquet should enhance the beauty of the wedding gown without dominating it. The bouquet should be proportionately sized to the height and shape of the blushing bride. The bolder bride may choose to make a bigger statement with a bountiful bouquet. Whatever style you choose, place importance on the design and color and not on every individual flower, since some flowers may not be in season on your wedding date.

Bridesmaids' bouquets no longer have to be minicopycats, with a scaled-down version of the big sister bridal bouquet. Each bridesmaid's bouquet can be uniquely her own, not repeating the same design, as long as palettes of colors and/or ribbons complement each other.

Bouquets are typically made in one of three ways:

- Every flower is **individually wired** and taped, so that the flowers can be bent and manipulated into design shapes. This is a more traditional, expensive, and time-consuming method.
- A commercial wedding **bouquet holder** consists of a plastic cage of wet foam and a plastic handle. Every stem must be inserted deeply into the form to stay.
- To create a **hand-tied bouquet,** stems are braided together in a spiral pattern, then bound with floral tape and ribbon where the hand grasps the stems.

Over the years, styles of bouquets—from the ballerina bouquet to the sheaf bouquet—have come and gone, but a few remain persistently popular:

- **Biedermeier** Features concentric rings of varied colors or blooms. Each ring is a single type of blossom.
- **Cascade** A large formal and traditional bouquet, tear-shaped, in which the flowers descend in a cascade of blooms below the main portion of the design.

- **Composite** A hand-tailored bouquet created by reassembling hundreds of real petals of the same flowers, then wiring them together to look like one huge flower.
- **Nosegay** A small, round, fragrant bouquet of mixed flowers, approximately 16 to 18 inches in diameter.
- **Pomander** Single flowers or multifloral clusters connected together to form a ball shape, suspended from a ribbon.
- **Posy** A petite bouquet, smaller than a nosegay, with larger flowers massed in the center and small filler flowers completing the edge of the bouquet.
- **Presentation** (aka **arm bouquet**) Long-stemmed flowers carried in the fold of the arm.
- **Round** Larger than a nosegay, round in outline, and mound-shaped on top.
- **Tussy mussy** A small posy is anchored in a silver cone-shaped holder dating from the Victorian age.

TO HAVE AND TO HOLD

WHEN YOU'RE WALKING down the aisle, remember that your bouquet is not a lollipop! Nothing ruins the details of a beautiful dress more than holding your bouquet at your chest. Instead, relax your shoulders and drop your arms and hands to the side. Now place your elbows alongside your hipbones, holding the stems of the bouquet in front of you by your belly button. Keep your elbows close to your body without raising your shoulders. There is no need to lock arms with anyone escorting you. Simply have him support your arm.

NAMING NAMES

HAVE THE FLORIST label the first name, last name, and role on each individual person's flower, not just "groomsmen" or "bridesmaids" (e.g., Andrew Carter, Best Man). It expedites a smooth distribution and there should be no missing boutonnieres or bouquets because the florist miscounted. All recipients appreciate knowing that a particular floral design is theirs.

WOMEN OF HONOR

TODAY, MOTHERS OF the bride and groom are choosing an array of styles and fabrics for their attire that are sophisticated and glamorous, taking an important role next to the couple. Correspondingly, they choose their flowers carefully to reflect their style, or sometimes forgo flowers altogether. For those who do select flowers, a posy bouquet (smaller than a bridesmaid's) is the preferred choice over ruining gorgeous fabrics with pinholes. (To free up her hands for hugging and having a cocktail, your wedding planner or a family member should take the posy from Mom upon her arrival at the reception and put it beside her place setting to enjoy throughout the evening.) If a posy is not selected, and a traditional corsage is preferred, ask your florist to use magnets to secure it, not pins. Another option to consider is a wrist bracelet.

MEN OF THE HOUR

MEN, TOO, CAN flirt with fashion as they eagerly await the pinning moment to receive their accessory, the boutonniere (French for "buttonhole"). Today's adornments can be made from unexpected materials such as feathers, grasses, and pods. To wrap the stems of the boutonniere, masculine elements such as leather or suede ribbon can also be used. With the gentlemen standing tall and handsome, boutonnieres are pinned on the left lapel from underneath using an ordinary corsage pin, so that the pin does not show. Or completely do the opposite and add a touch of style with a colored, jeweled antique stickpin.

Not all boutonnieres need to be the same. In fact, to distinguish the groom from the groomsmen and fathers and others, each grouping of gentlemen should have their own unique showpiece. What does need to be equal is lasting endurance. Select flowers, herbs, plants, berries that will pass the hugging test. The florist should have an extra boutonniere or two on hand just in case they don't all pass the test.

LITTLE LADIES AND GENTLEMEN

WHETHER THEY'RE BEDECKED with wreaths, pomanders, or baskets, flower girls relish their experience of a lifetime to share your moment. These adornments, especially head wreaths, should be appropriately designed to the size of the child, to make sure they are not too heavy or bothersome. Not required, but oh so darling, the ring bearer carries the rings on a pillow or box designed from fabrics and florals. Actually, it's advisable to have symbolic rings tied to the pillow or box and let the best man be responsible for the real ones.

CEREMONY FLOWERS

CONSIDER THE VISUAL aspect of your ceremony site from the guests' point of view. First impressions count. If you have selected a house of worship, no matter how ornate, greeting your guests with a garland on the railing leading up the stairs or floral wreaths on the doors certainly makes a warm and welcoming statement. Inside the hallowed halls, it is often dimly lit, so the altar or bimah decor should be large with bright, bold hues, to be seen from a distance and create focal points.

If your ceremony is nestled among grapevines, overlooking the ocean, or in some other natural outdoor setting, you don't need to compete with Mother Nature. Let the beautiful views be seen. However, if you don't have the perfect backdrop, look for focal points such as a majestic tree, a beautiful hedge of roses, or a stone wall to define your ceremony area. Or consider a canopy of fabric and florals, under which your ceremony takes place. This is actually a Jewish wedding tradition (called a chuppah), but couples of every faith are now adopting this custom into their own weddings.

No matter where your nuptials are taking place, here are decorating options to consider:

- garland along railings, or blooming plants along entry stairs or sidewalks
- front door treatments
- floral arches at the entrance to the ceremony area, or as an altar for outdoor ceremonies
- floral treatments attached to every 2 to 3 rows of pews or chairs, or in the aisle adjacent to the pews or chairs
- hand-painted, custom-designed aisle runners or banners
- altar arrangements
- votive candles or candelabras
- entry statues or baptismal areas
- fireplaces, mantels, windowsills

Reusing ceremony flowers at the reception is a nice idea in theory, but it works only under certain conditions. The complete wedding party and guests must vacate the ceremony site so that the florist can return to transport flower arrangements to the reception site. The transporting of arrangements should be considered only if guests cannot see this activity—in other words, if your dining area is located away from the cocktail reception and has a separate entrance. Altar arrangements can be repositioned at dance floor corners and pew decor can be repositioned at the backs of chairs. Evaluate the fees for the florist to transport these items before making final decisions.

THE RECEPTION

THE MAJORITY OF your flower budget should be spent at the reception—after all, this is where the party begins, and you'll be spending the most time here. The areas that you want to decorate are the main entry, an escort card/guest book table, cocktail tables, food stations, buffets, bars, dining tables, cake table, dessert stations, restrooms, and dance areas.

Following months of planning, the dining area is always my all-time favorite space to unveil the drama of a wedding with spectacularly designed tablescapes. Long gone are the days of total uniformity. Instead, tables and floral arrangements of various sizes, shapes, and heights take center stage. Floral "centerpieces" don't even need to be positioned in the center of a table but can be a composite grouping of containers. Think balance, scale, and proportion with the size of your tables and rooms. Mix low floral designs with tall taper candles and high arrangements with candles at the base.

Locating a Florist

ONE OF THE best places to find floral designers is through the American Institute of Floral Designers. Membership in AIFD is selective. To be accepted, a member must demonstrate advanced floral design abilities. Visit AIFD's Web site, www.aifd.org, and fill out the online form to get a list of members in your area. Also check out the floral arrangements in the lobbies of top hotels near you. If the arrangements speak to you, ask the concierge for the name and number of the florist.

Identify five florists to research initially and review their work on the Web. Look for florists who have experience doing weddings, which is very different from running a retail flower shop. Many of the best wedding floral designers do not have retail shops but instead have studios or warehouses where they exclusively design for weddings and special events.

Next, call the florists that interest you to see if they are available on your wedding date. They will want to know the location of your ceremony and reception, the total number of guests, the number of people who will receive personal flowers, and your approximate budget. As you engage in a conversation, ask yourself if they appear interested and knowledgeable. After your initial phone calls, pick three florists you would like to meet with personally, then make appointments.

The Consultation

FOR THE INITIAL appointment, bring your staging guide, and make sure it contains the following information:

- magazine clippings of floral designs you like (also make a list of any flowers you don't like)
- pictures and/or fabric swatches of your gown and bridesmaids' dresses
- a list of everyone who will receive personal flowers (provide their first and last names, as well as their role in the wedding)
- a sketch of the design you have developed for your save-the-date card or invitation (or an actual copy of the card, if it's available)
- pictures of the ceremony and reception sites

During the interview, look carefully at the floral designer's portfolios. Examine the use of colors, groupings, textures, and any unusual treatments in the design work. Does the portfolio demonstrate a style of design you are attracted to?

Here are some questions to ask the florist:

- What do you believe are your greatest design strengths? Is it groupings of color? Are you contemporary, traditional, avant-garde, or FTD?
- What current floral trends and new flower varieties could you incorporate in my wedding?
- Can you work with my budget? (Be realistic. Don't ask for $15,000 worth of flowers if your budget is $2,500. These are artists, not magicians!)
- Have you worked at my ceremony and reception site before? If not, are you willing to do a site inspection before submitting a proposal?
- Do you own an inventory of canopies, containers, table linens, candles, aisle runners, and props? If not, who will arrange for rentals?
- Who will actually design my bouquets and centerpieces? Who will be there the day of the wedding to set up? When will you return to the site to tear down?
- How long will it take for you to generate a proposal? (Understand that a designer's ideas are intellectual property, and if you are asking

for specific written design concepts for your wedding, there may be a consulting fee charge.)

The Proposal/Contract

EACH PROPOSAL YOU receive should contain a detailed description of flowers and designs to be provided by the florist. In some instances, sketches or photos should be included as well. Once you have received the floral proposals you have requested, ask yourself the following questions as you review them:

- Did the florist generate creative ideas from my magazine photos and theme?
- Can the floral designer translate my style and vision into workable floral designs within my budget?

If you are unfamiliar with the description of some of the flowers described in the proposals, you can find photos of most flowers on the Society of American Florists' Web site, www.aboutflowers.com, or the California Cut Flower Commission's Web site, www.ccfc.org.

The floral proposal should also include a breakdown of quantities and prices of bouquets, boutonnieres, centerpieces, rental items, and so on, plus delivery/on-site installation and tax. Do a detailed cost analysis of the proposals. Then decide which florist you would like to work with, based on his or her creativity and cost. You can always ask the florist to revise a proposal before you accept it, but never shop one floral proposal against another.

Request a contract from the florist, sign it, and send it back to the florist with the requested retainer fee (typically 50 percent of the total amount). The contract should include your name, date of wedding, times and locations of delivery, and setup. It should also contain a detailed description, photos and/or sketches of flowers, with prices and quantities of bouquets, boutonnieres, centerpieces, delivery, tax, cost of rental items and replacement cost on rentals in case of damage or lost items. The name and cell phone number of the person who will oversee the installation should also be specified.

For Brides on a Budget

A lavish floral display at your wedding could easily cost $20,000 or more. If you're trying to keep your costs down, I recommend using large groupings of leaves, candles, fruits, herbs, vegetables, seashells, ribbons, and other non-floral materials to enhance your decor—especially as centerpieces. Seasonal decorations such a gourds and pumpkins in fall, Christmas greens for the holidays, or potted plants for the spring are less expensive than flowers that need to be processed and arranged.

Another way to save is to avoid wedding dates when flowers and florists are in high demand, such as Valentine's Day.

Ultimately, floral designs can express your wedding vision more dramatically and enhance the beauty of your celebration more effectively than any other element of your wedding. Therefore, select a florist whose style you love and whom you can trust to make your wedding spectacular.

Decide on Music for the Reception

WHAT DO YOU want guests to experience and say about your wedding reception? It was "on fire," exhibited "edited elegance," or had that certain "cha-cha-cha"? Your day will go by in a flash, so savoring every moment is important. Whatever you want to hear, one thing is crystal clear: Your choice of reception music sets the tone of your wedding.

Styles of Music

NO TWO BANDS or DJs are the same, which is why it's important to define your music style at least six months before your wedding and before you begin your search for the perfect beat. I know you have your heart set on the music you love, but do remember that several generations will be represented at your reception. Make your music selections so that everyone crowds the dance floor, not just a handful. As the evening progresses, the golden oldies in your group may retire for the evening, so the tone of the music can get more contemporary.

Consider the following suggestions from Peter Berliner, owner of Innovative Entertainment in San Francisco:

- Make your wedding truly an elegant affair with the sounds of the big band era. Focus on classic standards, including dancing to fox-trots, waltzes, tangos, and cha-chas. If you hire a big-band orchestra, many of these groups can also play Motown, fifties rock and roll, and rhythm and blues.
- Whether it's called swing, jazz, jump or zoot suit, upbeat sounds made famous by Count Basie, Benny Goodman, Louis Prima, Duke Ellington, and Big Bad Voodoo Daddy get the joint jumping.
- Latin music is a diverse cornucopia of rhythm and sound, from cool jazz to spicy salsa, from a traditional mariachi band to the hip Cuban

style of the Buena Vista Social Club. This style definitely adds flavor and fun to your reception.

- From old-time country to contemporary country hits, down-home tunes from artists like Little Texas, Shania Twain, and Reba McEntire offer a surefire way to get those boots a-stompin'!

Your Reception Music Program

IT'S ALSO IMPORTANT to think about the flow of your reception and the type of music to go with each segment—i.e., first the cocktail hour, perhaps a dinner dance, then after-dinner dancing.

COCKTAIL TEMPO

YOUR COCKTAIL MUSIC should begin before the first guests arrive for the cocktail hour. The sound alone welcomes guests into the space for cocktails and lets the celebration begin. Since everyone is on a congratulatory high note, dispense with the solo musician. He or she will never be heard. Whether it's a duo, trio, or quartet of musicians, amplification is a must at this point. Typically, ceremony musicians differ from cocktail musicians, especially if your ceremony site is at another location from your reception site. Your cocktail musicians will probably play more upbeat, fun music and could possibly be a smaller subset of your reception musicians—or, if the budget allows, something totally different.

Here are some trendy ideas for cocktail musicians:

- a cappella group
- three strolling violins
- jazz trio or quartet
- barbershop quartet
- rhythmic gospel group
- French or Italian accordion players
- klezmer band
- multiethnic vocal or instrumental groups
- steel drums playing reggae music
- country fiddlers

During cocktails or for your after-dinner party, you might also want to consider adding a new dimension to your wedding with zany entertainers:

- gravity-defying jugglers
- spectacular costumed characters
- astonishing illusionists
- balloon animals or face painting for the kids
- a professional caricaturist to draw your guests and capture their likeness to take home as a wedding favor
- a "cigarette girl" with a box full of candy treats to pass out to your guests
- psychics, fortune-tellers, and tarot card readers to delight your wedding guests with good luck

SHOW TIME

IMMEDIATELY FOLLOWING THE cocktails, the banquet staff graciously invites your guests into the main reception area. Before the doors open, make sure your music—whether a band or DJ—is ready to strike the chord. As guests enter the room, music should be playing. Usually the type of music selected when the doors open helps create the right mood. If it is background music, guests immediately go to their tables.

One of my brides decided to have dancing before dinner, and the doors opened to "La Bamba." As guests entered the main reception room, everyone immediately hit the dance floor. It was an amazing sight to see! We couldn't get the guests off the dance floor for dinner because they were having such a fabulous time. When the catering staff was ready for dinner, I finally asked the orchestra to play something totally unrecognizable. That got everyone to their seats so the first course could be served.

Don't be upset if your guests want to dance before your first dance. Give your guests permission to have a great time at your wedding and let them dance. If you decide to have a dinner dance between the courses, you can start your first dance after all the guests are seated. You can be announced and go immediately to the dance floor for your first dance. Or if dancing is taking place in a separate area, you can have your first dance right after dinner.

Overall, one of the key decisions you need to make is when you want to have dancing, relative to the meal service. If you decide to have dancing before and during the meal, you can time the dance sets in between each course (please refer to the timeline in Week 47). Or you can save all the dancing for after the meal, perhaps in a seperate room with a night club motif.

Live Versus Recorded Music

THE NEXT MAJOR musical decision you need to make is whether you want your music to be provided by a live band or a disc jockey (DJ).

There are pluses and minuses for having a band. If you are looking for animation and live energy that fills the entire room, and you love the idea of a live performance, hands down it's a band. Whether it's a local doo-wop group or an electrifying dance band, there's nothing like a live performance to get your group stoked. From my experience and observations, here's the real bottom line: With a live band, more of your guests will dance. Even guests who stay glued to their seats all night would rather watch live musicians play than stare at a DJ's mixer board.

If you love everything from cutting-edge house and hip-hop music to Top 40s and classic oldies, then perhaps it's Dr. Spin for you. According to Dan Ohrman, general manager of Denon & Doyle Entertainment in Pleasant Hill, California, couples usually choose DJs in the following situations:

- DJs can cost a lot less than a live band. Rates for a DJ vary greatly across the United States, ranging from $600 to $3,500, with an average of $1,200 for a 4-hour booking. (Local bands, on the other hand, typically charge anywhere from $2,000 to $12,000, depending on their size and skill. Groups with a national "name" can run much higher.)
- If current music selections are at the top of your list, and you are set on hearing your favorite music exactly the way you've grown to love it, then a DJ is your answer.
- If you are looking for a "master of ceremonies" and a ringleader of the other vendors, some DJs can provide this service.

Tuning in to a Band

IF YOU DECIDE to go with a band, the best way to select one is by word of mouth from family or friends who danced the night away at a recent party or wedding. Your reception site may also have a list of referrals, and certainly other wedding vendors that you have secured— especially your wedding planner, videographer, or photographer—can make recommendations. Visit local nightclubs and ask the musicians on stage for their business cards. You can also call music agencies, or check out the Web site for the American Federation of Musicians, www.afm.org (click on "Find a Local").

Once you have a list of at least five possible bands, contact each band leader and ask for a presentation demo package. The package should include a CD, bio, photo of the band, play list, and testimonial letters. Look at the printed material carefully to see whom they have played for and where and what kind of music they list, and listen to the CD. The venues where the band has played are a good indicator of the band's level of professionalism.

If it all adds up, make it a point to see, hear, and talk to the band leader and members in person. Even if you are working with an agent, ask to hear and see the band play before hiring them. Not only listen to the sound of the band, but also pay close attention to their sense of timing and stage presence, and how they interact with the crowd.

Hire a band whose personality and musical taste correspond to yours. Always make sure that the musicians you meet will actually be playing at your wedding. Get their names and the instruments they play, and have that put in writing in your contract. Musicians have a tendency to jam around with other groups and substitute one musician for another, so be sure the band you saw and heard is the band that will play at your wedding. Remember, the band is providing an extremely important service. It can make or break the party atmosphere, and you don't want any divas or frustrated rock stars spoiling your reception.

Your contract with a band should include the following:

- Name, address, and contact phone numbers of music provider and purchaser
- Date, arrival time, setup time, performance time, and departure time
- Venue location name and address
- Names of all the members of the band, what instruments they play, and vocalists. (If one of the performers is unable to keep his or her contractual obligation, you must be informed immediately and approve any substitutes.)
- Hourly fee and overtime rates
- Number and length of the breaks, and specify the band break area
- Whose responsibility it is for needed equipment, electrical power, staging, dance floor, and lighting
- Attire that will be worn by performers and sound or lighting technicians. (Say no to "additional staff support," such as groupies or girlfriends!)
- Payment terms
- Cancellation policy

- Liability insurance coverage
- Responsibility for parking
- Provisions for meals and beverages. (There should be no alcohol allowed! After all, who else gets to drink on the job?)

HELPFUL HINTS

There is no set rule for the number of musicians to play at your wedding reception. According to Richard Olsen, leader of Richard Olsen Orchestras, here's a general guideline you can use:

100–150 guests	*5- to 7-piece band*
150–250 guests	*7- to 9-piece band*
250+ guests	*9- to 17-piece band*

Of course, the size of the venue space may influence your decision as to the number of musicians as well. Check with your reception site to see if there are any restrictions on the number of musicians that you can have, as well as any noise limitations.

At a minimum, if you want to keep costs down, in order to make up a band, you need at least three musicians—piano or keyboard, bass, and drums for rhythm. Ask if the musicians can also sing. If so, with just a trio you'll have a lovely combo of live performers for your wedding. After the initial three pieces, if you want a bigger sound, the fourth musician can play the guitar, the fifth a sax, and the sixth a trumpet. You definitely want a female and a male vocalist. Beyond six musicians it's simply a matter of adding more vocals and horns (saxophone, trumpet, and trombone) and strings to make for a fabulous orchestra.

All bands should provide their own sound system. The sound system should include a CD player, but inquire whether it is provided. You want to use the CD system when the band or orchestra goes on breaks. Break times are great for scheduling other activites as well (see timeline in Week 47). Also double-check that the band has wireless microphones that you can use for your toasts.

Typically a band plays for a 4-hour duration, consisting of four 45-minute sets or three 60-minute sets, with three 15-minute breaks. Ask the band if they are able and willing to play music continuously. If yes, individual band members alternate breaks so that music can continue at all times.

The price for bands is based on the number of musicians and the *number of hours of playing time. Prices vary per city from $200 to $500 per musician for local musicians and certainly much more for celebrity names. Overtime is usually time and a half, prorated in half-hour increments, but check with each band for their overtime rate. If you think you would like the band to play for 5 hours or longer, consider contracting the actual time up front. It may be cheaper than going into overtime.*

On your wedding day, carefully consider whether you want to go into overtime. Overtime is not just about your band. You incur additional fees not just for the music but also for the caterer, photographer, videographer, wedding planner, transportation company, and any other wedding provider that's on duty at your wedding. It can escalate into a considerable amount of money! Also, I always recommend ending your wedding on a high note. If you ask the band to play another set, by the time they're finished, everyone may have left!

Jockeying for a DJ

IF YOU DECIDE to hire a DJ, select a top-notch DJ company, not the kind that made you get up and do the Hokey Pokey at your cousin's bar mitzvah. For leads, check with the American Disc Jockey Association at www.adja.org.

After you have identified prospective DJs, contact them by phone. At a professional DJ company, you should get a live person during normal business hours, rather than voice mail. Ask some important questions:

- Are you using professional-grade sound equipment?
- Are you insured, and can you provide proof of liability insurance?
- Do you provide your own table/drapes?
- What type of attire will the DJ wear?

A professional DJ company will send you an information packet right away. Make sure you ask for up-to-date references, then contact those references.

Choose an Officiant

WHILE MOST OF your nuptial preparations may be focused on the reception, the real reason guests are gathering in your honor is to witness your union. A wonderful ceremony sets the tone for the rest of the day and remains in your memories forever. Therefore, the person conducting your service plays a crucial role in making your wedding fabulous, and choosing the "rite" officiant can be a crucial decision.

First read up on the basic requirements relating to marriages in your chosen locale. Within the United States, state laws typically allow any recognized clergy member, judge, or justice of the peace to pronounce you husband and wife. In some states, ministers must be certified or licensed. To get more information, go to http://northernway.org/marriage laws.html.

If you want a religious ceremony, you naturally begin your search for the celebrant by contacting appropriate churches near your wedding location. Check the Yellow Pages, or go to www.worshiphere.org for assistance. If you've decided to exchange vows in a house of worship (or if your religion requires it), your chosen church either offers some options from its clergy, or it simply assigns an officiant to your wedding. If you have selected a ceremony site that is not a church, ask the clergy members you contact whether they are willing to marry you in the location you have chosen.

For a civil ceremony, you can contact the county courthouse or city hall where you wish to be married. They can tell you which local government officials are authorized to perform a civil ceremony. However, many of these public servants may be able to serve you only at their locations. Furthermore, most mayors and judges tend to be too busy with other duties to have much time for matrimonial matters for people they don't know. So if you're looking for a personalized ceremony at a time and location of your choosing, this is probably not your best option.

Instead, you probably want to select an interfaith minister or nondenominational officiant who is licensed by the state to perform marriages. Depending on their individual backgrounds and practices, these individuals may be able to design a ceremony that is as spiritual or secular as you wish.

Your ceremony location may have a listing of officiants who have previously performed marriages there. These people are experienced in dealing with any idiosyncrasies associated with your site. Another alternative is to visit Web sites that provide nationwide listings of officiants, including

- National Association of Wedding Officiants, www.nawoonline.com
- www.weddingministers.com
- www.weddingofficiants.net
- National Association of Wedding Ministers, www.aministry.net

Various wedding Web sites, both national and regional, may also include officiants in their lists of vendors.

Once you have identified possible celebrants for your ceremony, telephone them to find out if they are available on your wedding date and to verify that they are licensed to officiate ceremonies at your location. Spend a few moments talking with your prospective officiants. See what kind of chemistry you have. Do they have a pleasant speaking voice? Are they considerate of your interests and preferences, or are they just telling you "this is the way I do it"? If they are affiliated with a house of worship, attend one of their services. If they are unavailable on your wedding date or unable to perform the kind of ceremony you want, ask if they can recommend any other officiants who might be appropriate.

After you have phoned all of the prospects on your list, identify your top two or three favorites. Ask to meet with them. Discuss the following subjects at your meetings:

- **Your program**   The officiant should be willing to work with you on the content of your ceremony. He or she should be able to provide you with sample readings and help you to incorporate any special celebrations that you want to include in the ceremony. The officiant should also offer you an opportunity to read or hear your ceremony before the wedding day.
- **Vows**   At the very least, the officiant should offer several choices of vows for you to select. If you want to write your own vows, discuss this with the officiant and make sure that he or she will allow you to do so.
- **The rehearsal**   Although this is often an additional fee, I recommend having your officiant at the rehearsal to help ensure that your ceremony runs flawlessly on your wedding day. If the officiant is not available, your wedding planner can conduct the rehearsal.

- **Backups**   In case of an emergency, the officiant should have a substitute who can step in and perform the service.
- **Attire**   It is important to find out what the officiant will wear for the occasion. If you are planning a formal wedding, he or she should be properly attired, preferably in a robe.
- **Working with other vendors**   Some officiants have restrictions. They may prohibit flash photography, or they may not allow the photographer or videographer to position himself or herself anywhere near the altar. This can be a deal breaker for many couples.
- **Attending the reception**   It is always a gracious gesture to invite your officiant to the reception (some officiants make this a requirement). If you want your officiant to give a blessing at your reception meal, he or she should be delighted to do so.
- **Price**   Make sure the quoted price includes all items you have requested (attending rehearsal, script writing, travel time, and so on).

HELPFUL HINTS

In some states, it is perfectly legal to have a friend or family member act as your "officiant," provided that he or she completes the necessary paperwork. This option gives you a uniquely personalized ceremony, while saving money at the same time. Make sure that the person you select is an eloquent speaker who really wants to perform this service.

In California, where I live, any adult of the couple's choice can be deputized to perform their wedding ceremony. Deputizing is done at the county clerk's office, which happens to be the same office that grants marriage licenses. So if your chosen celebrant tags along when you go to pick up your marriage license, he or she can obtain a Certificate of Appointment and Oath of Office to serve as a Deputy Commissioner of Civil Marriages on your wedding day.

No matter who is performing the ceremony, you can work with your officiant to create the kind of ceremony that appropriately reflects your love for each other. I discuss creating a beautiful personalized ceremony in Week 34.

Hire a Professional Calligrapher (or *Do Your Own*)

YOU HAVE SELECTED a save-the-date card that will make a statement with your guests, and you will soon be ordering fabulous invitations as well. But your guests actually get their first impression before even opening these mailings by noticing how their envelopes are addressed. That's why it's important to make the lettering on the outside just as enticing as the creatively designed materials inside.

In contemplating how you want to address your envelopes, you have two basic choices. You can hire a professional calligrapher or you can print them yourself. If you decide to go with a calligrapher, you need to line one up now, because your save-the-date cards are mailed at least 6 months before your wedding date. Below, I discuss the relative merits of each option and the steps to take in either case.

Calling All Calligraphers

THROUGHOUT HUMAN HISTORY, calligraphy has embellished regal documents, religious scriptures, and famous artworks. Calligraphy itself is often defined as "the art of the written word." If you employ an expert calligrapher to address your envelopes, you are not just adding a sophisticated touch of elegance. In this day and age of being spammed and junk-mailed to death, a calligraphed envelope shows your guests that you have gone to the trouble of personally inviting them to your wedding, and it motivates them to attend.

To look for calligraphers in your area, check listings in regional bridal magazines and Web sites. Also contact the Association for the Calligraphic Arts. Go to their Web site at www.calligraphicarts.org and click on "Freelance Calligraphers" to locate a calligrapher in your state.

If you are unable to find a calligrapher locally, don't despair. Many calligraphers service clients across the country, and you can search for them online. If you use an out-of-state calligrapher, you need to have your envelopes shipped back and forth, which requires a little more time and expense. Just make sure your envelopes are properly packaged for shipment.

Once you've identified prospective calligraphers, contact them to inquire about their background and experience. A professional calligrapher should have a degree or certificate in the arts and should be proficient in a wide variety of lettering styles. Show your invitation to each calligrapher you contact and ask for a font sample before you make a decision.

While black ink is a traditional choice, if your save-the-date card has a more contemporary style, ask about other colors that the calligrapher could use. In fact, if you have dark-colored envelopes (chocolate brown is the latest rage), ink may not work at all. Instead, make sure that the calligrapher knows how to use gouache, which essentially is an opaque water-based paint that can be produced in any color.

As you narrow down your choices of calligraphers, inquire about their availability and the turnaround time needed to complete your order. Most calligraphers need about 2 to 3 weeks' advance notice.

The typical charge for an envelope ranges anywhere from $2 to $10, depending on the calligrapher's experience and the intricacy of the calligraphy you're requesting. Like any other vendor you deal with, get a written agreement from your chosen calligrapher, indicating the agreed-upon price and completion date of your order.

Do It Yourself

IN LIEU OF hiring a calligrapher, you can do your own addressing. In proposing this alternative, I'm certainly not urging you to go out and buy your own quill pens and pot of ink. Instead, I'm suggesting that with today's computer technology, you can produce pleasantly printed envelopes that make your invitations and save-the-dates stand out.

There are three factors that may make addressing your own envelopes preferable:

- You do not have the budget for a calligrapher. (To save money, some couples use a calligrapher only for their invitations and print their own envelopes for the save-the-dates.)
- If you're following current trends in invitation designs, you're probably using very clean Roman or block lettering. You may wish to match this lettering on your envelopes, or you may want to have that perfectly printed look that computers and printers provide.

• Computer software and printers are more versatile than ever before, which makes it easier to create beautifully printed envelopes at home.

If you want to print your own envelopes, don't even think about using mailing labels. They are guaranteed to make your invitation look like an ordinary piece of junk mail. Instead, you need a printer that allows you to run the entire envelope through it. However, some printers don't work very well with certain papers, especially very thick envelopes. In particular, laser printers can be brutal on envelopes because of the heat generated during the printing process. So although lasers produce sharper lettering, ink-jet printers may be a better choice.

Once you have received your save-the-date envelopes, test one on printers that you have access to. (I hope you ordered extra envelopes, as I recommended in Week 14.) If the envelope gets jammed in the printer or has ugly spots and smudges, you may need to go back to the drawing board—of a calligrapher.

If your envelopes pass the test, think about how you want the printing to look. You may want to match the ink color and font that appear on your save-the-date card. If your printer has only black ink, that's okay as long as the envelope color is not too dark. Black generally works with any other colors.

If you wish to match the ink color on your printed material, you should be able to get quite close if you have word-processing software that allows you to mix your own custom colors. (Microsoft Word 2000 and later versions have this capability.) But it is a matter of trial and error, because the color on-screen usually does not match the color coming out of your printer. Keep adjusting your on-screen color and retesting your envelope. Vary the positioning of your test prints on the page, so you can keep reusing the same envelope, and label them something like "Test Print #1," "Test Print #2," and so on, so you can keep track of your trials. When you finally get a good color match, save the test file you've been playing with, so you can refer to it later.

As mentioned above, you may also want to match the font that was used for your printed materials. Ask your invitation designer/supplier for the name of the font. Or, if you love a particular calligraphic style of font that you've seen in print, research its name. Then go online to www.identifont.com to find the font. You should be given a list of Web sites where you can purchase and download it. You can then install the font on your computer as follows:

• In Windows, go to the Control Panel, click on the Fonts folder, then use the "File, Install New Font" command.

- For Macs, drag and drop the downloaded font into the Fonts folder inside the System folder.

If you can't get the name of your font, identifont.com has an "Identify a Font" page that can help you zero in on an appropriate choice. Or, if you can scan a copy of your font, go to myfonts.com and click on "What the Font" for an online analysis.

Address Lists

WHETHER YOU USE a calligrapher or do it yourself, you need to convert your guest list spreadsheet into an address list for your envelopes. In Microsoft Word, you can use the Mail Merge Tool to accomplish this task, although you must first set up your spreadsheet to have your column headings in Row 1 and first address beginning in Row 2.

Here is a step-by-step guide for creating your address list:

1. Create a new document, then click on "Tools, Letters and Mailings, Mail Merge."
2. A pop-up wizard will appear. Under "Select Document Type," click on "Directory." Then click "Next" at the bottom of the pop-up wizard.
3. Under "Select Starting Document," click on "Use the current document." Then click "Next."
4. Under "Use an existing list," click on "Browse," go to the folder where your guest list is stored, and select the appropriate file.
5. Click "OK" to return to the new Word document.
6. You will see a new toolbar appear on screen. Click on the "Insert Merge Field" icon to create a merge template for your address list. For the sample guest list that appeared in Week 7 the merge template would look like this:

   <<Salutation>> <<First_Name>> <<Last_Name>>
   <<Other_Names>>
   <<Address>>
   <<City>>, <<State>> <<Zip>>

   Note that you are inserting a comma and space between "City" and "State," as well as spaces between other fields that appear on the same line.
7. If you are submitting an address list to a calligrapher, put an extra blank line after the "City, State Zip" line on your merge template, so that it will skip a line between addresses. If you're printing your own

envelopes, use the "Insert Break" command to add a manual page break. You want each address (i.e., each envelope) on a separate page.

8. Once again, select "Tools, Mail Merge" and click on "Merge." Your guest list should be created as a new document called "Catalog1." You can then save it as another file name.

If you're printing your own envelopes, you need to reformat your newly created file so that the addresses print properly. When choosing the appropriate font and color, use the "Edit, Select All" command so that every address is changed at once. Use the "File, Page Setup" command to select the correct size, orientation, and margins for your envelopes. So that the addresses print out correctly on the envelope, you want the top margin to be at least 2 inches high, and even greater with a large envelope. I generally recommend centering the text horizontally, but with certain designs, left- or right-justified addresses may look better. I also like to make the text size fairly large, in order to make a statement with your guests, but this is a matter of personal taste.

Overall, whether you hire a calligrapher or address your own envelopes, choose a lettering style that fits the feeling you're trying to create with your wedding. If the printing on the outside is engaging, your guests open their envelopes with great excitement to see what is waiting for them inside.

Arrange Transportation for You and Your Guests

WHETHER YOU'RE GETTING married in a church or some other location, you need to get there on time. Carefully consider your transport needs for your big day and secure appropriate vendors to provide this service.

Transportation for Guests

FROM A TIMING standpoint, you need to think about transportation for your guests first, because you want to make any necessary arrangements before ordering your invitations. As I will discuss in Week 26, you should include information about transportation on an insert card that accompanies your invitations.

You should consider two critical questions in order to determine whether you need group transportation:

- *Is the parking at your ceremony and reception sites adequate for the size of your group?* Contact your site(s) to find out how many spaces are typically available for guests. Ask if there are other places in close proximity, such as parking garages, that can be used for parking. To estimate how many parking spaces you need, look at your guest list spreadsheet and count up the number of rows that you have designated as "Likely to Attend."
- *For your out-of-town guests, is parking readily available at the hotel where you have secured room blocks?* If you didn't do so when you made arrangements for the room blocks, contact the hotel(s) to inquire about this. If your hotel is in a large city, parking is likely to be very limited, very expensive, or both.

If you determine that parking at the sites and hotels is ample, there is no need to arrange transportation for your guests, and you can skip ahead to the next section where I discuss transportation for the wedding party. However, if parking is an issue, you want to arrange for appropriate vehicles to transport guests or secure the services of a valet parking company.

BUSING BASICS

BUSES (WHICH ARE more pleasantly referred to as "luxury coaches" by transportation companies) come in a variety of capacities, ranging from about 20 passengers up to about 55. To secure a coach, there is always a minimum rental period required—depending on the transportation company and the vehicle you want, the minimum can range from 3 to 5 hours.

Like buying groceries at a supermarket, the larger-size coaches cost more, but they are generally less expensive on a unit price basis. A mini-coach holding 20 to 25 pax (that's the industry abbreviation for "passengers") costs about $400 for a 3-hour minimum, while a large 50- to 55-pax coach costs about $600 for the same time period. If you're considering a larger coach, check with your ceremony and reception sites to make sure the access road leading to them can handle it.

If you're arranging transportation for guests to get to your wedding, you also need to transport them back to where they were picked up. Depending on the length of your wedding and how the transportation company prices its vehicles, you may or may not need to secure two separate transports. Sometimes it's cheaper to hire a coach for the entire day and pay for standby time while the coach isn't needed (during the reception) than to pay for two separate coaches at the beginning and end of the day. Ask the transportation companies you contact to do the math and let you know which alternative is less.

If you need to hire two separate vehicles, consider a shuttle arrangement at the end with a smaller vehicle to save some money. Don't take it personally, but some of your guests may want to leave early—especially the older folks, when your DJ transitions from big band to hip-hop. You can start shuttling your guests back to their original location about two hours before the official end of the festivities.

When Money Is No Object

If you have secured group air transportation for out-of-town guests flying in for the wedding, you can arrange for their ground transportation from the airport to their hotel (and then back to the airport again after the wedding). This works especially well when the hotel is located in an urban area where there are lots of things to do that don't require the use of a car. While it is certainly not necessary to pay for your guests' airport transportation, it is a lovely gesture if you have the financial means to do so.

VALET AWAY

VALET PARKING IS usually the best choice when most of your guests are driving from their homes to your wedding, and the parking is limited at this location. If your site is routinely used for weddings and events, the owners are well aware of your need for valet parking (and probably require it in the contract you signed). Your site should be able to recommend appropriate valet parking companies for you to contact. These companies are the best alternatives for you to consider, because they are already familiar with the site.

According to Rob Puccinelli, valet manager for California Parking in San Francisco, a valet parking company that has prior experience with your site knows how to appropriately staff your wedding, and therefore it will give you a more reliable price quote. Depending on the size and length of your wedding and the availability of other parking options near your site, valet parking fees can range from $750 to $2,000. If the valet company needs to use a commercial parking lot for the cars, that fee is extra. Most valet parking contracts for weddings are written with gratuities included in the total price. If that is the case, the valet parking attendants should not accept tips from your guests.

Transportation for Yourselves

SINCE THIS IS one of the most important days of your life, you certainly want to get to your own wedding in style. And to properly recognize your wedding party for the role they are playing (and for all their support), it's a great idea to arrange special transportation for them as well.

First, figure out the logistics—how many people you want to transport, where and when they will be picked up, and where they need to go at the end of the day.

Standard limousines typically come in 6-, 8-, and 10-pax sizes. However, the passenger rating is always higher than what is really comfortable, especially when you're all dressed up and holding a bouquet. So if you need to transport 6 bridesmaids, get an 8-pax limo. You have a real black-and-white choice when it comes to the color of your limo. White is often considered a traditional "wedding" color, but black appears to be the preferred choice of today's savvy brides.

A classic limo like a Rolls-Royce is a great choice for the bride, especially if you're having your ceremony and reception in different locations. You and your father can make a grand arrival at the church just before he walks you down the aisle. Then, after you're pronounced wife and husband, you and your groom can take your first ride together as newlyweds to get to your big bash in style.

Regardless of the type of vehicle you're considering, there is always a minimum rental period—usually 3 or 4 hours. Pricing usually ranges between $275 to $400 for a 3-hour period.

Many brides love the romantic and historic look of a horse-drawn carriage. This can be a great choice if you have a very short distance to travel. But do keep in mind that there were significant reasons why the automobile replaced the horse as the preferred method of transport about a century ago.

You may wish to consider other modes of transporting yourselves, especially if they fit with your overall wedding theme. For a lakeside ceremony, you could arrive by rowboat. Or for your grand getaway at the end of the evening, take off in a helicopter or hot-air balloon.

For Brides on a Budget

If your ceremony and reception are in the same location, there's no need to spend money on a limo. If the site has a nice bridal waiting room and allows you to arrive early, you can have photos taken there ahead of time, then duck into the waiting room before guests arrive. Even if you can't or don't want to get there early, nobody will see you making a grand entrance anyway—your guests are already in their seats waiting for you to walk down the aisle.

Instead of a limo, look into a town-car service that normally does runs to the local airport. Ask for a fixed price that you can pay in advance for a "one-way transfer" to get you to your wedding. Assuming you don't have a long distance to travel, the cost for the trip should be between $75 and $150. You and your groom can also hire the same kind of car to leave the reception at the end of the day.

On the subject of return transportation at the end of the wedding, your wedding party members need a way to get home if they arrive at the reception site by limo. Instead of spending more money on limos or coaches, here's a tip to eliminate this cost: The day before your wedding, have your attendants and parents drive a convoy of cars to the reception site. They should park some of these cars overnight at the reception site, then carpool together to the rehearsal (or rehearsal dinner) with the other cars that are not left behind. The next day, after they have been limoed to the reception, the cars that were left overnight are waiting for them to drive home at the end of the evening.

Selecting Transportation Companies

MANY TRANSPORTATION COMPANIES belong to the National Limousine Association (NLA), a nonprofit organization dedicated to the luxury chauffeured ground transportation industry. Members of the NLA agree to abide by a code of ethics that emphasizes professional conduct. The NLA Web site, nlaride.com, allows you to search for members by location (city, state, country) and by vehicle type (sedan, van, stretch, coach, SUV, specialty vehicle). These listings also provide links to the Web sites of the member companies.

Also contact your local convention and visitors bureau for referrals. Typically, the top transportation companies are members.

Once you've identified some prospective transporters, call them to obtain price quotes. Of course, they need to know specifics on types and sizes of vehicles you need, as well as the pickup and drop-off locations and the estimated times of service. Ask for a written quote first before you provide any deposit money!

Be sure to ask the following questions:

- How long has your company been in business?
- Do you own your own vehicles? (The answer should be yes.)
- How frequently do they undergo routine maintenance?

- Can you provide an insurance certificate for your vehicles?
- What training and licensing do your drivers have?
- What kind of attire do your drivers wear?
- Does your quoted price include all tax and gratuities?
- When do your vehicles typically "spot"? (The spot time is the time the vehicle shows up at the designated location in advance of the actual service. Most professional companies "spot" 15 minutes before the actual service time.)
- For limos, are there any extras included in the price, such as a bottle of champagne, sun roof, and so on?

If possible, make a trip to the company's lot to take a look at their fleet and note their state of cleanliness. Also, the vehicles should have livery plates, which means the cars are properly licensed by the state.

After you have selected your preferred transportation provider, request a contract if the written proposal doesn't also serve as a contract. Check all the details very carefully—the date, times, number of passengers, make, model, and color of vehicle—before signing and sending a deposit.

With the efforts you have made in advance to secure quality transportation, on your wedding day you can just sit back and enjoy the ride.

Select Musicians for the Ceremony

WHEN GUESTS ARRIVE at a house of worship or ceremony site to dead silence, it's an awkward feeling. But when the air is filled with music, they know "something special" is about to happen. That's why music always sets the tone for your ceremony.

There are hundreds of ceremony music selections beyond "Here Comes the Bride." Before searching for the perfect note for your walk down the aisle, stop to consider some important issues.

Ceremonial Circumstances

YOUR CEREMONY SITE may control the type of music selected for your auspicious occasion. If you are in a house of worship or your officiant is "of the cloth" in another location, you may be required to abide by the rules and regulations set forth by the church, synagogue, or clergy. Many denominations require that you choose only religious music for your ceremony, and many prohibit amplified music. Check with your ceremony site before you have your heart set on a particular selection of music and musicians.

If, on the other hand, your ceremony site is anyplace other than a house of worship, you may select just about any kind of music you love. However, keep the rap under wraps and keep the music in good taste.

Whether your selections include Gregorian chants, operas, Broadway show tunes, movie theme songs, ethnic selections, or classic ballads, your ceremony music is divided into five distinct components:

1. The **prelude music** typically begins 30 minutes before the ceremony. For example, if your invitation indicates a 2 P.M. ceremony, begin your prelude music at 1:30. The music welcomes and entertains your guests, and makes them realize they are about to experience something special. Even if no one has arrived yet, the musicians should start playing. From my experience, arriving guests always

ask me if they've come to the right place if they don't hear the music. Make it festive and untraditional if you are contemporary in style. If you are more traditional, select the favorite religious songs you sang in church growing up. No one requires you to use the tried-and-true "wedding tunes" that everyone has heard for eternity. Depending on the length of the songs, select up to 10 pieces for your prelude music.

2. The **processional music** is for the traditional bridal party or the contemporary wedding party to make their grand entrance. (Please see Week 34 for more information on the processional.) This is where the drama and pageantry come into play—you definitely want to get your guests' attention. You may want to select at least two to three music pieces. One could be for your officiant, readers, grandparents, parents, and groomsmen; another selection for your attendants; and a third selection for you. Keep it uplifting and majestic, and select something totally regal or bold that fits your wedding design concept, your personality, or your ethnic heritage. (For her Italian theme wedding, one of my brides chose to walk down the aisle to Verdi's Grand March from *Aida*). In any event, the energy of the music should increase with each selection.

3. With the **ceremony music,** you may have several opportunities to personalize your selections. You could have musicians playing if you choose to have family members light taper candles next to your unity candle, and again when you light the unity candle itself. If you're having Communion, perhaps a soloist may sing during this time. Always ask the musicians to play an interlude while readers are walking to and from their seats. Another great moment for music is immediately following your exchange of vows and rings.

4. The **recessional music** is played when the bride and groom walk down the aisle to exit as a married couple. Making this piece lively and definitely celebratory is the way to go. One of my favorite whimsical pieces is "Consider Yourself" (part of the family) from the musical *Oliver*. Select an award-winning piece that makes a statement and gets your guests primed for the reception. Your attendants and parents may or may not exit to this same selection. If not, select two recessional pieces.

5. The bucks you paid for musicians shouldn't stop here. They should continue playing the **postlude music** as your guests file out of their

seats. Festive music should continue for up to 10 minutes following the ceremony, or until all guests have departed the ceremony area.

Picking Your Pleasure

THERE ARE NUMEROUS combinations of musicians to consider for your ceremony music. Certainly your budget dictates the number of musicians you can afford. Most musicians contract for a 2-hour minimum and average $100–$250 per musician per hour depending on your location. You may also have to pay for travel time. Here are a few options to consider:

- a cappella singers
- organ
- piano
- choir
- solo harp, or harp and flute, or harp and cello
- bell ringers
- string quartet or quintet
- brass quartet or quintet
- classical guitars
- vocalists—solo, duo

I recommend live music whenever possible because a live performance is more animated, it establishes the mood, and it's easier to control. Once I had to deal with prerecorded music at a ceremony. Here's what happened: The groom had a special symphony piece that he loved. Because he could not afford to have a whole symphony, he decided to play a recorded piece at the ceremony. He asked a friend to start the music at the beginning of the processional, because I was busy lining up the entire wedding party in the processional line. For some reason, the friend could not find the starting point for the first processional song (although it had already been arranged and tested by me). So we waited . . . and waited. They had chosen three separate songs for the processional: one for the officiant, groom, and groomsmen; one for the attendants; and one for the bride. Once the music started, the first song was longer than expected and everyone but the bride went down the aisle to the first song. The bride then had to wait for another entire song before she could go. Yikes!

If you are going to use prerecorded ceremony music, the morals of the story are:

1. Make sure that the equipment operation is so simple a child could do it.
2. Accept that you can't adjust the length of prerecorded songs to match the length of time it takes to walk down the aisle.

On the other hand, with live music, the musicians can take a cue from the wedding planner or family member and end the song when it's appropriate.

Finding Ceremony Musicians

LIKE MOST WEDDING vendors, there are many ways to find your ceremony musicians. The house of worship may come with a music director already. Make an appointment to speak with him or her personally. If there is no in-house music director and you are getting married in a house of worship, its wedding administrator typically provides you with a list of preferred musicians.

Otherwise, consider contacting the local symphony, opera, or ballet companies and request a listing of the musicians who play for weddings and parties. Local music stores or musicians' unions are also excellent resources. Check out the American Federation of Musicians. Go to www.afm.org and click on "Find a Local."

Regional bridal magazines also have articles and ads for ceremony musicians. Additionally, you can go online to major wedding sites for listings of local wedding providers. Be sure to include the city where you are getting married in your search criteria.

For Brides on a Budget

Check out the music departments at your local universities for musicians. Many times the professors or students have a special program set up to perform and play for weddings and events.

Once you've found some potential players, request that a demo package be sent to you, which should include a bio, picture, and CD. If the musicians have Web sites, you may also be able to hear their music online. Whenever possible, meet with the prospective musicians and see a live performance before signing the contract. If you have some favorite ceremony music, make a list before selecting your musicians, then check if they know how to play the pieces. If not, find out if they can get sheet music for the pieces, or reconsider whether you have chosen the right instruments.

If you're working with in-house musicians at a church, keep in mind that they perform most, if not all, of the weddings at their site and may be in "auto-repeat" mode. Try to get them to think outside of the music box and suggest pieces they don't always play for every wedding.

Finally, make sure you understand what is included in the musicians' quoted price:

- Does the contract fee include time to consult on music selections?
- Will they be present at the wedding rehearsal? If not, what is the additional fee to attend the rehearsal?
- Will they proofread your wedding program regarding the ceremony music listings for the correct spelling of songs and composers?

Contract Considerations

ONCE YOU HAVE found the right musicians for your ceremony, get an agreement in writing. The contract should contain the following:

- Name, address, and contact numbers of all musicians. (Make sure they are the same musicians as in the demo package.)
- Wedding date, name, and address of ceremony site, arrival time, playing start time, ending time, the quoted price, and overtime fees.
- Equipment needed, such as armless chairs, lighting, protection for musicians and instruments from sun or inclement weather, and amplifiers/sound system.
- The attire you want the musicians to wear—i.e., tuxedos, concert attire, rock star wear, hula dancer skirts.

Your selection of skillful ceremony musicians will be music to your ears, and you'll definitely be a glowing bride as you walk down the aisle.

Order Invitations

YOU ALREADY GRABBED your guests' attention with an intriguing save-the-date card. Now it's time to make a really wonderful impression, with a fabulous official invitation to your celebration. The design you choose for your invitation carries through the concept you originated with your save-the-date card. Most important, the invitation sets the tone for your special day by giving your guests a captivating preview of what's to come.

Inviting Elements

IN GENERAL, A wedding invitation typically consists of several components:

- the invitation itself
- a separate reception card, if your ceremony and reception are in two different locations
- a response card (aka reply card), which allows your guests to indicate whether they will be attending the wedding
- a directions card, which indicates how to get to the wedding and also provides other important information that guests need to know
- an outer envelope (and an inner envelope for traditionalists) to hold the invitation and other components

Before you can go pick out your invitation, you need to decide how to word it. You have two basic choices: You can conform to the traditional rules of etiquette, or you can select more contemporary options. Either way, it can be a challenge to appropriately express yourself, so I offer some suggestions to help you wade through the ways of wording.

INVITATION CARD

IN PAST GENERATIONS, invitations all looked similar. Traditional invitations were written in the third person on a heavyweight, high-cotton-fiber card, white or ecru in color, with engraved printing in black ink and a delicate script font. The hosts' names, usually the parents of the bride, appeared first. The invitations were mailed inside two envelopes, and the inner envelope was not sealed because it had no glue.

These days, many outdated wedding rules are vanishing, particularly in the overall look of invitations. Nevertheless, the traditional ways of wording still appeal to many couples because they make a clear statement of impeccable elegance, backed by centuries of use. But with non-traditional family situations and multiple funding sources for the festivities, it is much more challenging to come up with wording to fit your particular situation. It is beyond the scope of this book to cover every imaginable combination of family circumstances (an excellent resource for further information on formal invitation wording is *Crane's Blue Book of Stationery*), but here is a general format for a traditionally worded invitation, with some common options italicized and explained:

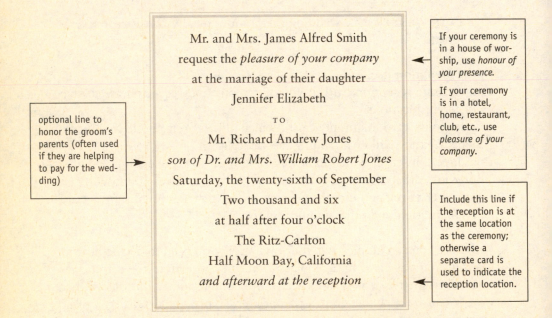

Mr. and Mrs. James Alfred Smith
request the *pleasure of your company*
at the marriage of their daughter
Jennifer Elizabeth
TO
Mr. Richard Andrew Jones
son of Dr. and Mrs. William Robert Jones
Saturday, the twenty-sixth of September
Two thousand and six
at half after four o'clock
The Ritz-Carlton
Half Moon Bay, California
and afterward at the reception

If your ceremony is in a house of worship, use *honour of your presence.*

If your ceremony is in a hotel, home, restaurant, club, etc., use *pleasure of your company.*

optional line to honor the groom's parents (often used if they are helping to pay for the wedding)

Include this line if the reception is at the same location as the ceremony; otherwise a separate card is used to indicate the reception location.

Note that full first names and middle names are used (no nicknames!), and nothing is abbreviated except titles like Mr., Mrs., Dr. and Jr. The bride's name is listed before the groom's, the groom has a title

(Mr.) but the bride does not. The British spelling of the word "honour" is used for a church ceremony. State names, years, dates, and times are all written out fully, and note that "half after four o'clock" is used rather than "four-thirty." Commas are used only to separate the day and date, and the city and state.

If your style is more casual or contemporary, you do not have to be bound by conventional phraseology, but you still want to create a feeling of elegance and sophistication. I recommend that you look through contemporary books of invitations in stationery stores for inspiring ideas. Overall, keep in mind that reverence for the institution of marriage is always considered proper. Here is one suggestion to consider:

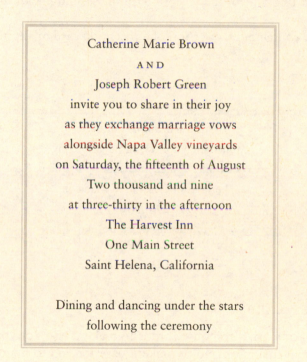

Catherine Marie Brown

AND

Joseph Robert Green

invite you to share in their joy

as they exchange marriage vows

alongside Napa Valley vineyards

on Saturday, the fifteenth of August

Two thousand and nine

at three-thirty in the afternoon

The Harvest Inn

One Main Street

Saint Helena, California

Dining and dancing under the stars

following the ceremony

RECEPTION CARD

YOUR INVITATION CARD indicates the time and location of the ceremony. If you are having your reception at a different site, a separate card indicates its location and time. In effect, the reception card serves as an invitation to a separate event. Here is a traditionally worded example:

> Reception
> immediately following the ceremony
> Kohl Mansion
> 2750 Adeline Drive
> Burlingame, California

If your reception site is not available until a certain time, and therefore you have a gap between the ceremony and reception, indicate the specific starting time of the reception on the second line of the reception card.

A more contemporary version of a reception card might be worded as follows:

> Our celebration continues
> immediately following the ceremony
> with cocktails, dinner, and dancing by the bay
> The James Leary Flood Mansion
> 2222 Broadway
> San Francisco, California

RESPONSE CARD

THE PURPOSE OF a response card is to make it easy for your guests to reply to your invitation and to make it easy for you to figure out who's coming. The RSVP deadline on your response card should be one month before your wedding date, so that you have enough time to determine seating arrangements, then have escort cards and place cards printed. Some old-school etiquette mavens are offended by the concept of response cards, because they believe a guest should reply to a wedding invitation with a personally written note. But I believe they're missing an important point—proper etiquette also involves showing sufficient respect for your guests to make things convenient for them. Here is an example of a traditional response card:

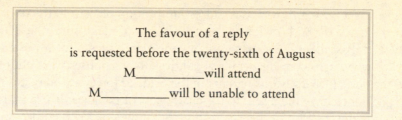

The favour of a reply
is requested before the twenty-sixth of August
M_____will attend
M_____will be unable to attend

Note the English spelling of the word "favour." Response cards never ask for the number of guests coming to the wedding. Instead, the specific names of guests who are being invited are indicated on your envelope(s), and those guests who can come to the wedding will so indicate by writing their names in the appropriate blank on the card.

Again, you are free to choose more contemporary wording for the response card. Many couples drop the traditional "M" in front of the blank line, so guests can write their names more casually. Also, if you're having a seated meal service at your reception with a choice of entrée, you need to design the response card in a way that allows your guests to clearly indicate their preferences, so that you can subsequently provide this information to your caterer. Here is one way to word your response card in this situation:

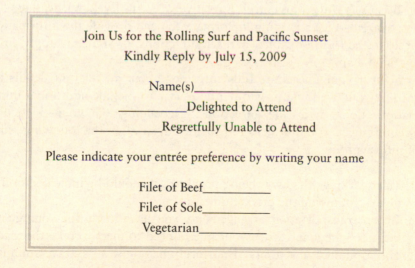

Join Us for the Rolling Surf and Pacific Sunset
Kindly Reply by July 15, 2009

Name(s)_____

_____Delighted to Attend

_____Regretfully Unable to Attend

Please indicate your entrée preference by writing your name

Filet of Beef_____
Filet of Sole_____
Vegetarian_____

It is not necessary to describe the preparation of the entrée. (Besides, you may elect to change how a particular entrée is prepared after you have a trial meal with your caterer—see Week 39.)

A preaddressed, stamped envelope accompanies the more conventional form of response card, but some contemporary versions are designed as a postcard, with the address and stamp placed on the back side of the card. If you go with the postcard option, make sure that it meets the U.S. Postal Service's sizing and layout requirements for a postcard—go to www.usps.com for details. Traditionally, responses were addressed to the hosts (generally, the parents of the bride). However, today it is more expedient to have them sent to the custodians of the guest list spreadsheet (usually the couple), so that the responses can be quickly recorded and efficiently tracked on the computer (more on this in Week 49).

DIRECTIONS CARD

BACK IN THE days when you married your high school sweetheart in your hometown, there wasn't much need for a directions card, because everyone already knew where the ceremony and reception sites were located (oftentimes street addresses weren't even written on the invitations). Nowadays, it's considered bad etiquette to assume that your guests can somehow manage to find their way to your wedding without directions. Despite the recent easy availability of online driving directions, it is still considered proper to make it convenient for your guests by providing directions with your invitations. Besides, Internet driving directions don't always provide the best route to get to a location.

Because a directions card is a relatively recent development, there are no stringent rules regarding its format. You can provide the information either in the form of explicit written directions, or you can supply an illustrated map.

So that your guests are fully informed about all relevant details regarding your wedding, it is often necessary to include additional information along with the directions. Depending on your particular circumstances, you may need to provide any or all of the following kinds of information:

- **Valet parking** If this is being provided, it should be indicated immediately following the driving directions.
- **Group transportation arrangements you have made for your guests** Indicate where and when your guests need to meet to take the transportation, and in setting a departure time, allow an extra 15 minutes to ensure an on-time arrival. If your ceremony and/or reception site has no available parking and therefore requires that all guests arrive by shuttle, make sure you clearly state this.
- **Child-care arrangements you have made** A great way to encourage guests with children to attend, while keeping the kids from crashing your party, if that's your preference.

- **Appropriate attire for the wedding** For example, black tie for a formal wedding, or "garden shoes suggested" for an outdoor wedding where you don't want the ladies aerating the lawn with spiked heels.
- **Weather information** If it's an outdoor wedding, a description of typical temperatures is helpful, and the location of a backup site you have secured in case of rain is essential.
- **Other things to do** If it's a destination wedding, you may want to provide information on area attractions.
- **Your personal wedding Web site address,** if you have one.

ENVELOPES

TO PROPERLY PACKAGE your invitation components, you need some sort of envelope to put them in. Centuries ago, both an outer and inner envelope were used because the outer envelope often got soiled while being transported via Pony Express. Today, most couples skip the inner envelope to save money, time, and a few trees. However, it is still popular to select a luxurious lining for the envelope that coordinates with all the components going inside.

The return address of the person(s) extending the invitation to the wedding is printed on the back flap of the outer envelope (i.e., if your parents are listed first on the invitation, use their address). Their names do not appear—only the street address, city, state, and zip—and of course, no abbreviations are used.

But Wait ... There's More

AT THE SAME time you select your invitations, it's a good idea to pick out other pieces of stationery you need. Depending on your situation, that may include thank-you note cards, wedding announcements, rehearsal dinner invitations, ceremony programs, escort cards, place cards, and menus.

THANK-YOU NOTE CARDS

IN STATIONERYSPEAK, THESE are known as "informals." You use these cards to thank guests who give you a wedding gift. They are probably the easiest item for you to select, because you don't have to worry about wording (at least until you start writing your thank-yous). Most couples simply place a design element from their invitation on their informals. Your return address is typically positioned on the back flap of a matching envelope.

The longer you wait to send out thank-you notes, the harder it is for you and the more resentful the gift givers become. One month from the wedding or your return from your honeymoon (if you took one) is the absolute maximum length of time you can stall. Three sentences will do it, and just be sure your thank-you doesn't sound like boilerplate with fill in the blank for the specific gift. For example: "Dear Aunt Sally, Thank you so much for the beautiful candlesticks. I hope Freddy and I will be having romantic, candlelit dinners for many years to come. I am so glad that you and Uncle Harry could share this joyous occasion with us. Love, Rachel." See how easy it is?

ANNOUNCEMENTS

YOU MAY WISH to send an announcement of your marriage to those on your original guest list whom you subsequently decided you could not afford to invite to your wedding. This is a completely optional item, but many couples who send an announcement utilize the same design as their invitation. The wording, of course, is different. Here is an example:

Jennifer Elizabeth Smith
and
Richard Andrew Jones
joyfully announce their marriage
Saturday, the twenty-sixth of September
Two thousand and six
Half Moon Bay, California

Never send announcements until the wedding has taken place. Since you may have a honeymoon to attend afterward, you can ask one of your attendants to mail the announcements for you. And in case you're wondering, there is no obligation for the recipient of an announcement to send a wedding gift.

INVITATIONS TO THE REHEARSAL DINNER
AND OTHER EVENTS

YOU PROBABLY HAVE not picked out a location for your rehearsal dinner yet (I talk about that in Week 33), but it's a good idea to start looking for appropriate styles of rehearsal dinner invitations. Many couples choose to have an informal rehearsal dinner so that it doesn't over-shadow the wedding day celebration, and in that case, a more casually styled and worded invitation may be appropriate.

Today, couples often have a series of events over a period of several days to celebrate their marriage—including the rehearsal dinner, a bridesmaids' luncheon, bachelor/bachelorette parties, a morning-after brunch, and so on. You can send all the invitations for these events to-gether in a single mailing, which includes invites for the parties as they apply to each guest. Some contemporary styles of invitations are de-signed with "pocket folds," which provide a very cool, clean, and conve-nient way to slip all of these enclosures into the overall package without making a mess.

Alternatively, you can send out separate invitations on different dates, so your guests get more and more excited as each invite arrives. (If other people are hosting some of these events, the invitation officially comes from them anyway.) You always send the wedding invitation out first. The rehearsal dinner invitation can be sent a couple days later, followed by the invitations for any other pre- or postwedding events.

CEREMONY PROGRAMS, ESCORT CARDS, PLACE CARDS, AND MENUS

OTHER PRINTED MATERIALS that are not utilized until the wedding day do not necessarily need to be ordered this soon in the planning pro-cess. However, you may be able to save some money by printing every-thing at once. In any case, it is important to consider the look and feel of these items now. You want to carry a consistent design concept through all your printed materials, from the save-the-date to the dinner menus. I cover this in more detail in Week 40.

Selecting Your Invitations

IF YOU'VE BEEN following the advice in this book, then you have already sent out a save-the-date card. As I suggested back in Week 14, all components of your wedding stationery ensemble should reflect your wedding visions and tie together to create a cohesive design. For each of these pieces, choose a printing method, papers, colors, and fonts that complement each other and fit the style you wish to express. Most likely, the stationery supplier or graphic designer that created your save-the-date card is the best bet for furnishing your other printed materials.

Once you have carefully considered the words you want to use and the pieces that you need to include with the invitation, take this information to your supplier/designer for his or her input. Bring along any fabric swatches or color samples that you have already decided to use in your wedding. With his or her experience, your stationery supplier/graphic designer will help you make the right fashion statement with your complete wedding stationery wardrobe.

It's always advisable to request proofs for each piece before the invitations are printed. Review the layout and recheck the spelling very carefully. (One old trick I learned is to read the text forward, then read it again backward. Also, give the proof to two other people to read, if possible.) The printer is not responsible for any mistakes you miss.

When examining various printing options, ask about the turnaround time required. You want to get your invitations back from the printer at least 3 months in advance of the wedding. That gives you 2 weeks to address envelopes that are going to international destinations, so you can send them out 10 weeks before the wedding. The domestic addresses can be completed 2 weeks later, so that all of your invitations are mailed at least 8 weeks before the wedding. If you did not send out a save-the-date card, you should get your printing done even earlier, so you can mail all of your invitations at least 3 months before the wedding.

Finally, to determine the appropriate quantities to order, count the rows in your guest list spreadsheet. In most cases, it's one card per family or per couple—not one per person. Make sure you add at least 10 percent extra to allow for keepsakes and envelope addressing errors, and keep in mind that many types of invitations are available only in increments of 25. When the order comes in, carefully examine and count the items before leaving your designer/supplier's shop, to make sure that everything is perfect ("perfect" is my favorite word!).

Choose a Cake Designer

WITH ALL DUE respect for Betty Crocker, most twenty-first-century professionals who specialize in fashioning wedding cakes prefer to be called cake *designers*, not bakers. This contemporary title is well deserved, because their creations are delectable works of art, made from top-quality fresh ingredients, and exhibiting meticulous workmanship and exquisite embellishments. (I feel obligated to mention that the most delicious ingredients in a wedding cake are not exactly the most nutritious. But nobody ever said that a wedding was a great place for a diet. This is a celebration, after all. Live it up and save the calorie counting for another day!)

To most effectively utilize the talents of a professional cake designer, your wedding cake should reflect your personal tastes (especially on the inside) and coordinate with your entire wedding vision (on the outside).

Like so many other elements of wedding design, your cake does not have to be the traditional white color. Instead of matching your bridal gown, you could choose a cake color to complement your bridesmaids' dresses, or pick some other shade that you want to feature in your wedding design. What makes your cake unique and distinctive (and sometimes expensive) are the adornments you choose for decorating it.

ONE COUPLE'S STORY

Jason proposed to Maureen while visiting her in Paris, where she was working temporarily. When they returned home to the United States, I worked with the couple to design a Parisian theme for their wedding. This theme was interwoven throughout every aspect of the wedding, including the cake. Handmade French fleurs-de-lis (lily flowers used as a French royal coat of arms) were placed on the sides of the cake, and on top, a miniature Eiffel Tower made a dramatic yet fun statement.

Before you start searching for a wedding cake designer, there are some sweet subjects you should familiarize yourself with.

Have Your Cake

YOU HAVE SEVERAL options to consider when choosing the cake itself. The most conventional wedding cake types are

- **Chiffon** A light sponge cake, best complemented with fresh fruit and mousse fillings.
- **Genoise** This classic French sponge cake is somewhat dryer and crumblier than chiffon. It works well with heavier, denser fillings.
- **French croquembouche** A tower of cream puffs iced with fine sugar frosting.

But feel free to break from tradition. Here are some other options to consider, especially if any of these are your favorite flavors:

- butter cake
- carrot cake
- cheesecake
- chocolate cake
- poppyseed cake
- pound cake
- fruitcake

Perhaps you're having trouble deciding among these choices because you love them all, or perhaps you have one favorite and your fiancé has another. No worries! Most cakes consist of multiple tiers (usually three), so you can each choose a different flavor for each tier.

Fill 'er Up

YOUR CHOICES FOR fillings include such diverse options as fresh fruits, flavored mousses, buttercream, light and dark chocolates, custard, and liqueur-flavored creams. Be aware that certain types of fillings, especially fresh mousses and pastry creams, may be inappropriate if your cake will be sitting out at the reception for a considerable length of time.

Fantastic Finishes

IN DECIDING ON a "finish" (that's cakespeak for icing), think about how you want it to look as well as taste. The most widely used finishes are

- **Buttercream** Made of sugar, eggs, and butter, buttercream is a soft yummy icing that can easily be tinted or mixed with various flavorings.
- **Fondant** A smooth icing made from sugar, corn syrup, and gelatin. Fondant is rolled out in sheets with a rolling pin, then placed over the cake.
- **Ganache** A rich mixture of chocolate and cream that holds up best in low humidity; sometimes poured over the cake as a shiny glaze.
- **Whipped cream** Light and luscious, but not the most practical choice for a wedding cake, because whipped cream should be kept refrigerated until it is ready to be served.

Until recently, fondant was the most popular choice for a wedding cake finish, because it can better withstand warm and humid weather conditions, and the cake needs no refrigeration. In fact, refrigerating fondant makes matters worse, as it beads up with moisture.

Nowadays, rolled buttercream has become the chic choice for covering a cake. It's just as smooth as fondant but much tastier! Plus, it's easier to add color or flavoring to buttercream. There is one drawback: If your cake is subjected to temperatures above 85°, a buttercream cake may melt. To deal with this problem, the designer usually frosts the cake in buttercream first, then adds a layer of fondant over the top.

DAZZLING DOODADS

TO COMPLETE THE fabulous design of your cake, a variety of beautiful decorations can be added. Some of these adornments can be very labor-intensive, and therefore the cost of your cake may increase significantly. The most commonly employed embellishments include the following confections:

- **Gum paste** A paste material made of sugar, cornstarch, and gelatin that is often used to create lifelike flowers and fruit, as well as other cake decorations.

- **Pulled sugar**   Sugar syrup that is heated to a molten state and pulled into such shapes as bows and flowers.
- **Royal icing**   A paste created by beating egg whites with confectioners' sugar. Royal icing is used to make intricate decorative elements, such as lace, beading, and buds.
- **Marzipan**   A paste made of ground almonds, sugar, and egg whites; most frequently used to mold edible flowers or fruit to decorate the cake. Marzipan can also be rolled in sheets and used as icing.
- **Modeling chocolate**   A mixture of white or dark chocolate and corn syrup that can be used to cover an entire cake, or to embellish a frosted cake with ribbons, ruffles, or chocolate flower buds.

Fresh flowers are the most popular type of adornment on a wedding cake. They make a beautiful but inexpensive addition. If you want fresh flowers on your cake, they should complement the designs your florist is providing for the reception. While some cake designers allow your florist to add flowers to the cake once it has been delivered on your wedding day, most prefer to position the flowers themselves. (They are the "designers" of the cake, after all, and by keeping control of the finished product, your cake designer can ensure that your fresh flowers are not poisonous or sprayed with pesticides.)

Beyond Cake

THE LATEST TREND at wedding receptions is not only to have your cake and eat it too, but also to scarf down even more confectionary creations. Typically, dessert buffets or stations are opened right after dinner and positioned in a separate room (so that your guests can get out of their seats and burn off a couple calories by walking to the dessert table). If you have a light, fruit-filled wedding cake, you can mix things up with a decadent selection of rich chocolates at a dessert buffet. You can even set up a dessert action station. At the time of this writing, "s'more stations" are a very hot item. A dessert station can be provided by your caterer or your cake designer, depending on their areas of expertise. Request a proposal from both vendors for this item.

Finding Cake Designers

IF YOUR RECEPTION is at an on-premise facility, first check into their requirements regarding cake. Do you have to get your wedding cake from the in-house caterer? If they allow you to select an outside cake designer, will they charge a "cake-cutting fee," and if so, how much is this fee? You may have some budgetary decisions to make at this point. Don't fret if you are locked into their cake provider. These people are generally very experienced at producing a quality product.

Assuming that you need and want to find a cake designer on your own, start by looking in regional bridal magazines and Web sites for designs that appeal to you. Look for photos of cakes from real weddings, rather than staged studio shots (sometimes fake cakes are used for commercial photographs). Start compiling a list of designers whose work you admire.

Ask for referrals from your caterer (if he or she is not trying to make you use an in-house baker), your reception site, and your florist. If you have hired a wedding planner, he or she will also provide referrals. Also ask recently married friends for their recommendations.

Once you have compiled a list of at least five prospects, visit their Web sites and look at the range of designs that are shown, as well as the craftsmanship shown in their work. Call the cake designers to find out if they have availability in their shops for your wedding day. Make appointments for a tasting with those designers who still interest you (many designers charge for tastings).

SELECTING A CAKE DESIGNER

WHEN MEETING WITH cake designers, try to visit the location where cakes are actually baked (i.e., their kitchens). Make sure their business license and health department certificates are posted. If not, ask for this information. Ask about the average number of wedding cakes they create each week and how long it typically takes to make a wedding cake.

Most designers can show you a portfolio of wedding cakes they've created. Pay attention to the execution of designs. Is the work clean and well presented, or do the details appear rough and amateurish?

The highlight of the meeting is the cake tasting (this was my husband's favorite part of planning our wedding!). At this point, you're not focused on the design of the cake anymore—just how it tastes. Savor each nibble of the cake samples and make notes about what you do and don't like. If you like the cake in one sample and the filling in another, ask if it's feasible to put your favorite cake and filling together.

To get an estimate of each designer's pricing, pick a couple of photos from the designer's portfolio and ask for the price of the cake shown. Typically, you can expect to pay somewhere between $8 and $20 per serving for a custom-designed cake made exclusively with fresh ingredients.

For Brides on a Budget

On average, about 25 percent of your guests will not eat cake. Take this statistic into account when you select the size of your cake.

Here's another way to save money: Order a smaller decorated wedding cake, accompanied by undecorated sheet cakes of the same flavors and finish. These can be cut and served discreetly from the kitchen. Serving slices instead of square chunks of cake makes this budget-saving trick less obvious to guests. Sheet cakes typically are about half the cost per slice.

If you are unable to afford a high-end cake designer, check out bakeries in your neighborhood. Many of them can supply wedding cakes at a lower cost ($2.50 to $7.50 per slice).

The Final Product

MAKE YOUR FINAL decision on a cake designer based on workmanship, taste, and price. Once you have made your selection and the details have been confirmed, get everything in writing. Your contract should describe the details of the cake—the number of tiers, their shapes and dimensions, the filling and icing flavors, colors, decorations, cake top, number of servings, delivery date, time, location, and setup. Confirm that all services, including delivery and tax, are in the final contract price.

About 6 weeks prior to the wedding, after your reception design details are all worked out, meet with your cake designer to finalize the look of your wedding cake. If you make any alterations or refinements to your design concept, adjust your cake design so that it remains compatible with your current plans.

When Money Is No Object

The "groom's cake," a perennial fixture in Southern weddings, is back in vogue across the country. Think dark, rich, decadent, and decorated to represent the groom's hobbies and interests—such as a cake in the shape of a football. A tasty sliver may be served alongside the wedding cake, or sent home with guests in a ribboned box.

Your wedding cake table is a focal point at your reception, so a creatively designed cake adds a special ambience to your grand celebration. It also brings a big smile to your face as you feed each other those yummy pieces of cake in front of your family and friends.

Select Attire for Maids, Moms, and Flower Girls

IF YOU AND your fiancé think of yourselves as the lead characters in a major motion picture, then the ladies in your wedding party certainly have key supporting roles. After all, the dresses of the bridesmaids, mothers, and flower girls are displayed prominently as they walk down the aisle—and then later on throughout the reception. Their attire should be harmonious with the overall wedding design, though it should never take the limelight away from the bride.

Bridesmaids

WHILE NOTHING IS more satisfying than serving as a bridesmaid in a dear friend's wedding, there is unfortunately nothing more horrifying than doing it while wearing an overpriced, outdated, and unflattering bridesmaid's dress. Therefore, just as you consider the needs and expectations of your guests as you plan your wedding, so should you consider the needs and wishes of your adoring attendants. Try to make it an easy process on them from the time they purchase the dress to the time they walk down the aisle. Remember: A happy bridesmaid means a happy bride!

Style

Bridesmaid dresses play a crucial role in setting the tone and style you want for your affair. After all, they are the first things your guests see after the ceremony flowers and, more important, they are a prelude to the bride's entrance. Their wardrobe should always complement yet never overshadow the bridal gown. For instance, if you're having an afternoon outdoor wedding in the spring and you have selected a tea-length organza gown, it is not appropriate for your bridesmaids to wear heavy satin ball gowns. A more suitable option for an outdoor wedding is a calf-length dress in a light fabric similar to that of the bridal gown—organza, cotton, or chiffon. For formal weddings, think dressier, heavier, and usually longer. Can't decide among two or three dresses? It is usually best to go with the more simple dress that has a touch of something special accenting it, such as a couple of rhinestone buttons or a beautiful scoop neck.

Color

Brides are no longer choosing the typical pastel and often muted bridesmaid dress. Today's bridesmaid dresses can be found in every shade imaginable—from fruity colors like juicy tangerine and lime green to neutral yet interesting colors like a shimmery taupe or chocolate brown. Not every color looks great on everyone, so opt for a color that looks good on the majority of your bridesmaids. For example, if most of your friends are desperately pale, avoid putting them in cream dresses in the middle of the winter (without a little self-tanner, that is!). Another great alternative is to let your bridesmaids choose from a variety of shades of one color, such as lilac or sage.

Body Types

The age-old question, "How do I find a dress that looks good on everyone?" is easy to answer: It's difficult. If you have plus-size friends in your wedding and you want that traditional, uniform look for your bridesmaids, then an A-line, waistless dress is a good choice because it is becoming on just about everyone. Another perfectly acceptable idea is to pick one designer and one color and let your bridesmaids choose what style they want to wear out of that line. (This is also a good option if you have a pregnant bridesmaid.) The variety makes for an appealing and interesting alternative for your guests to gaze upon during the ceremony.

Cost

Much like style and color, the cost of the bridesmaid dress should reflect the overall tone and theme of the wedding. As Dorcas Prince, owner of Low's Bridal in Brinkley, Arkansas, says, "If the bride is wearing an $800 dress, she is not going to ask her bridesmaids to spend $350 on Vera Wang dresses. On the other hand, if you are spending $7,000 on a Reem Acra gown, a $350 dress is appropriate for a bridesmaid to spend." A thoughtful bride always considers the budget of her bridesmaids, and because bridesmaid dresses can be very costly, brides are increasingly offering to help out with the cost either by paying for part of the dress or by buying some sassy heels to go with them. Another idea growing in popularity is to give jewelry or other accessories as gifts to your bridesmaids to wear with their divine dresses.

SHOPPING

BRIDAL SALONS HAVE always been the most popular place to shop for bridesmaid dresses because most bridal gown designers also offer dresses for attendants. Today, there are other options to consider as well. Major department stores and women's clothing shops, such as Ann Taylor, Bloomingdale's, Neiman Marcus, and Talbot's, offer fine lines of ladies' dresses that can easily double as bridesmaid attire. (And knowing that they're not buying a traditional "bridesmaid dress," your attendants might even wear them again!) You can also go online to shop. Check out www.ariadress.com or visit any of the major wedding Web portals.

Even if you end up making your selections in cyberspace, it's best first to look at bridesmaid dresses in person. If you need a little hand-holding, bring a bridesmaid or two along so that you can get an outside opinion and have an extra body to model the choices for you. Avoid inviting all of your bridesmaids, though. You don't want too many cooks in the kitchen.

Once you have made your decision on appropriate bridesmaid dresses for your wedding, your attendants should get their measurements taken and have their orders placed right away if the dresses are being purchased from a salon. It usually takes about 10 to 12 weeks for them to be made and delivered, and it may be necessary to make alterations before the wedding day.

HELPFUL HINT

Encourage your bridesmaids to be sized and get their alterations done at the store where they were purchased. The sales associates know the dress well and, more important, know how it should fit the body. If your bridesmaids are scattered about the country, give them a picture of someone properly wearing the dress to take to their alterations store. The last thing you want is for the train of a gown to be cut off because the seamstress thought it was supposed to be a tea-length.

Maid/Matron of Honor

TRADITIONALISTS SOMETIMES RECOMMEND that your honor attendant be set apart in her dress from the rest of the wedding party, though this is by no means the standard. These days, most maids or matrons of honor wear the same dress as the bridesmaids but are perhaps distinguished in a more subtle way, such as having a longer train, gloves, or a unique neckline. If your honor attendant is a shy sort who doesn't like too much attention, you can set her apart by the color, size, or style of her bouquet.

Junior Bridesmaid

ATTIRE FOR JUNIOR bridesmaids is similar to the bridesmaid dress in color and texture but is less revealing and usually less sophisticated than its older counterpart. These vibrant young ladies walk down the aisle with the other bridesmaids (which they love!) and are in all the pictures, so you want them to blend in nicely with the other attendants. Remember, however, that these girls are still children, so taste and discretion are advised in whatever you choose. Many designers now make this choice easier by designing modest yet stylish dresses for girls in this age range—Belsoi, Jim Hjelm, and Mori Lee to name a few. An important note: These preteens can sprout several inches and add several pounds over the period of an engagement, so think ahead when choosing their dress.

Flower Girls

PRECIOUS LITTLE GIRLS gliding down the aisle and tossing rose petals at admiring guests can add such a delightful touch to your ceremony. Traditional flower girl dresses are white, cream, or pastel in a satin or organza with a sash the same color as the bridesmaid dress. Contemporary flower girl dresses come in a rainbow of fabulous colors. These sweet dresses can be custom-made or found at a bridal salon or fine children's clothier. While picking out the dress may seem really fun, it is often advised to give this responsibility over to the mother of the flower girl, who knows the size and comfort factor of her daughter. Just be sure she gets your approval before making the purchase.

Mother of the Bride

MOTHERS ARE NO longer relegated to wearing dull and "styleless" dresses that make them feel, well, old. Today's hip moms are opting for more stylish and sophisticated attire than in years past, in part because they don't shop at the typical bridal salon anymore but in the evening wear sections of local department stores and smaller boutiques that offer something a little more distinctive. A mother of the bride's dress does not have to be the same color as the bridesmaid dress, but it should fit with the overall color scheme. For instance, if the bridesmaids are wearing hot pink, the mother of the bride might wear taupe or light rose.

Mother of the Groom

IT IS STILL considered polite for the mother of the groom to wait until the mother of the bride has selected her dress before she begins shopping for her own. (If your parents are divorced and your dad has re-married, the same courtesy is expected from your stepmother.) The key is courteous communication to avoid both moms wearing the same color or (gasp!) the same dress. The mother of the groom should harmonize with the rest of the bridal party yet never overshadow the bridesmaids or the mother of the bride.

For Brides on a Budget

Think creatively and you can save your bridesmaids a lot of money on their dresses.

- **Online auctions**   eBay has numerous listings from women who want to sell dresses they wore only once. If you do enough searching, you can likely find several of the same dress in the sizes you need. Just be quick to bid on those hot items!
- **Resale and thrift shops**   Many bridesmaids sell their used dresses to make a little extra cash. Check frequently at these stores, as merchandise is always coming and going.

> • **Discount stores** Loehmann's and Marshall's, for example, carry name-brand dresses at discounted prices. If you find a dress that works, you can call around to their other stores and find the correct sizes for your attendants.

Dressing your maids, moms, and little girls is fun, especially if you take the time to consider their needs, expectations, and budgets beforehand. Once you do this, it should come down to choosing the dresses you absolutely love. If you love them now, most likely you will love them years from now when you look back at all your dear and wonderful attendants in your wedding album.

Get Garments for the Guys

GUYS, ON YOUR wedding day, the bride should certainly be the center of attention. But it takes two to make a marriage, and the groom should stand out too—in a positive way, of course. In order for the groom and his guys to look like they belong on the same stage with the bride and bridesmaids, consider their choice of attire as carefully as the ladies' dresses.

Rigid requirements for guys' accoutrements have faded away in the modern world. There has been a strong trend in our society toward less formal clothing. In the workplace, traditional suits have been replaced by "business casual" attire. Similarly, in the world of weddings, the standard black tux is no longer required apparel. I'm certainly not advocating that you show up in a T-shirt and jeans. This is one of the most important days of your life, after all. Instead, the clothing you choose depends on the time and location of your celebration, the level of formality you wish to express, and the attire your lovely bride has chosen for herself and her attendants.

The table below gives you some general guidelines to match your look to the kind of wedding you want. If tuxedo terminology is all Greek to you, check out "Tux Terms" first.

	Daytime	Evening
Semiformal	A suit with a white shirt is suitable. Navy blue or charcoal gray suits work well any time of year, and khaki is cool for the summertime. You can either wear a nice necktie or go tieless. If the wedding takes place at the seashore or another relaxed venue, you might look great in a crisp linen suit.	Select a dark tuxedo and bow tie, worn with a cummerbund or vest. If that's too stuffy for your tastes, a tasteful dark suit will work. For summer weddings, try a white dinner jacket. You'll look just like Bogart in *Casablanca*.

| Formal | Choices abound—tuxedos, tailcoats, and gray strollers are all apropos. Match them with a vest, an ascot or a regular necktie, and a pocket square if you're feeling particularly dapper. If you want to go all-out, you can add a top hat, spats, and gloves. | It's black-tie at a minimum—a classic black tux with a white wing or spread-collar shirt, black bow tie, and matching vest or cummerbund. Or you can really wow them with a white-tie ensemble, which includes a black tailcoat and white bow tie. |

Tux Terms

IF YOUR IDEA of formalwear is a shirt with buttons, a trip to a tuxedo shop can be an intimidating experience, especially when the salesman starts spouting black-tie buzzwords. To help you find the outfit that fits best, here's a brief glossary.

JACKETS

- **Tuxedo** (aka **tux**)   This is the classic jacket, suitable for formal and semiformal events. It comes either single-breasted (with a 1- to 4-button front) or double-breasted (with a 2- to 6-button front), and is available with different types of lapels (see below).
- **Cutaway** (aka **morning coat**)   For formal daytime weddings. The cutaway coat is short in the front, long in the back, and tapers from the front waist button to a wide back tail. Cutaway jackets are either black or gray and worn with matching striped trousers.
- **Full dress** (aka **tails** or **tailcoat**)   This style jacket is cropped in front, with two tails in the back and a 2- to 6-button front. Generally worn at very formal evening weddings.
- **Mandarin** (aka **Nehru** jacket or **Mao** jacket)   This jacket features a stand-up collar with no lapel and is worn with a mandarin-collared shirt (see below).
- **Stroller coat**   This is a semiformal suit jacket cut like a tuxedo. Usually charcoal gray or black and traditionally worn at weddings that take place before 4 P.M.

LAPELS

- **Notched** Features a triangular indention where the lapel joins the collar. This is considered the least formal lapel style.
- **Shawl collar** A smooth, rounded lapel with no notch.
- **Peaked** This broad, V-shaped lapel points up and out just below the collar line.

SHIRTS

- **Crosswyck** This collar style crosses in front and is fastened with a shiny button.
- **Mandarin collar** (aka **band collar**) This collar stands up around the neck and is the most contemporary style of tuxedo shirt. Plus, you can wear it without a tie.
- **Spread collar** This resembles a standard button-front shirt but features a wide division between the points in front. The wider collar looks great with a Euro tie or a standard necktie tied in a Windsor knot.
- **Wing collar** The most formal choice and the collar style most often worn with tuxedo jackets, this stand-up collar has downward points.

NECKWEAR

- **Ascot** This wide, formal tie is usually patterned, folded over, and fastened with a stickpin or tie tack. Usually reserved for ultraformal daytime weddings and worn with a cutaway coat and striped gray trousers.
- **Bow tie** This is the classic accompaniment to a classic tux. Many rental shops carry only the pretied variety that hooks around your neck. But if you want to really impress your fiancée, buy your own bow tie and teach yourself how to tie it. Just make sure you practice enough that you could give a virtuoso performance at Carnegie Hall, because you'll be on stage for your wedding as well.
- **Euro tie** This is a hybrid between an ascot and a regular, run-of-the-mill necktie. It's a long, square-bottomed tie knotted at the neck and worn with a wing collar or spread-collar shirt. The Euro offers a more formal look that's not as all-out as an ascot.
- **Necktie** If your style is more casual, you can wear a classic tie with a suit or tux jacket. A silk tie in silver or blue is dressy enough to work with a tux.

Getting Your Getup

WHETHER YOU'RE PLANNING a dinner dance at a royal palace or a barbecue on the beach, you want to acquire your attire from an establishment that rents men's formalwear. Geographically speaking, your ideal choice is a shop in the vicinity of your wedding location. This facilitates the pickups and drop-offs before and after the big day. If your groomsmen are scattered across the country, don't automatically conclude that you need to find a shop with nationwide outlets near everyone. As a professional courtesy, most formalwear shops in the United States offer complimentary measurements to wedding party members, which your groomsmen can then send off to the shop of your choice.

It is important to select a store that can immediately and effectively deal with any problems that you or your groomsmen encounter when you pick up your attire. A shop that carries its own inventory is desirable, so that any problems with incorrect or incomplete orders can be quickly fixed. Also, if there is a tailor on the premises, he or she will be able to immediately repair any torn fabric or loose buttons. So, as you're seeking a suitable store, be sure to ask how it handles any last-minute problems with its products.

While many couples still abide by the tradition of the groom not seeing his bride in her gown until she walks down the aisle, it's not advisable to risk traumatizing her with a surprise selection of guy garb when she reaches the altar. Your fiancée should accompany you on your first visit to a formalwear store. She will help you select a style of attire that complements her wedding gown as well as the bridesmaid dress. (For instance, if her dress is ivory, your shirt shouldn't be bright white.) After you've found a formalwear store that you both like, you can round up your groomsmen, ushers, and fathers of the bride and groom for their measurements.

If you're renting a tuxedo, be sure to order the complete ensemble: jacket, pants, shirt, vest or cummerbund, cuff links, studs, tie, suspenders, and shoes. You provide your own matching socks (usually black). If you want a top-of-the-line tux, ask about thread count. A high quality jacket has about 110 to 120 threads per inch, while standard tuxes have thread counts of around 70 to 80.

You also want to pick a tuxedo that complements your body type, as well as the body types of your groomsmen, ushers, and dads. If you're lucky enough to be tall and slender, you could probably wear any style. Thin men look best in a double-breasted jacket. Shorter guys should go with a single-breasted jacket and smaller bow tie. The single-breasted, shawl-collar tux is a good choice for husky guys, with a single button around the belt line to make the torso appear longer and leaner. If you are on the heavier side, consider a vest over the traditional cummerbund.

Overall, your choice of attire should make you and the other male wedding party members look dashing and debonair, not stiff and uncomfortable. Choose a wardrobe style that best fits the style of your celebration. You will look great both on the wedding day and in the photos that last a lifetime.

Consult a Travel Agent About Your Honeymoon

WITH ALL THOSE details to take care of in planning your wedding, the honeymoon sometimes gets put on the back burner. While that's understandable, you'll definitely be ready for a relaxing respite once your big day is done. That's why it's important to plan ahead and make arrangements for a honeymoon that is as memorable as the wedding day itself.

Location, Location, Location

YOU FIRST NEED to figure out how much time you can afford to take off for your honeymoon. If you can spare only a week or less, that limits the distance you can travel because you don't want to spend the entire honeymoon on an airplane. In fact, you might want to consider taking just a brief break right after the wedding, then saving the real honeymoon for a few months later when you can better afford the time (and expense). On the other hand, if you have two or more weeks available to take off, it opens up a wider range of possibilities.

Sit down together over a glass of your favorite beverage and share ideas of where you would love to go for your honeymoon. For inspiration, look at travel magazines, or go to Web sites like lonelyplanet.com, roadandtravel.com, and roughguides.com, and click on their "destination" pages. In case you're wondering what places are hot for honeymooners, a survey published in the August/September 2005 issue of *Modern Bride* magazine indicated the following top ten destinations:

1. Hawaii
2. Italy
3. Tahiti
4. Anguila

5. Fiji
6. St. Lucia
7. Mexico
8. St. Barths
9. Jamaica
10. France

Next, think about the types of trips you have taken in the past. Do you like to travel quickly to your destination, then just chill by the beach or pool? Or do you prefer to take adventurous excursions and see as many sights as possible while you're away? If your fiancé answered yes to the first question and you voted for the second alternative, you've got some negotiating to do. A good compromise might involve a creative mixture of the two. For instance, he could pamper himself in a beach-front cabana while watching you take surfing lessons.

One thing to consider in picking a place for your honeymoon is the weather. Most honeymooners prefer locations where the weather is likely to be warm (but not too hot) and relatively dry. The following table shows the best months to visit some of the more popular honeymoon destinations:

Location	Jan	Feb	Mar	Apr	May	June	July	Aug	Sep	Oct	Nov	Dec
Alaska						✓	✓	✓				
Australia	✓	✓	✓						✓	✓	✓	✓
Bahamas	✓	✓	✓	✓							✓	✓
Bali				✓	✓	✓	✓	✓	✓	✓		
Belize	✓	✓	✓	✓	✓					✓	✓	✓
Bermuda					✓	✓	✓	✓	✓	✓		
Brazil					✓	✓	✓	✓	✓			
Britain					✓	✓	✓	✓	✓			
Canada						✓	✓	✓	✓			
Caribbean Islands	✓	✓	✓	✓	✓							✓
Central & South Africa				✓						✓	✓	
Costa Rica	✓	✓	✓	✓						✓		✓
Fiji					✓	✓		✓	✓	✓		
Florida			✓	✓			✓			✓	✓	
France					✓	✓	✓		✓	✓		
Greece					✓	✓			✓	✓		

Location	Jan	Feb	Mar	Apr	May	June	July	Aug	Sep	Oct	Nov	Dec
Hawaii			✓	✓	✓	✓	✓	✓	✓	✓	✓	
Ireland							✓	✓				
Italy				✓	✓	✓			✓	✓		✓
Jamaica	✓	✓	✓	✓				✓				
Kenya	✓	✓				✓	✓					
Las Vegas		✓	✓	✓	✓					✓	✓	✓
Maldives		✓	✓	✓								
Mauritius				✓	✓	✓			✓	✓	✓	✓
Mexico	✓	✓	✓	✓	✓					✓	✓	✓
New Zealand	✓	✓										
Pacific Coast – USA				✓	✓				✓	✓		
Seychelles					✓	✓	✓	✓	✓	✓	✓	
Spain and Portugal				✓	✓	✓	✓	✓	✓	✓		
Switzerland						✓	✓	✓	✓	✓		
Tahiti						✓	✓	✓	✓	✓	✓	
Thailand	✓	✓									✓	✓

If you prefer a ski vacation for your honeymoon, hit the slopes in the northern hemisphere between December and March, while southern hemisphere resorts typically have the best snow conditions between June and September.

HELPFUL HINTS

If you've decided to travel abroad for your honeymoon, make sure you have valid passports. If you need to apply for or renew a passport, do it now. The U.S. State Department, which issues passports, takes at least 6 weeks to process passport paperwork, unless you want to pay a hefty procrastination tax, which they call an "expediting fee." For information on passport application procedures, and to download application forms, go to http://travel.state.gov/ and click on "Passports." Or pick up an application at your local post office.

While visiting the State Department's Web site, be sure to check the "Travel Warnings" page for current information on countries that our government considers dangerous for travel. You may wish to bookmark this page so you can quickly recheck it shortly before departing for your honeymoon.

Hiring a Travel Agent

YOU CAN DO all the travel planning yourself, but there are plenty of travel agents that can help arrange your trip, and there are many benefits to using one. Travel agents offer the following advantages:

- expert advice on places to visit and stay
- access to discounts not well-known to the general public
- package deals for air, car, and hotel reservations
- additional time in your life to devote to other matters (like planning your wedding)

Once you've come up with some ideas on where and what you want, I recommend contacting an agent to obtain professional advice and help. The Internet has helped to create a niche market for some travel agents that specialize in honeymoons. Many of these specialists do not run a retail office, but they provide the personalized service of a brick-and-mortar travel agency. You typically correspond with these agents by e-mail, phone, and fax. Here are a few honeymoon experts for you to consider:

- Creative Travel Adventures, Colorado, 888-568-4432, creativetrav eladventures.com
- Just Honeymoons, California, 877-377-2200, justhoneymoons.net
- Honeymoon Consultants, British Columbia, 800-433-7364, honey moonconsultants.com
- Honeymoons, Inc., Georgia, 888-811-1888, honeymoonsinc.com
- Unforgettable Honeymoons, Oregon, 888-343-6413, unforgettable honeymoons.com

If you prefer to work with an agent in your area, or if you want to find someone with experience in a particular destination, look for members of the American Society of Travel Agents or the Travel Institute (formerly the Institute of Certified Travel Agents). To locate an appropriate agent for your needs, visit their Web sites—astanet.com and thetravelinstitute.com. Both sites allow you to search for agents by their location as well as the travel locations they specialize in.

To make sure you have found the right travel agent for your needs, request references and ask the following questions:

- Have you personally traveled to the location we have in mind? If so, what was your experience like?
- Given the kind of honeymoon we want, what specific suggestions do you have? Are there other destinations that you would also recommend? If so, what information can you provide us about these destinations?
- What is your preferred method of communicating with us, and what is your normal response time when we have questions?
- Can you advise us on how to obtain the necessary visas, immunizations, or any other clearances we need prior to traveling?
- If we have a problem with our travel arrangements while we're on the honeymoon, what will you do to help us? How can we contact you?

For Brides on a Budget

According to the Travel Institute, the average couple spends more than $4,000 on their honeymoon. If that figure causes you to consider the nearest campground for your getaway, here are some tips to keep you from breaking your bank:

- **Travel at off-peak times.** Do the opposite of what my weather chart says, and you could save a bundle at your chosen location. Just make sure you understand why your favorite location isn't as popular during its off-season. For instance, August through October in the Caribbean is hurricane season. Also, if your schedule allows you to fly on off-peak days—typically Tuesday through Thursday—your airfare could be a lot less.
- **Forgo the view.** It's better to select a nonview room at a nice resort rather than a superb view at an ugly location.
- **Cash in your chips.** This is the perfect opportunity to use those frequent-flyer miles and hotel points you've accumulated.
- **Set up a honeymoon registry.** For couples who are content with their current collection of housewares, consider a honeymoon registry, where your guests purchase a portion of your travels, instead of towels and toasters. Check out www.honeyluna.com, www.thebigday.com, or www.thehoneymoon.com.
- **Look at all-inclusives.** Depending on your interests, the complete offerings at an all-inclusive resort like Club Med, Sandals, or SuperClubs may be more economical than individually purchasing your particular preferences at other locations.
- **Publicize your position.** Everybody loves lovebirds, and if you politely make your circumstances known when making your reservations, you may score some free upgrades or extra perks.

Finally, keep in mind that the honeymoon is the start of your married life together. Make sure that your travel plans won't have you continually running from one hot spot to the next, but instead will allow you plenty of time to focus on each other.

Pick Out Rental Items

SAY YOU'VE DECIDED to have your wedding in your parents' poolside garden, or maybe at a pastoral barn setting in the countryside. Where will all the lovely tables, dishes, and surroundings come from? The answer: a rental company. With the freedom of being able to customize every aspect of your wedding—from the size of your tables and style of your chairs, to the china, stemware, flatware, and even the lighting to be used—comes the added task of choosing rental items that mesh with your design concept.

Finding the Right Rental Companies

YOUR CATERER IS probably the best source for referrals on rental companies, because it likely has vast experience dealing with rentals. In fact, some caterers make it a contractual requirement to handle your rental items. Other caterers take care of ordering your rentals for an additional fee. It may be well worth that added expense. By having your caterer contract with the rental companies, it assumes responsibility for checking the rental items on arrival and securing them at the end of the day (something you certainly don't want to deal with). Just make sure your caterer allows you to select the specific colors and designs you want.

Alternatively, if you have hired a professional wedding planner, he or she will help you find the right rentals for your needs. If you need to secure a rental company on your own, check out the Web site of the American Rental Association, www.ararental.org. Click on "Find a Rental Store" and enter your zip code. You'll get a listing of rental companies in your area, complete with links to their Web sites.

The Internet, however convenient and easy, is not the way to select these important items for your wedding. Rental companies may have depictions of chairs, china, stemware, and flatware—and even attempt to describe in words and pictures the fabrics of their table linens. But this is never a substitute for an in-person visit to the showroom, where you can see, feel, and physically put these components into place with each other, to get a feel for how they will look in final form.

Gear Up

HERE IS A brief list of rental items you may need if you are having your wedding and/or reception at an off-site location:

CEREMONY

- aisle runner
- arbor/canopy
- chairs or benches for guests
- decorative shrubbery
- floral arrangement pedestals

RECEPTION

- barware
- chairs for cocktails and dining
- china
- dance floor
- flatware
- hedging (for privacy)
- lighting
- napkins
- portable restrooms
- seat cushions
- staging
- stemware
- table linens
- table number stands
- table votives (your florist might supply these instead)
- tables for cocktails, food stations, and dining
- tenting

Shopping for Rentals

WHEN CHECKING OUT rental companies, take into account the quality (and quantity) of their items. If upon visiting a showroom you notice only a few linen and china patterns, very basic stemware and flatware, and rental chairs that appear chipped and tired, you probably won't be happy working with them, regardless of price. Instead, your rental company should have a vast selection of linens, china, flatware, and stemware. Keep in mind the number of courses you're serving (if it's a sit-down meal) and select appropriate table settings for each course. Don't be afraid to grab linens, drape them over a table, and play around with your tabletop design—this is the only way you can really get a feel for how it will look.

To give your tabletops a truly trendy look, here are my top design tips:

- For linens, look at bold colors, beading, and embroidery, multiple-color linens, and sheer overlays.
- Choose colored glass plates and glasses or nontraditional plate shapes such as triangles, squares, rectangles.
- Use unmatched pieces of china, flatware, and stemware that coordinate in color and style.
- Vary the china and flatware patterns for each course, but select a beautiful charger, which is a base plate that is part of the decor and is kept down throughout the entire service, removed only when the entrée plate is cleared.

You also need to decide whether you want your guests seated at round, square, or rectangular tables, or some combination of all three. Rounds are usually 60 or 72 inches in diameter, and comfortably seat 8 or 10 people, respectively. Squares are a more recent development, coming in 48- and 54-inch options, which can seat 6 or 8 people comfortably. "Banquet" tables are 30 inches wide and come in lengths of either 6 feet (seat 3 per side) or 8 feet (4 per side). A popular variation of the traditional banquet table is the 48-inch-wide "kings" table, which better accommodates floral centerpieces.

The linens you need for each table depend on the table sizes you choose. All sit-down dining tables are 30 inches high, and linens should always go to the floor. So if you're using 72-inch round tables, think like this: The tabletop is 72 inches across and 30 inches high on each side, which totals 132 inches; you need a 132-inch round tablecloth to reach to the floor. If you're envisioning full-length linen with an accent or "overlay" linen on top, the second one can be 102, 108, or 120 inches. If you've selected "banquet" tables, you need either a 6-foot or an 8-foot table drape, depending on your table size. And don't forget the linens for the cake table and napkins as well. The rental company professionals can help you with ideas and measurements.

Usually chiavari chairs (aka ballroom chairs) go well with these table arrangements, and you may want to rent color-coordinated seat cushions and jeweled chair caps as well. But if you're planning a contemporary wedding in an urban loft, consider sleek metal chairs instead. For outdoor ceremonies on the lawn, standard wooden folding chairs are less likely to sink into the ground when your guests sit down, but consider natural wood over the tired white look.

Other Rentals

UP UNTIL NOW I have touched on only the "standard" rental items, but of course there are many other areas where rentals may be needed. For example, if you have the financial means, you might want to rent a tent as part of your private venue wedding. Some companies that rent standard items also supply tents, or there are companies that strictly specialize in tent rentals. Tenting can range from an open push-pole tent to the more substantial frame tents with covered sides and see-through "clear walls." Frame tents are self-supporting with no poles in the middle, allowing for more usable interior space. Also, to soften the look of the interior of your tent, a billowing fabric lining can be attached to the ceiling and walls for an amazingly beautiful (and expensive) effect. Linings come in a variety of colors, so don't feel bound by "bridal white"— pick a color that matches your motif.

Additionally, you may want special lighting to illuminate your fabulously designed space, in which case you need to engage the services of an event lighting company to create the proper effects for your wedding. Event lighting companies can transform any space into a ballroom by suspending sparkling chandeliers from the ceilings (or from wires or trees if you're outdoors). Walls, columns, statues, shrubs, or any other objects worthy of being accented can be dramatically uplit with lights placed on the floor pointing upward. And you can showcase your cake table as well as floral centerpieces at each dining table by positioning "pin spot" lights from overhead. "Projection lighting" can even be cast on floors and walls, with the couple's initials or names stenciled on a "gobo."

One of the less glamorous rentals you may have to consider (although vitally important) are portable restrooms. Depending on where you are holding your wedding or reception, portable restrooms are not only a convenience, they may actually be required. Certain outdoor facilities mandate that you rent portable restrooms in order to use their space for your wedding. But don't cringe as you envision the blue plastic cylinders often seen in front of home remodeling projects. There are other more elegant portable restrooms to choose from, including elevated bathroom "suites" with porcelain sinks, mahogany vanities, and marble countertops. Of course, these "executive" restrooms are more expensive than those typically used by construction crews. There are a number of "portable" companies online that you can contact for details and pricing. They deliver these restrooms to your venue and pick them up afterward, just like any other rental item.

Quantities, Payments, and Contracts

TO DETERMINE HOW many of each kind of rental item to order, start with your current estimate of guests likely to attend, as shown in your guest list spreadsheet. Add a few extras to allow for breakage, damage, or loss. Ask your caterer for input on appropriate quantities to order for beverage glasses during cocktail hour, and plates and silverware for food stations. For portable restroom rentals, you generally need at least one restroom for every 50 guests.

To secure the rentals, you may need to place a deposit (typically ranging from 25 to 50 percent), then make a final payment shortly before the wedding once you have an accurate head count (see Week 51). The rental company contract should indicate the name and phone number for the rental company representative whom you can contact on your wedding day if there are any problems with delivered items. It should also include the name and phone number of the contact person at your venue who is overseeing delivery and pickup of the rentals.

Delivery of rental items normally takes place the day preceding the event, and pickup is normally the day after, with the exception of Sunday, which can incur extra charges. Make sure that all these details are spelled out in the rental agreement.

Select a Hairstylist and Makeup Artist

EVERY BRIDE WANTS to look and feel beautiful on her wedding day. You certainly want your hairstyling and makeup to hold up throughout the day while you're enjoying the celebration (and while your photographer is snapping away). Because this is one of the most important days in your life, seek out the services of professional hairstylists and makeup artists who have the skills and knowledge to make you look marvelous!

On your wedding day, you don't want to be running all over town to get your hair and makeup done. Either choose a full-service salon that can do both hair and makeup inside the salon, or have your chosen hairstylist and makeup artist travel to your location. It may be more expensive for them to come to you, but it is a time-saver, because you can slip into your gown immediately afterward.

Your attendants, your mom, and your future mother-in-law may also want to get their hair and makeup professionally done. This provides a great opportunity for a bridal bonding session. You can secure hairstylists and makeup artists to take care of all the ladies. Specific circumstances may vary, but in most cases, you need to secure 1 hairstylist and 1 makeup artist for every 4 to 5 people in your group.

When Money Is No Object

If you choose to arrange for professional hair and makeup for other members of your wedding party, there are no set-in-stone etiquette rules on who pays for their services. If your budget allows, it is a gracious gesture to pick up the tab. Also, it is much less of a hassle for everyone if the hairstylists and makeup artists can collect a single payment from you, rather than having each wedding party member write a check.

Qualifications

FIND HAIRSTYLISTS AND makeup artists who are state-licensed cosmetologists/aestheticians. Licensed stylists and artists have been through many, many hours of training and certification. The right hairstylist and makeup artist enhances your natural beauty rather than covering you up with a mask. These beauty experts help you truly look your very best on your wedding day. Their prices vary considerably across the country but typically range from $175 to $700 for the bride and much more for the complete bridal party.

You may be wondering whether makeup artists who work at department store cosmetics counters are an appropriate cost-saving choice. Keep in mind that these people usually are not professional makeup artists. Typically, they are trained only on the products the stores carry and are behind the counter primarily to sell the line of cosmetics they represent. They are generally not required to blend or create specific colors needed for a professional quality of makeup and are limited to the colors and products they have in stock.

On the other hand, seasoned makeup artists have skills and expertise beyond what most behind-the-counter artists are required to learn. The professional licensed makeup artist works with both professional makeup and consumer products, custom blending and color matching whenever necessary. As Jeni Fong, owner of Grace Image in San Francisco, points out, "Their goal is not to sell you more makeup, but to beautify your face on your wedding day."

Finding a Hairstylist and Makeup Artist

THERE ARE SEVERAL ways to find qualified beauty professionals:

- Talk to recently married friends whose hairstyles and/or makeup you admired. Just make sure they have a similar hair and skin texture to yours.
- Your photographer can be an excellent source for referrals. Photographers work frequently with hair and makeup professionals, both on wedding and fashion photo shoots.
- If you are using a wedding planner, definitely ask him or her for recommendations and referrals.

- If you purchased your wedding gown in a local salon, it may have appropriate referrals.
- Check out regional bridal magazines and Web sites.

Once you have compiled a list of prospective hairstylists and makeup artists, telephone to inquire about their availability on your wedding date. If you want them to travel to another location, such as your home or a hotel room, verify that they are willing to do this. Look at their Web sites or go to their salons to examine portfolios of their work. Be sure to ask for pricing information.

For Brides on a Budget

If you absolutely, positively cannot afford to have your hair and makeup professionally done, you can do your own. If you must apply your own makeup, follow these suggestions from makeup artist Jeni Fong:

1. Start out by covering blemishes with a concealer that matches your skin.
2. Next, even out your complexion with foundation that matches your skin. Take care to go over your eyelids and lips for longer wear.
3. Set your face with a translucent power. This adds staying power to your makeup application.
4. Spice up your regular look by emphasizing your eyes and adding some sparkle to your skin. Some inexpensive choices are Max Factor Dual Finishing Powder, L'Oréal lip gloss, Cover Girl lipstick, and Maybelline Pure Blush.

SELECTING A HAIRSTYLIST AND MAKEUP ARTIST

AFTER YOU HAVE spoken to all of the stylists and artists on your list, narrow down your selection to two or three of each. Then make appointments for a trial run with each stylist and artist remaining on your list. Try to schedule these appointments so you can first have your hair done, then your makeup immediately following. (This is the sequence you will use on your wedding day).

To prepare for the appointments, look for pictures of hair and makeup styles that you like in bridal magazines, then bring copies with you. You can also bring photographs of yourself that show your hair and makeup in styles that you prefer. These photos will help the hairstylist and makeup artist to develop a look that is just right for you. Ask them what they feel should be done to your hair and face, including what features they would enhance and which they would downplay.

Feel free to express your opinions about what you like and don't like. According to Hillary Clark, owner of Blush Beauty in San Francisco, "*You* know your hair best. Don't let someone try to force your hair into a style that won't work. If your hair doesn't hold curl well, don't expect it to look great down with large barrel curls. The curl will relax and could look stringy."

If your wedding gown is white, wear a white shirt to your trial appointments so you can get an accurate idea of what your hair and makeup might look like on your wedding day. Ideally, the shirt should have a neckline similar to that of your gown because the neckline of the gown can influence the hairstyle and makeup you choose. If you have already purchased a headpiece to accompany your bridal gown, bring the headpiece to your appointment as well.

Also take along your camera and a notebook. If you really like what the hairstylists and makeup artist do, ask them to snap a few photos of you. Write down the names of all products they used, as well as how these products were applied. You want to be certain that whatever you like is repeated on your big day.

Make your final choice of hairstylist and makeup artist by carefully considering how you look and feel after each trial appointment. Once you have reached a decision, pay a deposit to secure their services. I recommend that you have a written agreement as well.

You may need to do some rough scheduling at this point to determine an approximate time frame that their services will be required. Backing up from the start of your ceremony, allow ample driving time to get to your ceremony location, at least 90 minutes prior to that for dressing and photos, and if necessary, the driving time to get from the hair and makeup salon to the location where you are dressing. This gives you an approximate time when your makeup needs to be *completed*. Your hair must be finished one hour earlier. (For additional information, see Week 47, where I explain how to create a detailed timeline for the wedding day.)

Finally, arrange to see your chosen hairstylist and makeup artist once or twice more before your wedding day. (Bridal showers provide an excellent opportunity for getting your hair and makeup done again.) This will give you an opportunity to fine-tune the look you want well in advance of the wedding, and you will also become more comfortable with your hairstylist and makeup artist.

HELPFUL HINT

Do not try any new skin care products or makeup of any kind right before your wedding! If you have an allergic reaction and develop a rash, it could take a month or even longer for it to heal. If you must try a new product, do so at least one month prior to the wedding.

Reserve the Rehearsal Dinner Location

AS FAMILY MEMBERS and attendants gather in preparation for your fabulous wedding, the rehearsal dinner provides a wonderful way to commence celebrating in a more intimate environment. Those you hold most near and dear have an opportunity to socialize and relax before the big day, and you also have a chance to express your gratitude to them for all of their support over the years.

Who and How Much?

THE FIRST STEP in planning the rehearsal dinner is determining whom to invite. At a minimum, your guest list includes yourselves, your parents, immediate family members, the entire wedding party, and their significant others. If you're having flower girls and ring bearers in your wedding party, their parents should be invited as well. Usually, you also want to invite your grandparents and your officiant. It's always a gracious gesture to include guests coming from out of town, since you may not see them very often. For a destination wedding, invite all of your guests, since everyone's an out-of-towner.

Once you've come up with a rough head count, you can start to ballpark a budget for the rehearsal dinner. Depending on whether you want a very informal meal at a nearby ethnic restaurant or an exquisite chartered yacht cruise, the cost could range anywhere from $25 per person to $250 per person. Just keep one point in mind when considering the kind of rehearsal dinner you want: It should never be so over the top that it upstages the wedding itself.

Traditionally, the groom's parents host the rehearsal dinner. But like most old wediquette rules, this one does not need to be followed. Nowadays, anyone can play host, including the couple, the bride's parents, another family member, or a close friend. No matter who is nominated to fund the festivities, you will probably be responsible for doing most of the legwork in finding an appropriate place for the dinner.

When?

PRIOR TO THE rehearsal dinner, you and your wedding party of course need to rehearse by meeting at the ceremony location for a dry run through your program. Before you can start looking for rehearsal dinner sites, you first need to schedule the date and time of your rehearsal. If you haven't already done so, call your site and officiant to make those arrangements.

Usually, the rehearsal takes place the day before the wedding. It's preferable to pick a late afternoon start time if one is available. Allow one hour for the rehearsal to be completed. With that in mind, the start of the rehearsal dinner should be based on the travel time from the rehearsal to the dinner location you choose. By the way, try to keep that travel time to a maximum of 30 minutes.

Where?

MANY COUPLES OPT for an informal and nontraditional rehearsal dinner by planning a clambake at the beach or a barbecue in the backyard. These ideas are definitely fun and festive, but they can also be a lot of work. You already have a wedding to plan, so unless you can enlist a trusted family member or friend to take the lead in planning your rehearsal dinner, you might want to stick to simpler options. Restaurants are the most popular choice because they score lowest on the hassle scale.

To find an appetizing restaurant in the vicinity of your ceremony location, contact the local convention and visitor's bureau or chamber of commerce. Ask for information on restaurants with private dining areas. If you have a favorite ethnic cuisine, look for a restaurant of that genre. If there are no private dining rooms, another possibility is to buy out a restaurant—take over all the seats for the entire evening. However, this can be quite expensive.

If you live near your wedding location, visit any restaurants of interest to check out their ambience and regular menu offerings. For those that look good to you, plan a romantic evening with your sweetie and sample their cuisine.

If you don't find any restaurants to your liking, hotels are another option to consider. If you have blocked hotel rooms for your out-of-town guests, check to see if the hotel has any available banquet facilities. It is certainly convenient for your out-of-towners, plus you may be able to get more favorable pricing, given that you're bringing them other business as well.

What?

ONCE YOU'VE LOCATED some potential rehearsal dinner sites, call and ask for menu proposals. You don't want this meal to resemble anything you're serving at your wedding. If your wedding dinner features a filet mignon, choose a chicken or seafood dish for the rehearsal. Some restaurant owners may be willing to offer two or three choices of entrée at a fixed price, while others will even allow you to order off their regular menu.

Preferably, the locations you're considering have a separate space near the dining area where your guests can enjoy a round or two of cocktails prior to being seated for dinner. The cocktail hour format gives your guests a chance to mingle and socialize first and also permits a more flexible arrival time for any invited guests who don't need to attend your rehearsal.

Base your final decision on a rehearsal dinner site on the convenience of the location, the ambience and relative privacy of your designated dining area, the price quoted, and last but certainly not least, the quality of the food.

HELPFUL HINTS

Some bridal publications advocate turning the rehearsal dinner into a spectacular theme party, complete with casino tables, video game arcades, or karaoke competitions. I believe that such special effects are unnecessary and can even be counterproductive. With this extraordinary gathering of your closest friends and family members, the energy flows naturally from within your group. Everyone is very excited to begin celebrating this major milestone in your life, and you don't need a lot of external stimulus to make it an entertaining event.

Nevertheless, you can take some specific steps to ensure that the rehearsal dinner is a particularly enjoyable occasion:

- *If the families are meeting for the first time, consider an icebreaker activity during the cocktail hour to encourage introductions and mixing.*
- *Vary the seating arrangements from the wedding. For example, if your reception head table includes only your attendants, then seat your parents next to you at the rehearsal dinner.*
- *The more intimate atmosphere of the rehearsal dinner makes it the best time for guests to get their personal stories out. In particular, encourage guests with a proclivity for verbosity to give their toasts and roasts during the rehearsal dinner. (On the other hand, toasts at the wedding should be short and sweet.)*
- *Offer your own toasts to your guests, thanking them for their support and friendship. The rehearsal dinner is also an excellent time to present your gifts to attendants and parents.*
- *Take very small sips with each toast. You don't want to be hungover on your wedding day!*
- *End the evening early, so you can get a good night's sleep before the big day.*

For Brides on a Budget

If you can gather your group earlier, have a rehearsal lunch instead of dinner. Your food costs are less, and you're more likely to get to bed at a reasonable hour on the night before your wedding. If you choose to have a lunch, reschedule the rehearsal for late morning.

If you are set on having a dinner, consider Thursday evening instead of Friday. Many restaurants may offer a lower price, since it's at an off-peak time. Of course, first make sure that your attendants and important family members can join you a day early.

Finalize Your Ceremony Program

TAKE A MOMENT to consider the real reason why so many of your friends and family will be gathering on your wedding day. Yes, they want to party. But more important, they want to express their love and support for you, and witness one of the most significant milestones of your lives. Your wedding celebration may be mostly about the reception, but your marriage is memorialized by the ceremony.

Ceremonial Substance

YOU HAVE ALREADY chosen the "rite" officiant and ceremony site. Now it's time to make an appointment with your officiant to discuss your desired ceremony flow and length. Work closely with the officiant to determine and write out the content and sequence of your ceremony.

Carefully consider and select songs or readings to make your wedding ceremony personalized and meaningful to you and your guests. Ask the most important people in your lives to be a part of your ceremony—as readers, candle lighters and, if they are suitably talented, musicians. Honor deceased family members with a special song, reading, or prayer.

Are you having a religious, secular, interfaith, or nondenominational ceremony? Your answer helps you determine the sequence or flow of the ceremony. In most religious ceremonies such as Roman Catholic, Protestant, or Jewish, the ceremony is already structured according to the particular rituals of that religion. If you are having an interfaith or nondenominational ceremony, you typically have more control over the content of your program. Make sure you clearly indicate your preferences to your officiant and work closely with him or her to create a ceremony that expresses your spirit.

While significant denominational differences often exist, most religious ceremonies contain some or all of the following elements:

1. **Prelude music**   Starts 30 minutes before the ceremony.
2. **Processional**   With the traditional bridal processional, only the bridesmaids and bride walk down the aisle. In a contemporary wedding processional, the whole wedding party participates—readers, groomsmen, the groom with his parents, bridesmaids, and the bride with her parents.
3. **Words of welcome**   The officiant introduces the couple and makes the guests comfortable.
4. **Opening prayers or readings**
5. **Declaration of consent**   Similar to a contract, to be sure that both parties (bride and groom) are entering into this agreement of sound mind, free will, and an understanding of what they are about to do— as in a lifelong commitment!
6. **Presentation of the bride and groom**   The officiant asks the guests to affirm their support of this marriage.
7. **Readings from the Bible**   In most Christian weddings, there may be a total of three readings: one from the Old Testament, one from the New Testament (both of which are read by family or friends), and a third from the Gospel, read by the officiant. Many times the Gospel reading is followed by a personal message from the officiant to the couple.
8. **Exchange of the vows**   This is the moment you have all been waiting for. Consider writing your own vows to make them more personalized. But keep them short, especially if you are memorizing your vows (something I highly recommend, so you can repeat them every year on your anniversary).
9. **Blessing and exchange of the rings**
10. **Unity candle lighting**   The two of you take taper candles that were previously lit by your family members, and together you light a single larger candle positioned in the middle.
11. **Declaration of marriage**   The officiant pronounces you husband and wife.
12. **Final prayers and blessings**   Could include a song and the Lord's Prayer.
13. **Presentation of the couple**   To rousing applause from your guests.
14. **Recessional**   Walking back down the aisle as newlyweds to lively music.

HELPFUL HINTS

In a traditional Christian ceremony, the bride's family and friends are seated on the left and the groom's on the right. At a traditional Jewish wedding, it is the opposite—the bridesmaids and bride's family are on the right, the groom's on the left.

For a very contemporary processional, line up your wedding party in the following order:

1. *Clergy member, officiant, rabbi, or priest*
2. *Readers*
3. *If grandparents are healthy, it's a lovely gesture to include them in the processional—the groom's go first, followed by the bride's*
4. *Groomsmen, usually paired together*
5. *Groom with parents; groom is in the middle*
6. *Bridesmaids—can be in single file or paired with groomsmen*
7. *Flower girl*
8. *Ring bearer (may go together with a flower girl)*
9. *Bride with parents; bride is in the middle*

Typically the bridesmaids and groomsmen are lined up according to height, with the shortest attendants entering first, and the maid/matron of honor and best man going last. Children under 6 years of age should be snatched by a parent or family member as they reach the end of the aisle and be seated with the guests. All eyes then turn toward the bride, including the attendants, who face out toward the bride as she approaches.

When the bride reaches the groom, I recommend they slightly face each other as well as the guests. The wedding party is positioned in a semicircle or diagonal line facing the guests with the first attendants situated farthest from the wedding couple. Your guests are there to witness this event, and your photographer and videographer are supposed to record it, but they can't do that with your backs turned to them. If your ceremony will be more than 20 minutes, don't torture your attendants by making them stand. Kindly give them chairs to be seated.

For the recessional, it's typically last in, first out. In other words, the bride and groom go first, followed by maid/matron of honor and best man. Then the bridesmaids and groomsmen are paired together, followed by the bride's parents, then the groom's.

Religious and Ethnic Variations

IT IS BEYOND the scope of this book to write about the unique aspects of every type of wedding ceremony in the world. However, below

I provide a brief glimpse at some of the more prevalent types of religious and ethnic weddings.

ROMAN CATHOLIC

FOR A MARRIAGE to be recognized by the Roman Catholic Church, it must take place in a Catholic church. The marriage ceremony can be performed with Communion, called a nuptial mass (approximately 60 minutes in length), or without Communion, called a nuptial blessing (lasting about 45 minutes). Gone are the days of kneelers and banns; instead, there are numerous ways to enrich and personalize your ceremony through music, readings, and rituals. For a more contemporary Catholic ceremony, check out the Maryknolls, Christian Brothers, Jesuits, or Newman Center priests on university campuses.

JEWISH

BEFORE THE CEREMONY begins, the groom and his designated witnesses gather with the rabbi for the signing of the *ketubah,* the traditional Jewish marriage contract. At the start of the ceremony, the couple sips ceremonial wine from the first of two kiddush cups and receives a blessing from the rabbi. After the exchange of the rings, the *ketubah* is usually read aloud and officially presented to the bride by the groom. Then, after the couple drinks wine from the second kiddush cup, the rabbi gives the Seven Blessings, usually reading them both in Hebrew and English.

During the ceremony, the bride, groom, rabbi, and parents gather under the chuppah, a canopy representing the Jewish home as well as the tents of nomadic ancestors. The chuppah is typically made of four slender poles, decorated with flowers and greenery. The fabric top is made of silk, satin, or even a prayer shawl.

The best-known part of the Jewish ceremony is the breaking of the glass, a joyous conclusion that encourages merriment. This ritual serves as a reminder of the destruction of the Temple in Jerusalem, as well as the fragility of human relationships. As the groom stomps on the glass, guests shout "Mazel tov!" in celebration.

AFRICAN AMERICAN

MANY AFRICAN-AMERICAN weddings feature the Libation Ceremony, which is designed to call on the ancestors of the couple. Your officiant, family elder, or honored guest pours water or wine into a bowl or gourd, and the names of the ancestors are announced. These ancestors are called on to bless the marriage and ward off evil spirits.

Crossing Sticks is a wedding blessing that originated in the early 1900s. You show your commitment to each other by leaning long sticks or branches on the floor and crossing them against each other in the middle. The sticks represent the vitality and strength of trees—and your marriage.

The most popular ritual is Jumping the Broom, which usually takes place just before the recessional. In times of slavery, African Americans weren't legally entitled to be married and live together. The slaves, therefore, invented their own ceremony, which featured the bride and groom jumping over a broom to the beat of drums. The broom symbolizes the sweeping away of an old life and the beginning of a new life for the new couple. Tradition says that whoever jumps over first will be the boss of the household.

HISPANIC

IT IS A Mexican tradition for both the bride's and the groom's parents to serve as the official hosts of the wedding. Guests are sent two identical invitations, one from the bride's family and one from the groom's family. The parents bless their children in their homes before the ceremony. Six sets of godparents, known as *padrinos,* sponsor and actively participate in the wedding.

The bride and groom use special kneeling pillows during the Catholic mass, usually provided by their padrinos. A large rosary called a *lasso* is wrapped in a figure eight around the couple's shoulders and hands during the ceremony to symbolize the union and protection of marriage. A key ritual is the blessing of the *arras,* where the groom presents a gift of 13 gold coins to his bride. These coins, symbolizing Jesus and his 12 apostles, represent his commitment to support her throughout their lives.

Filipino weddings feature these same rituals. In addition, during a Filipino ceremony, the sponsors place a ceremonial veil over the groom's shoulders and the bride's head. This veiling ceremony symbolizes the unity of the two families into one, and it is also a prayer for health and protection during the couple's married life.

ASIAN AMERICAN

MOST ASIAN-AMERICAN couples opt for a Christian ceremony, but some choose to invoke Buddhist scriptures. These Buddhist ceremonies feature the *o juju*—a rosary of 21 beads in two different colors. These beads represent the couple, their parents, and one for Buddha. They are tied on a string to symbolize the joining of the families, and the bride and groom use them as they offer prayers to Buddha.

Matrimonial Odds and Ends

MARRIAGE PREPARATION

MANY RELIGIONS REQUIRE engaged couples to go through counseling prior to their wedding. Regardless of your religious beliefs, every couple about to enter marriage should seriously consider premarital counseling. It is an opportunity to deepen your level of commitment and communication with one another by discussing your attitudes about money, children, sex, your roles in the family and community and, of course, who takes out the garbage. If your house of worship does not offer marriage preparation counseling, look online or in your Yellow Pages for leads.

MAKING YOURSELVES HEARD

YOU ARE INVITING your guests to witness your wonderful ceremony. They really want to hear it as well as see it. Unless you're both accomplished Broadway performers, it's doubtful that your guests will all be able to hear your exchange of vows, especially if you're in a large church or an outdoor location, without some sort of amplification. I therefore highly recommend that you use a sound system for your ceremony. Specifically, I suggest two lavaliere microphones that can be clipped, one onto the officiant and the other on the groom. Also, have a wireless hand-held microphone for readers.

Check with your ceremony site to see if there is a sound system you can use. If your ceremony and reception are at the same location, your reception musicians or DJ may be able to provide a sound system for a modest fee. Alternatively, you can contact an audiovisual company to provide this service.

With so much emphasis placed on the reception, the ceremony can sometimes get overlooked. As you're planning the details of your ceremony, keep this mantra in mind: A wedding is a day, a marriage is a lifetime.

Register!

A TIME-HONORED TRADITION in our society, wedding gifts have historically been given by guests to show their support and to help you begin married life on a stronger financial foundation. But picking the perfect present for anyone is no small feat, and that's why wedding registries were devised. A registry enables your guests to select gifts that you're sure to enjoy.

Of course, your guests are not obligated to buy you a present just because you invited them to the wedding. Many couples balk at registering because they don't want to be perceived as greedy and materialistic. However, the vast majority of your friends and family genuinely want to send you a token of their esteem, whether you register or not. So you might as well give them the opportunity to purchase something that you actually want.

The Cutting Edge of Reg

WHILE BRIDAL REGISTRIES may be steeped in tradition, they have also experienced dramatic changes in recent years. No longer are you restricted to selecting the formal china, crystal, and silver collections at major department stores (although these choices remain popular). Now you can register anywhere from Amazon.com to Z Gallerie, and you can pick any kind of merchandise you want, including patio furniture, sporting goods, electronic equipment, home improvement supplies, and artworks. You don't even have to register for physical products. Other possible options include honeymoon travel (see Week 30) and donations to charities (check out the I Do Foundation at www.idofounda tion.org).

The process of registering has been greatly simplified in recent years due to technological advances. Most of the major retailers provide hand-held scanners that allow you to create your registry list by simply walking through the store and zapping the bar codes of items you want. It's certainly much quicker than writing everything down (which is what we did in the olden days), and your fiancé can enjoy a game of laser tag with your favorite set of china. Later, when a guest purchases an item from your registry list, the store's computer system automatically records the purchase and updates your list of remaining items, so that the next shopper can't choose the same thing.

Perhaps most important, technology is now actually making it easy for your guests to buy a gift that you've registered for. The powerful combination of a personal wedding Web site and online shopping has made it ridiculously simple and convenient. A task that used to take days for a guest to accomplish can now be completed in a matter of minutes.

Here's how it works: On your personal Web site, you provide registry information, including hot links directly to the stores' online gift registries that you have signed up for. These online registries have real-time listings of the items you have registered for, and they work like any other e-commerce site. Your guests simply visit your Web site, jump to the registry's Web site, select an item to purchase, provide a credit card number, have the package shipped to your address, and they're done!

A wonderful by-product of this technological breakthrough is the elimination of two of the most vexing etiquette problems that have plagued couples for decades—informing guests where you have registered and handling gifts that are brought to the wedding.

Until now, it has always been considered socially unacceptable to inform guests about your registry locations unless they specifically ask you. Otherwise, you would be considered a "gift grubber." (Especially verboten is the notion of listing on your invitations where you're registered.) Instead, etiquette experts advocate that you appoint your parents and attendants to serve as "surrogate gift grubbers" and spread the word on your behalf. One problem with this politically correct approach is that another cardinal rule of etiquette is being broken: You don't make it very easy for your guests when you employ this convoluted method of communication.

Now, with a personal wedding Web site, you can provide your registry information to your guests directly but tactfully. I am certainly not suggesting that the home page of your wedding Web site have flashing dollar signs and arrows pointing to large neon-colored wording that says, "TO BUY US A GIFT NOW, CLICK HERE." Instead, your Web site should mostly contain information about you and your fiancé—how you met, how he proposed, and some cute photos. The registry information can be placed on a separate page or tastefully displayed in a not-so-prominent position on your home page.

So that guests find out about your Web site, include an insert card about it with your save-the-date card or invitation. Besides disclosing your Web site location, this insert serves other important purposes, such as providing information on hotel room blocks, local attractions, driving directions, and so on. Simply say something like, "Please visit our wedding Web site at whatever-your-location-is.com," without mentioning anything about where you're registered. (That is still considered tacky by today's etiquette standards.) As guests become more accustomed to them, they will realize that personal wedding Web sites are the best way to find out where you're registered. Guests who are cybernetically challenged can still call your parents to get this information, so be sure to keep your parents in the loop on your registration locations.

Finally, by using an online registry, guests should be motivated to stop the exasperating practice of schlepping gifts to your wedding. In the olden days, guests would have your gifts carefully wrapped with a lovely card attached. Although it has always been considered proper etiquette to have gifts sent to your home, some guests instead brought them to the reception. There, they were stacked on an unattended table for hours. At the end of the evening, all of the gifts (assuming they hadn't been stolen by then) got crammed into the trunk of a parent or attendant's car, causing most of the accompanying envelopes to detach from the gifts. Upon your return from the honeymoon, a huge pile of mangled packages and envelopes was dumped on your doorstep, leaving you to sort out the mess.

Now, guests can simply ship their gifts directly to you at no extra cost, saving themselves the unnecessary additional effort and saving you an enormous headache. In the subsequent thank-you notes that you'll write, the appreciation you express will be totally sincere.

Registry Recommendations

REGISTERING FOR YOUR wedding gifts can be a lot of fun, but it is often difficult deciding what to select, especially if you are already trying to figure out how to merge your stuff together with your fiancé's.

The best strategy is to start with a standard checklist of household items that couples commonly register for, and compare that list to the items you already own. (I provide a standard checklist below.) Go through your possessions, room by room, and compare them against the standard checklist. Decide what items you want to keep in your married life, what you want to sell in a garage sale or on eBay, and what you don't already own that you would like to have.

This should give you a rough draft of your registry list, as far as traditional items are concerned. Nontraditional items are limited only by your imagination.

Next, pick out shops that you love and go online to preview their offerings. This should help you zero in on those stores where you really want to register, as well as the specific styles, colors, and patterns that interest you. It's generally advisable to select about three registry locations. This enables you to register for a wide variety of items without making it too complicated for guests to browse the registry Web sites for gifts. If you find that your personal preferences require you to select more than three stores, I recommend that you utilize an online service that provides one-stop shopping for your guests, such as findgift.com or myliferegistry.com. Alternatively, you can try the consolidated registry services offered by the large wed sites like theknot.com and weddingchannel.com.

Ideally, you should go to the store in person to make your actual selections, because items you like in a Web site photo may not look the same when you see them live. At most stores, you need to schedule an appointment to register, and you should avoid weekends and holidays if possible. Some stores assign you to a registry specialist, who can provide helpful suggestions and answer any questions you have.

The number of items on your registry list should exceed the number of invitations you send out for the wedding, so that your guests have options to choose from. In case you're feeling self-conscious about this, please understand that having a large registry list does not make you look greedy. You're actually helping your guests by giving them more choices. You also want to offer a wide range of prices for your registry items, to ensure that everyone can find a great gift within his or her budget. Finally, check your registry periodically to make sure that items at all price levels are still available for your guests to purchase. If your registry runs out of items at a certain price range, try to come up with additional choices at this price.

Gift Checklist

WHILE THERE IS a much greater diversity of acceptable choices for registry items in the twenty-first century, most couples select at least some of the "traditional" goods. To help you decide whether you need or want to stock your new household with any of these items, I offer the following checklist for your use.

Item Description	Quantity
China and Dinnerware	
Butter dish	1
Cake plate	1
Candlestick holder	2
Casual place setting (dinner plate, salad/dessert plate, soup/cereal bowl, coffee mug)	12
Charger	12
Coffeepot	1
Espresso cup and saucer	8
Formal china place setting (dinner plate, salad/dessert plate, bread and butter plate, teacup and saucer)	12
Gravy boat and stand	1
Salad bowl	1
Salt and pepper shaker	1
Serving bowl	3
Serving platter	2
Serving tray	2
Soup bowl/pasta bowl	12
Soup tureen	1
Sugar bowl and creamer	1
Teapot	1
Flatware	
5-piece casual setting (dinner fork, salad fork, tablespoon, teaspoon, knife)	12
5-piece formal setting (dinner fork, salad fork, tablespoon, teaspoon, knife)	12
Butter knife	12
Demitasse/espresso spoon	6
Ladle	1
Salad server	1
Serving fork	2
Serving spoon	2
Slotted serving spoon	1
Glassware	
Beer mug or pilsner	6
Casual drinking glass	12
Champagne flute	12
Cocktail shaker	1
Dessert wine	6
Double old-fashioned glass	12
Highball	12
Ice bucket and tongs	1
Iced beverage	12

Jigger and bar tools	1
Juice glass	6
Margarita	6
Martini	6
Shot glass	6
Water goblet	12
Wine glass	12
Kitchen Item	
10- or 12-inch skillet	2
1½-quart saucepan with lid	2
3-quart saucepan with lid	2
4- or 5-inch skillet	2
Baking sheet	1
Blender	1
Bread knife	1
Cake pan	1
Casserole dish (1 small, 1 large)	2
Chef's knife	1
Coffee grinder	1
Coffeemaker	1
Colander	1
Dish towel	4
Double boiler	1
Dutch oven (4 to 6 quarts)	1
Food processor	1
Hand mixer	1
Hot Pad	2
Juicer	1
Kitchen shears	1
Measuring cup	2
Measuring spoons	1
Microwave oven	1
Mixing bowls (1 small, 1 large)	2
Muffin tin	1
Omelette pan	1
Panini grill	1
Paring knife	1
Roasting pan	1
Salad spinner	1
Sharpening tool	1
Slow cooker	1
Steak knives	12

Stockpot with pasta insert	1
Teakettle	1
Toaster	1
Vegetable steamer	1
Waffle iron	1
Table Linens	
Napkin rings	12
Napkins	12
Place mats	12
Tablecloth	2
Bedding	
Bed skirt	1
Bedcover	1
Blanket	2
Decorative pillow	2
Duvet or down comforter	1
Mattress pad	1
Pillow	4
Sheet set	2
Bath Items	
Bath mat	1
Bath sheet	6
Bath towel	6
Electric toothbrush	2
Guest towel	4
Hamper	1
Hand towel	6
Scale	1
Shower curtain	1
Washcloth	4
Luggage	
Duffel bag	2
Garment bag	2
Tote bag	2
Upright suitcase	2

ALTERNATIVE WEDDINGS

If this is your second or third marriage, or if you're tying the knot later in life, you probably have accumulated more household items than the average bride and groom. If you've always wanted a set of fine china, silver, or crystal but couldn't afford it in your younger years, this may be an ideal time to go for it. Or how about something a little more up-scale than standard home furnishings, like that cappuccino maker they use in your favorite coffee shop?

Regardless of your personal tastes and needs, remember that the wedding registry is actually a service for your guests, not a plea for gifts. If you make it easy for them to buy you a gift that you can use, everyone will be happy.

Choose and Order Your Wedding Rings

UNDOUBTEDLY, THE MOST memorable and heartfelt moment on your wedding day is the actual rite of marriage. The centerpiece of this ritual is the exchange of rings, whose unbroken circular shape represents your unending love for each other. Since you will wear these cherished symbols of your marriage every day, it's important to choose your wedding rings carefully.

Style Options

TRADITIONALLY, THE BRIDE'S wedding band matches her engagement ring, and the groom selects a band similar to hers. But today you're free to do as you please. You can decide to wear your engagement ring on your right hand and your wedding ring on the left. Your groom does not need to select a similarly styled ring; it doesn't even have to be made of the same metal. Instead, you should each choose rings that best fit your style and personality.

The first thing to consider in your choice of a wedding ring is the metal. You have four principal options:

- **Yellow gold** is the most traditional of ring metals, often viewed as a symbol of the warmth and love of a marriage. While 24-karat is the most pure, it is also the softest, so choose 14- or 18-karat for durability. Look at the mark inside the band to check the karat count.
- **Platinum** has become the most popular choice because it is a very hard metal, which makes it extremely resistant to damage. Unfortunately, it is also the most expensive metal used in ring making. Although a beautiful silver in color, jewelers often describe platinum as "white," to avoid any confusion with the "silver" metal.

- **White gold** is a popular trend in wedding rings because it has the look of platinum but is less expensive. White gold is not a natural material but is instead made by coating regular gold with a metal called rhodium. Over time, the rhodium plating can fade, so the ring may need to be replated.
- **Titanium** is increasing in popularity, especially among men, because it is even harder than platinum but less expensive. However, due to the hardness of this white-colored metal, it is not easy for designers to work with, and therefore most bands do not have intricate details.

If you're having trouble deciding between a gold or "white" color, you can compromise and get both. Rings made of mixed metals have become very popular in recent years. For instance, you can have 18-karat yellow gold sandwiched between two narrow bands of platinum, or vice versa. A bit of decorative detailing on one of the colors can add even more punch to the design.

If diamonds are your best friend (next to your fiancé, of course), consider them in a "channel setting" for your wedding ring, where a row of small stones are set into the metal all the way around the band. This style of ring gives you a very glitzy look that coordinates fabulously with your engagement ring. Flush-mounted diamonds have become quite fashionable on men's wedding rings as well.

Here's another way to make a statement—you can have personal messages engraved on the inside of your bands. There are numerous inscription options, including your wedding date, your initials, or an inspiring phrase proclaiming your love for each other. Whatever you choose, that special message from your spouse will be with you whenever the ring is on your finger.

Overall, in deciding what wedding ring style(s) may work best for you, there are some practical issues to consider. Because you're going to be wearing this ring every day, it should work well with your lifestyle. If most of your jewelry is gold, a platinum ring may not be the best choice. If you love sports, or work with your hands a lot, you probably should pick a "comfort fitting" ring with rounded edges. When in doubt, it's best to select a ring with a more classic styling. After all, you will be wearing this ring for a long time, and you want to still love it on your fiftieth anniversary.

Finding and Purchasing Your Wedding Rings

WITH THE EXPERIENCE of shopping for an engagement ring already under your belts (see Week 2), you will probably find it easier to purchase your wedding rings. Before you visit any stores, it's best to start by looking at photos—in magazines and online—to make some preliminary decisions on the styles and metals you are interested in.

You have already identified the best jewelry stores, so visit these stores again to shop for your wedding bands. Bring any photos that interest you when you go shopping. The salespeople in reputable stores can quickly identify any of their offerings that closely match your interests, or they may be able to suggest other similar styles that you were not aware of.

Prices for simple gold bands start at around $125, and can be $500 or more if they have intricate design details on them. For the same style of ring in platinum, expect to spend anywhere from $500 to $1,200. Of course, if diamonds are introduced into the equation, the prices can jump significantly (often into the thousands), depending on the quality and quantity of stones in the setting. Whatever you end up paying, use a credit card, if possible.

While you have many decisions to make for your wedding, your choice of wedding rings will be with you for years to come. Remember that you'll be wearing your ring every day, so it should not just fit properly on your finger, it should also fit your personality and lifestyle.

Purchase Memorable Mementos

ALTHOUGH YOUR WEDDING reception lasts only several hours, the memories that remain afterward are important to preserve. Several items are typically displayed at your reception, then taken home as a keepsake to remind yourselves and your guests of the wonderful celebration. These items include favors, a guest book, a cake knife/server, and toasting glasses.

Finding Favor

GIVING YOUR GUESTS a favor on your wedding day is a long-standing tradition, as a way of showing appreciation for their support. In today's wedding world, favors are still considered a lovely gesture, but they are not mandatory, especially if you're on a tight budget. If you decide to have them at your celebration, they should be unique mementos for your guests to enjoy. Giving them a traditional tulle sack of Jordan almonds to break their teeth on is not a particularly imaginative choice (unless you also happen to be a dentist).

To begin thinking about favors for your wedding, first consider what happens when guests take them home afterward. They do one of five things:

- display them in their homes
- use them for their intended purpose
- eat them
- stash them in an out-of-sight storage area
- throw them away

Obviously, you don't want your guests to pick either of the last two possibilities, so give them a favor that's beautiful, useful, or edible.

With these overall parameters in mind, think again about your wedding design concept and whether it can be expressed through a favor. In particular, ask yourself if there is something you can buy or make for your guests that fulfills your vision and the ambience you are creating, and also fits within your budget.

For edible favors that can't reasonably be shared, it is advisable to have one for every guest at your wedding. Otherwise, one favor per couple is generally sufficient. If you're having children at your wedding, consider providing special candy favors for your young guests. In any event, before you go shopping, look at your guest list to guide you on the appropriate quantities to purchase or prepare, and allow for a few extras to keep for yourself.

Many online businesses specifically sell "wedding favors," including, favorfavor.com and myweddingfavors.com. However, you can find some of the most interesting ideas for favors in "regular" shops, including home furnishings stores like Ikea and Pottery Barn, import stores like Cost Plus and Pier 1, and gourmet food shops like Dean & Deluca and Williams-Sonoma.

If you're still not inspired with an idea for favors, consider the altruistic approach: Make a donation to a favorite charity in the name of each guest. For more information and ideas regarding charitable favors, visit www.idofoundation.org.

In lieu of buying favors, making your own is a wonderful way to personalize your wedding, and having a "wrap party" with your bridesmaids can be a great bonding session. However, you certainly don't want to be baking and boxing the night before your wedding. Make sure the favors you fabricate have a reasonable shelf life, so you have plenty of time to wrap them carefully and calmly.

Finally, don't be constrained by thinking the favor must be a certain size or shape, so that it can fit on your dining tables with the place settings. Instead, you may be able to reuse your guest book table to display your favors. Your wedding planner, caterer, or a family member can put them out on the table during dinner, and guests can pick them up as they depart. Or you can ask your caterer to have the waiters distribute the favors to your guests as the festivities are drawing to a close.

ONE COUPLE'S STORY

———

*F*or ethnically mixed marriages, favors that bring the two cultures together provide a wonderful way to honor the couple's heritage. Susan a
Chinese bride, and Lawrence, an Italian groom, had beautifully wrapped
boxes positioned at every guest's place setting. Inside the boxes were two
very simple, yet very meaningful gifts—a fortune cookie and a biscotti
cookie.

Great Guest Books

TODAY, YOU HAVE many choices beyond the traditional guest
book with its signature lines arranged in tidy little rows. As one well-
known wedding expert would say, that's a good thing! The purpose of
the guest book is not to collect perfectly arranged autographs but rather
warm wishes from your guests that you can treasure for a lifetime.

Once again, start thinking about the kind of guest book you want by
considering your wedding visions and design concept. Perhaps the cover
of your book can be creatively adorned to complement your decor (or if
you're lucky, maybe you can find a book that's already appropriately
decorated). Perhaps the perfect thing for your guests to write on isn't a
book at all but an object that embraces your ambience.

If you can't think of a way to reflect your wedding theme in your
guest book, try personalizing it by using photos. My favorite is the Polaroid photo book, where you give a Polaroid instant camera to your
wedding planner or a friend or family member to photograph each guest
at your wedding. Then your guests attach their photos to a blank page
with double-sided tape and inscribe messages alongside. Another popular
choice is to display a large matted photo of the two of you at the reception. Guests can write directly on the mat.

You can purchase conventional guest books at stationery stores or
through a multitude of Web sites. Before you buy, it's advisable to look
online first, so you can familiarize yourself with the choices of guest
books that are available.

On your wedding day, prominently display your guest book so that
your guests will be sure to write some rosy remarks. During the cocktail
reception, place it on a beautifully decorated table alongside the escort
cards. To ensure that everyone sees and signs the guest book, you might

have your wedding planner or one of your attendants take the guest book around to every dining table during the reception.

Toasting and Cake Cutting

THE CHAMPAGNE TOAST and cake-cutting ceremony are reception traditions that remain popular to this day, and your toasting glasses and cake server provide a permanent reminder of this ritual.

If you registered for formal dinnerware at a major department store, you will likely find that they also have a fabulous selection of toasting glasses and cake knives and servers. You may even wish to match them with the patterns you've already registered for. Also, in lieu of a two-piece cake knife and server set, consider a single-piece pie server with a cutting edge—you don't really need a separate knife to slice through a wedding cake. My husband and I actually use our pie server every time we have a dessert that needs slicing. In addition to serving dessert gracefully, it is a lovely reminder of our wedding.

Numerous Web sites sell toasting glasses and cake/pie servers. For a wide selection of brand names, go to www.exclusivelyweddings.com. If you wish, you can usually get your purchase engraved with your names and wedding date for a nominal charge.

Although you can have your toasting glasses placed at your head table for use during the best man's toast, I recommend that you put them on the cake table and save them for the groom's toast, which you can give just prior to the cake cutting. Guys, this is the first opportunity for you to toast your lovely bride. You also want to thank your guests for attending your wedding (especially those who traveled a great distance to be there) and for their support throughout your lives. Ladies, although old traditions didn't contemplate a bride speaking at her own wedding, feel free to reciprocate your groom's toast.

Cut your cake with the lady's hand placed on top of the gentleman's, so that the bride's ring is prominently displayed for photos and video. After cutting the cake, feed each other the way you expect to treat each other throughout your married life. Then take this opportunity to honor your parents by cutting and serving pieces of cake to them. But now I'm getting a bit ahead of myself!

Overall, the wonderful memories of your wedding day are enhanced with keepsakes such as favors, guest books, toasting glasses, and cake/pie servers. These items may be small tokens in the grand scheme of things, but they play a big role in making your wedding a unique and unforgettable occasion.

Shop for Wedding Gown Accessories and Celebratory Clothes

IN PREPARING FOR your wedding day, purchasing your gown was a major event. So that you look and feel fabulous as you walk down the aisle, you need to pick out some additional elements of your wedding day wardrobe. And you want to look marvelous not just on your wedding day but also at other special occasions in your honor—showers, the rehearsal dinner, and your honeymoon. That's why it's time to go out and outfit yourself so you are ready to celebrate in style.

Wedding Gown Accessories

TO COMPLETE YOUR bridal ensemble, you need to accessorize. The most important enhancements to a wedding day wardrobe are the headpiece, veil, and shoes. First, take a look at photos in bridal magazines to see what kinds of accessories appeal to you, and flag any photos of interest. When you go shopping, make sure you bring along a swatch of your gown fabric, or at least a photo of the gown. Images of preferred bouquet colors and styles can also be helpful in making selections.

HEADPIECE

A HEADPIECE CAN be worn alone simply as a lovely adornment, or it can serve the important purpose of securing a veil. Your choice of headpiece should be compatible with the way you want to wear your hair on your wedding day. Therefore, if you haven't already done so, first choose a hairstylist and decide how you would like to have your hair done (see Week 32).

There are a wide variety of options for headpieces, but here are some of the more popular:

- **Backpiece** A barrette or comb that is fastened to the back of your head, often adorned with beads, bows, or flowers. A backpiece is a good choice when you want to accent your ensemble but don't want all attention drawn to the accessory. Backpieces can be worn with a variety of hairstyles, and they work especially well with a low bun or French twist. A veil can easily be attached to the backpiece.
- **Bun ring** A complete circle of crystals that is worn around an updo, providing a classic styling.
- **Hat** Typically trimmed with lace, pearls, or flowers, a hat may speak to your sense of style. You can choose a variety of sizes, from large brims to pillboxes.
- **Headband** This less formal headpiece works well if you want to wear your hair down, because it is a great way to keep hair away from your face. A headband can also be worn to accent an upswept hairstyle, by wrapping it around the bun.
- **Tiara** A jeweled or beaded semicircle worn on top of the head. Tiaras are as versatile as they are beautiful: They can be worn with or without a veil, they work well with most styles of gown, and they complement longer as well as shorter hairstyles.

If the salon where you bought your wedding gown also carries headpieces, it may be to your advantage to purchase yours there. Using the display model of your gown, you'll be able to see clearly how well the gown coordinates with the various headpieces offered. Be aware, however, that most bridal gown designers do not design their own headpieces, so there may be no such thing as "the matching headpiece."

Instead, when choosing a headpiece, look for something that complements the ornamentation or design elements in your dress.

If you don't find anything to your liking in your salon, ask if they can refer you to any specialty shops or designers in your area. Or look in the Yellow Pages under "Bridal Accessories" for leads. You can also go online to search for headpieces—check out bridalheadpieces.com or glamgal.com.

VEIL

FIRST, CONSIDER WHETHER you even want to wear a veil at your wedding. While it is certainly a revered tradition, a veil is not necessary. And if this is not your first marriage, pay no attention to those traditional etiquette rules that say you should walk down the aisle sans veil. Go ahead and get a veil if you want one.

Your options in veils are generally categorized by their length. Here are the typical choices:

- **Blusher**   A short, single layer of fabric worn over your face as you walk down the aisle, subsequently flipped over your head or removed.
- **Flyaway**   A veil that just brushes the shoulders. It is less formal than other styles.
- **Mantilla**   A Spanish-style veil that encircles and frames the face, usually secured with a comb.
- **Elbow**   As the name suggests, this veil extends down to your elbows.
- **Fingertip**   Also cleverly named, this style reaches your fingertips when your arms are fully extended downward.
- **Waltz** (aka **ballet**)   A veil that ends above the floor but below the knee.
- **Chapel**   A formal veil that extends to the floor and is often worn with a sweep train for added effect.
- **Cathedral**   The longest and most formal veil. It falls 3½ yards from the headpiece onto the floor. The name indicates the best place to wear one.

In shopping for a veil, two factors have the greatest effect on your choice: the style of your wedding gown and the shape of your face. If your gown has lots of detail and ornamentation, select a plain veil that won't take attention away from the gown. On the other hand, you can select a more elaborate veil if you're wearing a simpler gown.

To find a veil that best fits your face, look for a style that complements your features. If your face is round and full, pick a veil that drops straight down along the sides of the face, which will make it look narrower. If you have an oblong face, look for a veil that provides some width, perhaps with multiple layers.

As with your purchase of a headpiece, you may wish to start your search for a veil at the salon where you bought your wedding gown. The same advantages and caveats apply. Otherwise, check out local specialty suppliers and designers, or go online to veilshop.com or weddingveil.com.

SHOES

ON YOUR WEDDING day, you'll spend hours on your feet—walking down the aisle, posing for photographs, greeting guests, cutting the cake, and dancing the night away. So above all else, your shoes should be comfortable. The heel height of your wedding shoes is very important, because your gown will be fitted to accommodate their height. I recommend picking a heel height similar to what you normally wear, because this is what you are most comfortable in. If you want a little added height on your wedding day, but you don't normally wear heels, consider platform or lower kitten heels.

While silk or satin are traditionally the two most popular choices for wedding shoes, pick a pair that reflects the style of your wedding gown (which presumably also reflects your personal style and tastes). For instance, if you're having an evening wedding and wearing a glamorous gown, strap on a pair of chic evening sandals. Satin shoes coordinate well with shiny fabrics, while crepe shoes complement dresses with a matte sheen. If your wedding gown has lots of lace, look for lacy shoes.

If you expect to wear hose on your wedding day, be sure to have it on when trying on your bridal shoes. When searching for shoes, it's preferable to shop later in the day, because your feet tend to swell a bit over the course of the day, and you certainly don't want to pick out shoes that are too small.

Today's most popular designers of bridal shoes include Vera Wang, Kenneth Cole, Jimmy Choo, Stuart Weitzman, Anne Klein, and Gina Shoes. Many of these designer shoes are sold in major department stores. While most allow you to purchase their shoes online, I don't recommend it, because a good fit is extremely important with shoes.

HELPFUL HINTS

About a month before the wedding, wear your new shoes around the house for several days in a row, to break them in. A Band-Aid on your heel to cover a blister is not the look you are aiming for.

Be sure to use some sandpaper on the soles of your shoes so they are not slippery. You don't want to fall while walking down the aisle.

LINGERIE

IT'S BEEN SAID (by my editor and perhaps someone more famous, as well) that "clothes make the man, but lingerie makes the woman." Go out right this minute and buy brand-new pretty undergarments—for the wedding and your honeymoon. Here are some things to keep in mind. Your gown is likely strapless or spaghetti-strapped, and low cut, and you probably have no idea what size or kind of bra you need. Most lingerie stores and the lingerie departments of department stores have fitters. Have the fitter help you choose the right bra. I know this is embarrassing, but be assured that she has seen them all and yours are not new or strange to her.

If the bottom of your dress is tight and slinky, you don't want the elastic of your underpants to show. The best bet may be to buy cotton-crotch panty hose to avoid this fashion no-no. (Buy at least two pairs of panty hose, in case you accidentally put your thumb through the first pair.)

The wedding lingerie needs to be white so it doesn't show, but you can go wild on your honeymoon accessories. Red! Black! Leopard print! Thong! Push-up!

Other Occasions

WHILE YOU'RE OUT shopping for accessories is a great time to pick out new outfits for other pre- and postwedding events, such as a shower, rehearsal dinner, and the honeymoon.

SHOWER

APPROPRIATE ATTIRE FOR today's bridal shower is in keeping with the contemporary and more relaxed way of approaching fashion in general. Check out a sleek silk sheath with a coordinating three-quarter-length coat. Or try on a knee-length circle skirt in a fun, brightly colored fabric with a 1950s-inspired jewel-accented cardigan sweater, buttoned almost to the top. Look to places such as Banana Republic, Bebe, Ralph Lauren, and Anthropologie for some wonderful looks. Keep in mind that you are dressing to suit the occasion.

With many showers now morphing into couples' cocktail parties or relaxed BBQ gatherings in the warm months, your groom may also need to update his wardrobe. He would do well with the stylish but relaxed look that takes him from the office (sans button-down shirt and tie) to a chic evening gathering—a crisp pair of slacks, beautifully tailored (sometimes fitted) shirt, and unstructured sport coat. Olive greens and browns/blacks mixed with hot-hued shirts are fun and festive. B/R, Kenneth Cole, and Boss (Hugo Boss) are the places to go when dressing for a special event.

REHEARSAL DINNER

DEPENDING ON THE location you have chosen for the rehearsal dinner, the appropriate attire could be formal, casual, or somewhere in between. However, plan on coordinating your clothing with your fiancé so that you're both dressing in the same degree of formality. That doesn't mean you should look like twins, but your clothing choices should complement each other.

For a more formal rehearsal, a cocktail dress is probably the best choice for the bride, and a suit and tie for the groom. You and your fiancé can shop together for your rehearsal dinner apparel at major department stores like Bloomingdale's, Nordstrom, or Macy's. If your rehearsal dinner is in a less dressy location, the attire types and shops described above for showers would work equally well.

You may want to take one of these new outfits with you on your honeymoon. Make sure you set aside something for the rehearsal dinner so it doesn't get prematurely packed away in your suitcase.

CLOTHES FOR THE HONEYMOON

IF YOU'RE HEADED to a tropical resort for your honeymoon, your days will probably be spent lounging at the beach or by the pool. In the evening, you may want to go out for dinner, and maybe spend a night or two on the town. So you want to have a wide variety of clothes, but they all need to fit inside your suitcase.

For beachwear, it's best to take two swimsuits with you, so you're not wearing the same thing every day, and perhaps more important, each swimsuit can dry out on its "day off." If you need a new bathing suit, you generally get a better deal at home than at the resort. Consider a light sarong or wrap to wear over your swimsuit during the day. Ideally, it coordinates with a tank top for evening wear.

For casual daytime activities, take several T-shirts in a variety of bright colors, preferably made of cotton blends that can easily be hand-washed and worn again. Also, make sure you have a couple pairs of cotton slacks and shorts, preferably khakis or lightweight denim. And you should have a pair of sandals that are very comfortable yet dressy enough to wear out on the town.

Ladies should also have a sundress and a sleeveless black dress, both of which look fashionable in the daytime or evening. Guys could pick up a couple of high-end Hawaiian-style shirts, so you look like you belong in paradise. If you can't find Hawaiian shirts locally, look on the Web at paradisefoundhawaiianshirts.com or shirtsofhawaii.com. If Hawaiian shirts are not your style, loose-fitting cotton shirts in solids or patterns should do the trick.

Finally, the most important garments for the honeymoon may be those not worn in public. You can charm your husband with a new selection of sexy sleepwear and lingerie. Check out the offerings at Frederick's of Hollywood and Victoria's Secret.

Meet with the Caterer for a Trial Meal

YOUR WEDDING MEAL should be a fabulous feast that everyone savors and remembers. To ensure that you and your caterer are on the same page, it is important to schedule a trial meal (not to be confused with a tasting), so you can finalize your menu selections. Plus, the trial meal is great fun—just like going out to a new restaurant.

To schedule a time for your trial meal, you need to give your caterer a minimum of about 4 weeks' advance notice, sometimes more if it's a busy time. The same chef who will be running the kitchen on your wedding day should supervise the trial meal. You should taste every item on the proposed menu, including hors d'oeuvres, breads, and desserts. In addition, ask the caterer to prepare not just the menu items that you tentatively selected when you signed the contract, but also one or two alternate items that you considered. Often, runner-up items can become your top choice after you've had a chance to see and taste them.

The caterer typically limits the number of people at a trial meal to 2 or 4. Of course, you and your fiancé should both attend, and if possible, your parents should join you so that you can have additional input on the meal selections. (Also, it's a great way to show your appreciation of their support). Sometimes, the groom's parents are also invited, especially if they are making a significant financial contribution to the wedding.

Before the trial meal takes place, have a set of the table linens, china, flatware, and stemware you selected from the rental company delivered to the caterer. You want to see how the menu items look with the rental items you have chosen, so you can make adjustments to your choices, if appropriate. The caterer should be able to arrange for the delivery of the rental items.

You also want to see how the menu items pair with the wines you have tentatively selected. If your caterer is supplying the dinner wines for your wedding, verify that he or she will be serving the wines you've chosen at your trial meal. Or, if you're purchasing your own wine, bring a bottle or two with you to the trial meal, and perhaps a couple of alternate choices as well.

Bring a camera, notepad, and pen to the trial meal, so you can keep track of your observations and thoughts about the various items being served. With each item, pay close attention to the visual presentation of the food on your rental plates, the smell and temperature, and of course the taste. Don't be bashful about offering your comments, first among your dining partners, then to the caterer. If the sauce is too salty, or the vegetables are overcooked, nicely bring it to the chef's attention. Record all comments and decisions on your notepad.

After the tasting, follow up with the caterer in writing. Review your notes, summarize your comments, and indicate your final selections of menu items, as well as rental items, so that the caterer has written documentation of your preferences.

If there was a particular menu item that did not turn out to your liking during the trial meal, ask for an opportunity to retaste it with an alternate method of preparation, or an entirely new item, if necessary. It's important that every menu item meets with your approval and that any problems be ironed out in advance.

Overall, your trial meal should be a delightful dining opportunity that makes you relaxed yet very excited about what you and your guests will experience on your wedding day.

Order Your Ceremony Program, Escort Cards, Place Cards, and Menus

YOU HAVE FINALIZED your ceremony program content with your officiant and made menu selections at your trial meal. Now it is time to purchase programs, menus, and other printed materials that you will use on your wedding day. Of course you want to make sure that the look and feel of these materials are consistent with the style of the other wedding stationery you have already selected. That way, you weave your design concept through every element of your wedding.

Program

ALTHOUGH IT'S NOT a requirement to have a printed wedding program, it does add a lovely personal touch and helps set the stage for your big day. It identifies and recognizes those people who are participating in your ceremony, while enabling your guests to follow along with the various rites, readings, and music you have selected. Your program also serves as a wonderful keepsake.

A program can range from a single sheet that provides a summary of your ceremony, to a booklet that's many pages long, where you write out the full text of all readings, prayers, and song lyrics. The length of your program is a matter of personal preference. If the majority of your guests are of different religious faiths, they may not be familiar with the rituals of your ceremony, so it is helpful to include explanatory information to make them feel more comfortable with the proceedings.

The conventional layout of a program is a folded card stock cover with the ceremony details printed inside, held together with a ribbon or tassel if multiple sheets are used. However, you can certainly choose other creative alternatives, especially if they embrace your overall design concept. Other popular options include rolled-up scrolls tied with ribbon or raffia, trifold wraps of handmade papers, and pouches made of card stock or fabric, with the program information tucked inside on custom-cut sheets.

A typical wedding program contains the following basic elements:

1. **Title page or section**   Indicating the bride's and groom's names, as well as the location, date, and time of the ceremony.
2. **Identification of the wedding party members, officiant, readers, and musicians**   It's important to honor everyone who is participating in the ceremony, as a way of thanking them for their support. If all members of your wedding party are in the processional (something I strongly recommend), you can list them in the order in which they enter the ceremony. It's also advisable to indicate your relationship to each member of the wedding party (e.g., "brother of groom," "friend of bride," and so on).
3. **Actual sequence of the ceremony**   As mentioned above, this can be in as much or as little detail as you want. See Week 34 for more information on the typical elements of a ceremony.
4. **Acknowledgments**   You may wish to express thanks to your guests for attending, or if you have a close relative who has passed away, you can include a special memorial.
5. **New address**   If you will be living somewhere else after the honeymoon, indicate your new address.

An important decision you need to make at this juncture is whether to have your entire program or only the cover professionally printed. If budget is not a concern, you can have the whole program done by a stationery company or commercial printer. Keep in mind that a 16-page program can get very costly. As an alternative, consider purchasing the cover from your stationery shop/graphic designer, then printing the detailed text yourself using a laser printer and/or copy shop. Either way, choose a font for your detailed text that is relatively easy to read—a flowing script that looked lovely on your invitation may not be legible for longer text.

Before going to press, review the text of the program with your officiant to make sure you have your service in the right sequence, and check with your lead ceremony musician for the correct spellings of music selections and composers. You also want to get a proof from the printer and review it carefully before the programs are printed.

Escort Cards

ESCORT CARDS ARE displayed at the cocktail reception (often alongside the guest book) and inform your guests where they will be sitting during the meal. Usually, escort cards are arranged on a beautifully decorated table in alphabetical order to allow guests to quickly locate their cards.

Traditionally, the escort card was a small (approximately 2½" by 3½") piece of card stock with the words "You Are Seated at Table Number ____" preprinted on it, and it included a matching blank envelope. More recently, designs for escort cards have become very creative. A cleverly constructed escort card that expresses your wedding motif is particularly memorable. For instance, if you're having a destination wedding in Florida, how about having a calligrapher write your guest's name and table assignment on the outside of an orange, then carefully arrange the oranges in a decorative orange crate? (Or you could take it one step further—bring in a live orange tree to the cocktail reception and have your guests pick their escort cards.)

Even if you decide to use a more traditional form of escort card, think of something more inspiring to print on the card than "You Are Seated at Table Number ____"—preferably a cleverly worded welcome that incorporates your design concept. At the very least, you can express your appreciation to your guests with a simple "Thank you for sharing this special day with us" before indicating the table assignment.

While having separate matching envelopes and cards is another old tradition that some couples also find dated, it does have one very practical advantage over the one-piece escort cards: If there are last-minute cancellations by guests due to illness or other unforeseen circumstances, you can easily shuffle around your seating assignments without needing to have any new escort cards printed.

Depending on the style of escort card you choose, you may need a calligrapher to handwrite your guests' names and table assignments, or you can run your escort cards through an ink-jet or laser printer. Consider these options as you select your escort cards. Test your printer to see if it can handle smaller-sized cards. If you need a calligrapher, make these arrangements now, so the calligrapher can set aside appropriate time in his or her schedule about two weeks before the wedding.

Place Cards

A PLACE CARD has the guest's name printed on it and is positioned at the exact place setting where the guest is to be seated during the meal. The conventional place card is folded in half and set down like a tent above the place setting, with the guest's name printed on the side facing the chair.

Some couples think that place cards are too formal or too expensive to bother with. I had a bride who was adamant about not using place cards at her guest tables, but she later regretted that decision. She assigned her parents to a table next to her head table, but with no place cards, they did not have designated seats. When the guests entered the dining area, her parents were busy socializing and accepting congratulations from other guests, and they were the last ones to make it to their assigned table. The result: Her parents got the worst seat positions at the table and spent the whole night with their backs to their daughter.

As stuffy and expensive as place cards may seem, they serve important, practical purposes—more than just ensuring that your VIP guests are facing your way. Many times, guests you have assigned to a particular table are meeting for the first time, and place cards can facilitate introductions and make it easier to remember people's names. Also, assigned seating eliminates the awkwardness that a couple may experience if they are the last to arrive at their table, and the only two seats left are on opposite ends of the table.

You don't have to go with the traditional "tent card." You can hang it from the back of the guest's chair using a ribbon, or you can have it positioned to poke out of a creatively folded napkin. The place card doesn't need to be a "card" at all. The guest's name could be printed inside a small picture frame or on top of a gift box, so the place card doubles as a favor.

Finally, if your are offering a choice of entrée for the meal, place cards are a necessity. The catering staff should not have to go around asking each guest which entrée choice he or she ordered. Instead, you can identify the choice the guest has made by using different colors of ink when writing the guests' names on the place cards.

Menus

HAVING A PRINTED menu at each place setting provides an elegant touch and gives your guests a memento of your delectable wedding meal. However you choose to describe your culinary selections, don't ruin it by putting the word "Menu" at the top of the page. Your guests are smart enough to figure out what they're looking at. To make your menu a more charming memento, you might begin with something like this:

Nicole and Paul's Wedding Celebration

Saturday, June 26, 2010

Stonepine Estate

Carmel Valley, California

If you love the look of hand calligraphy, you can hire a calligrapher to write out your menu. Then take it to a professional printer to be reproduced onto a custom-designed card. Another option is a personalized menu card, which doubles as a place card. The menu is laid out on the page with a blank space, which allows you (or, better yet, a calligrapher) to write in the guest's name.

Other Printed Pieces

IN ADDITION TO escort cards and place cards, you need to appropriately identify each guest table in the dining area, so your guests can find their way to the right location. Consider custom-printed table names or numbers that coordinate with your decor and other printed materials.

Generally, I recommend that you name your tables instead of numbering them, because it usually gives you another way to creatively incorporate your design concept into the reception. However, one disadvantage of naming your tables is that it's harder for your guests to find their table location, because there's no obvious sequential table layout when you use names instead of numbers. So you may also want to create a diagram of the room that pinpoints the location of each table. This diagram can be blown up, mounted on a poster board, and placed on an easel outside the dining area.

If you're having a cocktail party with food stations instead of a sit-down dinner, perhaps you are pleased that you don't need to pay for escort cards, place cards, and menus. However, it's a good idea to provide your guests with some information about the food they will be eating. Well-placed, artfully designed signage that describes the items being served at each food table is greatly appreciated by your guests.

Making Your Selections

TO PURCHASE ALL of these printed materials, you generally want to go to the same designer or stationery company that printed your invitations and save-the-date cards. It is in the best position to provide a styling that complements the previous pieces and fits with the overall design of your wedding.

Purchase one program and one escort card for each couple, or one per family if you're putting children at the table with parents. For place cards and menus, you need one per person. In all cases, order plenty of extras to have as keepsakes and to allow for errors in printing or calligraphy.

It is the details that really separate one wedding from another. With a beautifully and consistently designed wedding stationery wardrobe, you definitely create a celebration that is uniquely your own.

Have the Engagement Portrait Session with Your Photographer

TRADITIONALLY, COUPLES HAD formal portraits taken by their photographer several weeks prior to the wedding, so they could submit a photo along with a formal wedding announcement to their local newspaper for publication. Since formality has fallen out of favor in recent years, some couples now view an engagement photo session as a waste of time and money. However, it can be beneficial for you to spend this time with your photographer before the wedding. Your photographer will also find it valuable to have the opportunity to work with you before the big day. For this reason, many photographers offer an engagement photo session with their wedding packages.

By having engagement photos taken, you get to know your photographer better and become more familiar with how he or she works. That familiarity should translate into an increased comfort level on your wedding day, and you therefore will probably be more photogenic. Meanwhile, your photographer learns from the engagement photo shoot which poses and camera angles work best, and he or she develops a better understanding of what kinds of photos you like and dislike. Ultimately, you and your photographer both benefit from this session—the likely result is an improvement in the overall quality of your wedding day photos.

What to Do

NOW THAT I'VE convinced you of the value of an engagement photo session, the first thing you want to think about is where to have it. I recommend that you pick a favorite location, preferably outdoors, or perhaps the place where you and your fiancé first met. A site you love makes you more inclined to smile for your photos. If you want to have a formal portrait to send to your local newspaper for a wedding announcement, ask your photographer if that can be done in his or her studio, either at the beginning or end of your session.

You next question is probably, "What do I wear?" Your choice of clothing may depend on the location you choose for your photos. A "dressy casual" look works for outdoor photos, but more formal attire is more appropriate for indoor/studio shots. You may wish to bring a change of clothes with you so you look your best in both kinds of settings. In general, you and your fiancé should pick outfits that complement each other in style, color, and formality. Wear cool colors—medium and light blues generally work well—and avoid busy patterns. Most important, be sure to wear something comfortable so you look at ease in your photos.

It normally takes about 2 to 3 weeks for your prints from the engagement photo session to be ready. If you want to send one to your newspaper for a wedding announcement, choose your favorite and submit it along with any forms the newspaper requires. If you're sending a physical photo instead of a digital image, and want to get your photo back, include a self-addressed, stamped envelope. Place a piece of cardboard in the envelope, so the photo won't bend.

Your engagement photos can serve many other purposes as well: You can give them as gifts to family members; you can use them on the cover of your wedding program, for a "guest book" (see Week 37); or you can have them framed and displayed in your home.

ONE COUPLE'S STORY

*S*everal of Christy and Peter's engagement session photos were used in creating a wedding favor for their guests. The favor was a specially made CD containing some of their favorite music, and their photos graced the front and back of the CD case.

Other Matters to Consider

WHILE YOU ARE with your photographer for the engagement session, take this opportunity to discuss some important details regarding your wedding photos. To prepare for this discussion, you need to think about a few things ahead of time.

First, although the photojournalistic style of wedding photography has become very popular and prevalent, you want to have some posed photos on your wedding day. Even Denis Reggie, who pioneered the art of wedding photojournalism, acknowledges the importance of certain posed photographs "for family historical purposes." According to Reggie, there are five essential shots:

- you and your groom alone
- the two of you with all your attendants
- the two of you with both sets of parents
- the two of you with the bride's immediate family
- the two of you with the groom's immediate family

Depending on your personal preferences and circumstances, you may wish to have additional posed photos with other groupings of relatives and close friends. In any case, give this subject some thought by preparing a preliminary list of group photos you desire before getting together with your photographer. Share this list with your photographer, but make it clear that the list may change once you receive your final RSVPs from family members and friends. In compiling your list, keep in mind that your photographer needs about 5 minutes to arrange and snap each posed photo, so if you want 12 different groupings of people, allow one hour.

Also consider when you would like to have these posed photos taken. To make a decision on that subject, you need to address a more fundamental question: Do you and your fiancé want to see each other before the ceremony? In my experience, couples are pretty evenly divided on this issue.

Couples who choose not to see each other before the wedding place a high value on the sense of anticipation and excitement that comes with the first sight of each other as the bride walks down the aisle in her gown.

Couples who do see each other before the wedding typically want to get most of their group photos out of the way ahead of time, so they can proceed directly to the reception once the ceremony is complete and spend more time with their guests.

Whether or not you choose to see each other beforehand, you definitely want your photographer to start shooting before the ceremony begins. Photos of you dressing with your bridesmaids and your fiancé with his groomsmen tell a wonderful story of your special day.

So when you meet with your photographer for your engagement photo session, discuss your thoughts and preferences and the various options you have. Come up with an approximate schedule for your wedding day photography. This schedule can be tweaked and finalized as you sit down to prepare your detailed timeline for the day (covered in Week 47).

Overall, the engagement photo session is very worthwhile for both you and your photographer. Perhaps most important, spending this quality time with your photographer makes you feel much more at ease having your photo taken on your wedding day.

Purchase Gifts for Your Attendants and Out-of-Town Guests

A GIFT IS a wonderful way to express your appreciation to members of your wedding party and other special guests. Your parents and all of your attendants have been helping and supporting you throughout your engagement (and your lives), and it's important to recognize their efforts with a token of your appreciation. Likewise, guests who are traveling far to join in on your celebration feel exceptionally appreciated—and special—if you have a welcoming gift awaiting them upon their arrival.

Wedding Party Gifts

THE IDENTICAL TRINKETS once given to bridesmaids and groomsmen have (thankfully) been replaced by more imaginative options. Presenting your attendants with gift certificates for spa treatments, sports tickets, or gift cards to their favorite shops tells them not only how much you appreciate their participation in your wedding but also how individual and special they are. Get personal with your purchases. Think about each person's tastes, style, and interests, and choose accordingly. That way, they all know you made the effort to pick out something just for them. One popular personalization technique is to put a monogram on the gift. Just keep in mind that it sometimes takes several weeks to get your gifts monogrammed.

Otherwise, there is only one rule of etiquette you still need to follow: Try to spend about the same amount on each gift for your bridesmaids and groomsmen. But with every rule, there is also an exception: You can spend more on your maid/matron of honor and best man because they have a greater responsibility at your wedding. As far as your budget is concerned, you can spend hundreds of dollars, or just a few, if that's all you can afford. In general, though, most couples spend somewhere between $50 and $150 per gift. Regardless of how much you actually spend, make sure you write a personal note to each of your attendants to express your thanks and appreciation, and include the note with your gift.

Generally, you want to give your gifts at the rehearsal dinner, or you can give them to your attendants at whatever variation they might be having of the traditional "bridesmaid luncheon." Either way, it's a great opportunity for you to speak to each recipient about how much his or her support means to you.

When giving a gift to your parents, you can choose a more private moment. The monetary amount is much less important than the depth of meaning and expression of love and gratitude for all they have done for you (besides helping with your wedding day). Consider a small album of photos of yourself with your parents as you were growing up (family vacations, holidays, and so on), or perhaps a small scrapbook of notes they sent you while you were away at summer camp or college.

When Money Is No Object

If your attendants are financially constrained but you're not, keep in mind that their wedding-related expenses can quickly mount. Instead of following the tradition of making them pay for the attire that *you* are asking them to wear, put it on your tab. If they have to travel a great distance to be with you at the altar, pick up their airfare and hotel accommodations. They will value this expression of your friendship more than any other gift you could provide.

Welcoming Gifts for Out-of-Town Guests

IT'S A GRACIOUS gesture to surprise your out-of-town guests by delivering a gift to their hotel rooms before they arrive in town. After their long journey, your guests will be most appreciative of your thoughtfulness. For a destination wedding, all of your guests are on equal footing because everyone is an out-of-towner. In this case, you certainly don't have to incur the expense of providing welcoming gifts for everybody, unless your budget can handle it.

You don't need actually to purchase your welcoming gifts this soon in the planning process. In fact, for certain types of perishable items, it's definitely too soon to buy them. Plus, you don't know how many out-of-town guests are coming until you receive all of your responses from your invitations. However, I recommend that you shop around now and decide what you want to buy. You can then quickly make your purchases once you have a confirmed head count. As you're researching items to buy, note the shipping time required for any online or catalog purchases, so you know when you need to place your order.

Typically, when travelers arrive at their destination, the things they value most are little snacks and beverages, as well as information on the local area. You may want to welcome your guests with candies, fruits, nuts, crackers, bottled waters, sodas, or even a bottle of wine. (If you provide a bottle of wine, make sure that the welcoming gift also includes a corkscrew and that the hotel can furnish wineglasses in the room.) Also include a road map and tourist brochure so they can check out local attractions during their visit.

For other ideas, consider the amenities that are available in the hotel rooms. If the rooms come with microwave ovens, a selection of herbal teas or a package of popcorn might be appropriate. If there is a nice Jacuzzi in the room, how about some bath salts, body lotions, and aromatherapy products so your guests can really unwind after their trip?

You have two fundamental choices for furnishing welcoming gifts: You can purchase them preassembled or you can create your own. If you buy precomposed packages, such as the tried-and-tired gift baskets, expect to spend at least $30 each. You may be able to save some money if you assemble your own gifts, but you need to decide if the hassle is worthwhile.

If you want somebody else to package them for you, I recommend that you first consider a local company that's in the business of creating welcoming gifts. That way, you can provide your guests with a selection of notable products from your area. Look in the Yellow Pages under "Gift Baskets" for leads. If you don't find anything, there are some national online networks of gift companies that may be able to help you find a local provider. Check out globalgiftnetwork.com and gift-basket-superstore.com.

Otherwise, many gift companies ship nationwide. Go to www.harryanddavid.com or www.winecountrygiftbaskets.com. Or, if you're a member of Costco, they sell prepackaged gifts at various times throughout the year for very reasonable prices.

If you decide to make your own, you need a supply of gift boxes, bags, or other containers, as well as wrapping, shredded fillers, ribbon, and of course the items to go inside the container. Several Web sites offer a wide variety of useful and creative packaging options. Check out bags andbowsonline.com, nashvillewraps.com, papermart.com, and veripack .com. Or you can call 1-800-GIFTBOX.

For food items to include with your welcoming gifts, your local supermarket or gourmet food store is probably the best place to look. I don't recommend that you pick perishable items, because you will have to wait until the last minute to wrap your welcoming gifts. However, if you feel strongly about giving your guests some fresh fruit and cheese, make sure you have a small army of volunteers standing by to wrap up your packages.

To find bath and body products, visit stores like Bath & Body Works, The Body Shop, or Crabtree & Evelyn. For tourist brochures and maps, contact your local convention and visitors bureau or chamber of commerce. Because they're in the business of promoting tourism and commerce, they often provide them for free!

To determine how many welcoming gifts you need, call the hotel where you blocked rooms. Ask for a copy of their "pickup" list once their cutoff date has passed. This list identifies every guest who has booked a reservation under your room block. You may want to call other out-of-towners who have RSVP'd to find out where they are staying. But in my opinion, this is not necessary. They didn't take advantage of your efforts to secure a room for them, so there is no reason for you to expend any additional effort tracking them down.

Finally, write a warm, personal note to accompany each welcoming gift. This note should welcome and thank your guests for traveling so far to attend your wedding. On a separate piece of paper, you may wish to recap some important nuptial details, such as driving directions or transportation arrangements.

For Brides on a Budget

It really is the thought that counts. If you can't afford the expense or effort involved in supplying an elaborate welcoming gift, a simple box of chocolates or nuts is appreciated by your guests. But don't skimp on the personal welcome note.

Mail Your Wedding Invitations

IT IS ALWAYS an exhilarating day when you mail your wedding invitations. Not only does an invitation officially announce your upcoming nuptials to family and friends, it also becomes a historical document that commemorates your marriage long after the fact.

Picking Your Postage

IDEALLY, THE POSTAGE on your outer envelope also serves as a coordinating element of the design for your invitations. The U.S. Postal Service does not always offer stamps in matching motifs or color schemes, but it's worth investigating. Once you find out how much it will cost to mail your invitations, you can examine your postal options and select appropriate stamps.

Nearly all wedding invitations weigh more than 1 ounce and therefore require more than a standard stamp to mail. On the other hand, your reply card generally takes a regular first-class stamp if it has an envelope, or a postcard stamp if it does not. To determine how much postage your invitations need, gather up all the pieces for one invitation (reception card, response card, directions, envelopes, and so on), then go to your local post office to get the entire ensemble weighed. If your outer envelope is square, verify the correct postage with a postal worker. Sometimes there is an additional charge for nonrectangular shapes.

If your post office carries stamps in the amount you need and a design you like, consider yourself lucky. You can immediately buy your stamps while you're there. Don't forget that you need stamps for both the outer envelope and your reply envelope/postcard. Also, if you are sending any invitations to foreign countries, you need to get the appropriate additional postage for your outer envelopes. But an American stamp on the response envelope/postcard is useless to your foreign guests, so leave the postage off those replies.

In my experience, most post offices don't carry a particularly wide selection of stamps, and you may be better off studying your alternatives online before making a purchase. The standard "love" stamps can be a good choice but may not necessarily be the best option for you. For example, if you are having an outdoor, rustic wedding, a stamp with birds or trees may be more fitting. Or a contemporary chic wedding in an urban loft might call for a stamp with great pop artwork. Keep in mind that any more than one stamp on the outer envelope often looks cluttered and detracts from the elegance of your invitation. It's better to have a single stamp with an unflattering design than five that perfectly match your style.

The Postal Service's Internet stamp store (http://shop.usps.com) sells all the different designs and denominations of stamps that are currently available, and they will ship your order for a minimal freight charge. You can go online, view images of the offerings, then place your order. Or, at the Stamps.com Web site, you can now submit your favotie photos to create custom "Photo Stamps" that are sure to give your invitations a distinctive look.

Assemble Your Ensemble

YOU CERTAINLY WANT your invitation to make a statement when your guests receive it. That's why it's important to assemble everything carefully so it looks perfect upon arrival. When your guests open your beautifully packaged invitation, they will get even more thrilled about your upcoming wedding.

When assembling a traditional invitation, the left side of the invitation card goes into the envelope first, with all enclosures placed faceup in front of the invitation in decreasing order of size. This allows all pieces to be seen when they are removed from the envelope. If you have a response card with a matching envelope, turn the envelope over (stamp side down), then tuck the card faceup under the back flap of the envelope.

If you have both the traditional inner and outer envelope, insert the invitation and other enclosures in the inner envelope as described above. The inner envelope is then placed unsealed in the outer envelope with the addressed side facing out, so when your guests open the invitation, their names are immediately visible when the inner envelope is pulled out.

Contemporary invitations typically do not use inner envelopes. Moreover, the stuffing sequence is often reversed. The invitation is placed on top so it is completely visible as soon as it is pulled out of the envelope. The other inserts follow behind the invitation in order of size.

If you have purchased wedding announcement cards to send to acquaintances whom you are unable to invite to the wedding, this is a good time to stuff and stamp those envelopes as well. Of course, you don't mail these announcements until after the wedding has taken place, but if you get them ready now, you won't need to spend time on this while you're trying to catch a plane for your honeymoon.

Getting Your Words Out

AFTER YOU'VE CAREFULLY assembled your beautiful wedding invitations, don't just drop them into the black hole of a big blue mailbox. The postal service's electronic canceling machines will smear your crisp envelopes with ugly pinstripes in no time. To avoid this brutal treatment of your invites, take them to a post office and request to have them hand-canceled. To be sure they are treated gently, ask if you can use their hand-canceling stamp yourself while you stand beside their window (you may have to beg!). In my experience, the large, busy post offices are the *least* accommodating. Instead, search for a small, out-of-the-way station that doesn't get a lot of traffic. You will leave the post office feeling confident that your invitations will keep their elegance.

Finally, while you're getting the official word of your wedding out to guests, this is a great time to update your personal wedding Web site, if you have one. You can now add all the detailed information that you have revealed in the invitation—time and location of the wedding, driving directions, transportation arrangements, typical weather conditions, and so on to your Web site. In case your guests accidentally misplace your invitation before your wedding date, they can find the information they need online.

Your fabulous wedding celebration is now just two months away, and the anticipation really starts to build as your guests receive your wonderful invitations. It will be a very exciting time for you over the next few weeks, as you start to receive the responses.

Meet with the Band Leader and Get Ready to Dance

THERE IS NO better way to turn your wedding reception into a festive celebration than to have fabulous dancing. To ensure that you have a great time on the dance floor, pick out your favorite songs and practice your dance moves before the big day.

Meeting the Music Maestro

MEET WITH YOUR band leader or DJ to go over the reception music logistics and selections. During the meeting, reconfirm everything already written in the contract and provide a detailed description of what you expect to see and hear at your reception.

SINGING YOUR SONGS

YOU DON'T WANT to be that bride who tells her band to "play whatever you want," then cringes in horror when she hears the macarena cackling through the sound system. Ask your band leader or DJ to send you his or her song list in advance of your meeting. Go through this list, circle or highlight songs you'd like to hear, and cross out any that you don't want played.

During your meeting, be very specific about the types of music you want to hear (Motown, oldies, hip-hop, and so on), and when you want to hear them. To aid in conversation and digestion, softer music is always a better alternative during dining. But you may choose to start the dancing before the first course is served, or to have a dinner dance between courses. Experienced bands and DJs know how to get the room shaking and how to slow things down, but you need to give a vision of your reception and how you expect the music to flow throughout the night.

Also make specific selections of songs you want played for all of the special dances:

- **Your first dance**   Pick a song that you especially love, or has particular meaning to you and your fiancé.
- **The second dance**   It traditionally begins with the bride's father dancing with the bride, while the groom dances with the bride's mother. Halfway through the song, the groom's father cuts in to dance with the bride, while the bride's father cuts in on the groom to dance with his wife. The groom then asks his mother to dance.
- **The third dance**   This dance was traditionally reserved for your attendants, but I usually suggest that you pick an upbeat dance tune that will get everybody out on the floor.
- **The last dance**   End the wedding on a high note with a memorable final song.

Bring a list of your choices to your meeting, discuss them with your band leader or DJ, then make a final decision on these special dance selections.

BREAK DANCING

IF YOU'VE HIRED a band, your contract stipulates how many breaks they take during the reception. As soon as the band stops for a break, your dance floor clears almost immediately, but that doesn't mean the mood has to turn dull. Have your band put on some recorded music before they break, which is a great way to incorporate songs into your reception that your band may not be able to play. For example, if you have a Motown band but your fiancé is a die-hard country music fan, have your band play his favorite country CDs during the break.

Also keep in mind that you can creatively fill the break time with important events like the toasts by the best man, maid/matron of honor, and father of the bride, as well as the cake-cutting ceremony. These activities hold your guests' attention while the band chills out; then everyone is ready to rumba when the band fires back up again.

ONE COUPLE'S STORY

At Patty and Ross's wedding, we found a creative way to keep their guests entertained during a band break. To honor her ethnic heritage, Patty hired a traditional Korean dancer for a 15-minute performance. Guests were enthralled as the dancer, wearing traditional Korean garments, performed a beautiful fan dance and energetic drum dance. Most important, Patty's parents were genuinely thrilled and touched by the way she chose to honor them.

OTHER POINTS OF INTEREST

DURING YOUR MEETING with your band leader or DJ, discuss and verify the following:

- **Location/layout of stage and dance floor** Your reception venue may have more than one suitable area for dancing. If your band/DJ has worked at your site before, they may have a specific preference as to where they want to be situated. Often, the deciding factor, especially with bands, is the availability of sufficient electrical power. Ask your band leader about the power requirements and take this information when you do a site walk-through with your caterer (see Week 45 for more). Also discuss whether the band needs to be up on a raised platform, or whether they can live without one. An elevated stage is sometimes more dramatic. However, if you are in a smaller room with a low ceiling, a stage is not appropriate. Also if your budget is tight, ask the band if you can avoid this additional rental expense.
- **Attire** Most likely, their dress is stipulated in the contract, but it is always good to confirm that their intended apparel is appropriate for your reception venue.
- **Clarify their role** I do *not* recommend that you have your band leader/DJ act as an emcee throughout the night. If you hired a wedding planner, or have someone designated to control the flow of activities behind the scenes, only the entrance of the wedding party and cake cutting-ceremony need to be announced. A family member or someone with closer ties to the bride and groom can make these announcements more personal.
- **Confirm the point person** Whether it is a wedding planner or trusted friend, someone who knows the timeline needs to be the point person

for communication with the band/DJ on the day of the wedding and can remind them of important events such as the first dance.

The bottom line is that your band/DJ plays a central role in the success of your reception, so communication with them is crucial. You want to get everything nailed down *before* the big day.

Put on Those Dancing Shoes

UNLESS YOU MAJORED in dance when you were in college, it's unlikely that you and your fiancé are professional waltzers. Since all eyes will be on you for your first dance, you don't want to be stumbling across the dance floor. Now that you have chosen a first dance song, think about what kind of dance you prefer to accompany it and how much you need to practice beforehand.

There are numerous types of dances to choose, from the romantic waltz and fox-trot to the sexy salsa and rumba. Whatever style you pick for your first dance, make sure that it is consistent with your first dance song and your personalities. If you really want to impress your guests à la Fred and Ginger, consider taking dance lessons. Look in the Yellow Pages under "Dancing Instruction" for studios near you. Work on your first dance together several times before the big day. When practicing, wear a dress and shoes similar to what you have selected for the wedding, so you can do twists and twirls that work with your attire.

HELPFUL HINTS

Most brides practice dancing with their fiancé before the big day but often overlook another important dance partner—their father. A thoughtful gift for your dad is to take him out for dinner and dancing a couple of weeks before your wedding. It is a nice break from the brouhaha as well as a way to practice your special dance together—not to mention a fond memory for both of you for years to come.

A few final tips: Remember to stand up straight, keep a solid frame and, most of all, look at each other and smile as you are sweeping across the room. Relax, have fun, even let loose a little, and your music and dancing experience will be one to remember.

Set the Stage at Your Site

AS YOUR WEDDING date draws closer, walk through your ceremony and reception locations with those vendors who have the primary responsibility for making your site beautiful to behold. Schedule a meeting to discuss how and where to place decor, tables, bars, food stations, and so on, so that your wedding looks and feels just the way you have been envisioning it.

Ideally, your caterer, florist, and facility manager for the site all attend this meeting. If you have secured the services of a wedding planner, a lighting company, or a tenting company, they should also be invited to walk through the site. Ask the facility manager for a preprinted floor plan of the site that you can use to mark down the locations of key elements that are discussed during the walk-through. If none is available, bring a pad of paper so you can sketch out a plan. Also bring a tape measure and camera to facilitate the preparation of proper floor plans.

Ceremonial Spaces

IF YOU'RE GETTING married in a house of worship, only your florist and wedding planner need to walk through your ceremony location with you. Identify where florals should be positioned on the altar, at the front entry, and alongside the pews. In addition, recheck the church's policies and requirements regarding the placement of this decor. Keep in mind that you don't want to obstruct any guest's view of your ceremony, and remember that you are not required to decorate every nook—your budget and taste determine your selections.

If your ceremony and reception are at the same location, your caterer and site facility manager should join the meeting. In this situation, the caterer usually has responsibility for placing the chairs at the ceremony. Also, you may wish to serve a welcoming beverage to your guests prior to the ceremony. In this case, you need to determine where the caterer will provide this service.

Most important, your wedding ceremony needs a visual focal point to mark the location where you exchange your vows. In a place of worship, that focal point is the altar. In a secular setting, you should still create a spiritual center for your ceremony. If you're outdoors, you can utilize a natural feature such as a majestic tree, or you can have your florist create something like a fabulous floral canopy. Brainstorm with your vendors to determine the best location for your ceremony. Consider the time of day your ceremony is taking place and whether the location is in the shade or the sun at that time (a shaded area is always preferable for a summertime wedding.)

No matter which location you choose, make sure you have enough room for your guests. Leave about 3 feet of space between each row of chairs, to allow for easy access. The aisle needs to be 7 feet wide if both parents are escorting you during the processional.

Cocktail Considerations

AFTER THE CEREMONY, your guests proceed to the cocktail reception. Can you guess what's the most important focal point when they arrive at your cocktail area? No, it's not the bar or a food station—believe me, your guests won't need any help finding those tables. It's not even the cute little tables where you can hang out and munch on hors d'oeuvres while sipping on a beverage.

Instead, it's your escort card and guest book table(s). You want to make sure your guests find their dining assignments and that they have an opportunity to make some momentous remarks in your guest book. That's why the escort cards and guest book should be the first things your guests see when they enter the cocktail reception area. Position them where they are easily accessible but not where they create a bottleneck. To draw attention to your escort cards and guest book, have your florist create a focal point with festive decor that complements your overall wedding design.

Place the bar(s) and food station(s) for the cocktail reception on opposite sides of the space, so guests naturally circulate. Keep these tables away from entryways so that they don't cause a traffic jam.

Cocktail tables for your guests should be either 30-inch round or 30-inch square, so that they each hold a maximum of 4 people. The cocktail reception should be designed primarily for mingling, not sitting, so provide cocktail tables for only about one-third of your guests. Vary the height of your tables by selecting a mixture of standard tables (which need 4 chairs) and "kiosk" tables (aka "stand-and-sip" tables or "highboys"), which do not need chairs. Standard cocktail tables are 30 inches tall, while kiosk tables are 42 inches high.

Reception Reconnoitering

TO CREATE A breathtaking reception area, first consider the entrance to the space. The ambience should make guests feel like they're being transported to a whole new location. Carefully examine the physical features of the space. As they say in real estate, "accentuate the positive." What elements should be played up with beautiful decor and/or lighting? What elements should be downplayed? Venues with high ceilings may call for tall dramatic centerpieces, while pavéed designs may be better suited for lower ceilings. In either case, vary the composition of your florals by having a combination of tall and low centerpieces.

While some designers suggest that you make the color scheme of your decor fit with the colors in your reception room, I believe this is totally unnecessary, especially if your reception is in the evening. By accenting the elements that you want to highlight, any undesirable elements automatically fade into the background.

To give your dining table settings more variety, use a mixture of round, square, and rectangular shapes, and consider multiple (but compatible) colors of linens as well. Make your head table special by using a unique shape, linen color, or style of decor. In laying out all of your table locations, allow at least 5 feet of space between tables—enough room for guest chairs to be placed and waitstaff to pass through.

If you're having a dinner dance, the dance floor becomes the center of energy for your party. Make sure it's centrally located. To the extent your room configuration allows, lay out your dining tables evenly around the dance floor and place your head table in the center.

Don't tuck your beautiful wedding cake in a back corner of the room. Instead, it should be a focal point. Place it near your head table so you and your guests can admire it throughout the evening. If you're having a dinner dance, position it near the dance floor. Guests can easily witness your cake-cutting ceremony by gathering around out on the dance floor.

To make sure your dance floor is appropriately sized, allow 3 square feet of space per guest. A band needs about 25 to 35 square feet per band member. If the room has high ceilings, you may wish to put the band on an elevated platform (usually about 15–16 inches high) by renting staging from your rental company. Most important, in the area where you're planning to place the band, make sure that there are enough electrical outlets to operate the equipment.

Finally, locate all the fire exits, make sure they are clearly indicated, and actually test the doors to see that they are not locked.

Miscellaneous Situations

DEPENDING ON YOUR particular circumstances, there may be a few more positional issues to deal with. If you're pitching a tent for your festivities, walk the grounds with the facility manager and your tenting company representative to determine the best location. Ask him or her to mark the layout of the tent with lawn flags or measuring tapes, to help you visualize it. If your site does not have a kitchen for the caterer's use, discuss with your caterer where the staff like to position themselves. You may need to rent screens or an auxiliary tent to keep the catering prep area out of your guests' view. If you need portable restrooms, you need to pick a convenient but somewhat out-of-the-way location for them. If the portable restrooms need water and electricity to operate, make sure plumbing and electrical hook-ups are available.

Preparing the Plans

AS YOU WALK through your ceremony and reception sites, make detailed sketches and notes of all the decisions you make. Take measurements as needed and take photos of every area and room to keep ideas fresh in your mind. After your meetings, sit down and draw up detailed floor plans of each area.

It's often much easier to make modifications and consider alternative layouts if your floor plans can be prepared on your computer. (If you don't have access to a computer for preparing floor plans, draw them in pencil.) Ask your facility manager if there is a diagram of the site available in electronic format (or, if you have a scanner, you can convert a hard copy into an electronic format). I recommend using a basic computer graphics program like PowerPoint to draw tables, bars, food stations, dance floors, etc. (You can use the "ruler" and "guides" in PowerPoint to help you draw things to scale.)

Here is an example of a reception site floor plan I created. The site map was provided in electronic format, and the guest tables, bar, stage, and dance floor were drawn in.

FLOOR PLAN FOR DINNER RECEPTION

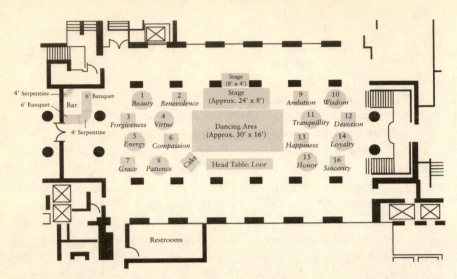

Overall, the site walk-through is an important step in the process of designing your fabulous wedding. Bringing your vendors together in this manner helps generate lots of creative ideas to turn your wedding dreams into reality. Developing detailed floor plans ensures that these ideas are carried out to perfection on your wedding day.

Have Your Fittings and Floral Meetings

BY NOW, YOUR wedding gown presumably has been fabricated and shipped by the designer and is ready for you to try on at your salon. The same for your bridesmaids' dresses. It's therefore time for both you and your bridesmaids to schedule appointments for a fitting. In addition, following last week's walk-through of your sites, schedule a meeting with your florist to finalize the design and color of your arrangements.

Fantastic Fittings

HAVING YOUR WEDDING gown fitted is almost as important as picking it out in the first place. In order for it to look truly amazing when you walk down the aisle, your gown should fit perfectly. That's why it's essential for you to have a fitting with an experienced seamstress. Your bridesmaids should also schedule a fitting for their dresses. If you purchased everything from the same salon, you could all go as a group and have a fitting party!

You and your bridesmaids should bring all the undergarments you will wear to the fitting, including bras, slips, underwear, bustiers, body-shapers, and so on. If you're not sure what to wear under your dress, go to a reputable lingerie store for help or ask the salesperson at your salon for advice. Be sure to choose undergarments that don't show and are comfortable enough to be worn up to twelve hours or more on your wedding day.

Also bring the shoes you and your bridesmaids purchased for your wedding, as well as a camera. If your bridesmaids can't join you at your fitting, ask your mother or a trusted friend who can give you an honest opinion about your fitting.

When you arrive, first check your gown carefully to make sure it is in perfect condition. Are any beads missing or are there seams that were not correctly or completely sewn? Then ask the seamstress or salesperson for advice on how to get into the gown. After you have put on your gown, the seamstress should look for the following things:

- Does the gown fall in the correct places?
- Does it need to be taken in or let out anywhere?
- Does the hemline need to be shortened or lengthened?
- Does it need bustling?

As you look in the mirror, ask yourself whether there are any significant changes you want to make, such as shortening the sleeves, adding beading, or removing the straps.

In most cases, some amount of alterations will have to be done, so you need to schedule a follow-up fitting with the seamstress once those alterations are completed, preferably about a month before the wedding. At this second fitting, verify that everything looks fabulous and falls properly, and make sure there is no bunching or unusual crinkling in the dress. The dress should not be too tight or too loose—you want to be able to sit down, stand up, and dance without any problems. If you still see something that is not to your liking, speak up and get it corrected while there is still time.

HELPFUL HINTS

If your gown has a train, make sure you bring your mom or a bridesmaid to your second fitting, so she can learn how the gown is bustled. Have her practice bustling the gown so she can quickly help you with it on your wedding day—and you can spend more time enjoying your reception.

Also carefully check the quality and quantity of hooks, loops, and snaps that have been installed for bustling purposes. I have seen numerous situations where the seamstress either skimped on the number of fasteners, or did not stitch them into the gown firmly enough. The item that gets used most frequently from my bridal emergency kit is the 2-inch safety pin, which I usually use as a makeshift bustling device.

Finally, schedule a time to pick up the gown about a week before the wedding. You may want to give it a final steaming or ironing before the big day (be sure to ask the seamstress for recommendations). Keep the gown in a safe place before the wedding—preferably hang it from a high clothes pole so it doesn't puddle too much on the floor—and don't let anyone disturb it!

Meet with the Florist

IF YOUR FLORIST attended the walk-through of your ceremony and reception sites last week, he or she should now have a great understanding of the kinds of designs and decor that will work best for your wedding. It's a good idea to take it one step further and meet with your florist to make final decisions on design details.

To prepare for this meeting, contact your rental company and ask to borrow a table linen and a place setting (china, flatware, stemware, napkin, and chair) that you have selected for your reception. Some rental companies consider "borrowing" to be the same thing as "renting," so they may charge you for this. Bring these rentals to the florist's studio. Also make sure you bring your camera, as well as an extra copy of the floor plan you just created, so you can go over it with the florist.

Meanwhile, your florist should prepare a prototype of the centerpiece design that you have been considering. This prototype should be constructed with the specific flowers and the container/vase you plan to use. Dress a table in the florist's studio with your rental items, then place the prototype on top. If the florist is doing a special napkin treatment, this should also be staged. You can clearly see how the textures and colors of the centerpiece actually work together with the linen, china, flatware, and stemware that you have selected. Take photos so that you have a visual record of this creation, and be sure to send copies of your photos to the florist.

If you don't like the look of certain flowers in the arrangement, this is your best opportunity to request changes. If you're lucky, the florist will have some other flowers on hand in the studio that may work better—in which case they can be quickly substituted on the spot. Otherwise, perhaps the florist can modify the prototype within a day or so by purchasing other appropriate flowers.

Alternatively, perhaps you love everything about the centerpiece but decide the linen is not quite right. Often, a couple picks a linen color that is too close to the color being featured in the centerpiece. Typically, though, you want the centerpiece to visually "pop" out from the linen, so a contrasting color of linen may be a better choice. If you find yourself in this situation, ask your florist for suggestions on linen colors, then check with your rental company for alternatives.

During your meeting, have the florist demonstrate what your personal flowers will look like—especially your bouquet. It's not necessary for the florist to construct a full "prototype" of the bouquet (it is costly to do so). But simply by gathering up the flowers you want and holding them together in a bunch, your florist can easily demonstrate what your bouquet will look like. Take photos of these gatherings. Your florist can also show you the types of materials available for tying your bouquet—different kinds of ribbons, pins, and so on.

By the end of your meeting, you should have a clear picture of how the floral designs you've been dreaming about will actually look at your wedding. This sneak preview from your florist should make you feel very excited and confident about your big day.

Begin Preparing Your Wedding Day Timeline

AS THE SAYING goes, timing is everything. What is most important on your wedding day is not the quantity of time, but the quality of time that you and your guests spend together. Guests do not notice when the timing is working well. They notice only when it's not—the bride is late for the ceremony, the cocktail hour runs too long, the dinner takes forever to be served, and the cake hasn't been cut when they're ready to go.

But making your special day run smoothly is not easy, because weddings are very complex events. Activities are usually taking place at multiple locations. You are dressing at home or in a hotel room, the ceremony may be in one place and the reception in another. Typically, you have hired at least 10 different vendors to create and memorialize your fabulous celebration; sometimes, 20 or more vendors are needed. To ensure that everything comes together correctly, it's important to plan carefully and schedule the activities that need to take place.

The Lowdown on Timelines

THE WEDDING DAY timeline is a schedule that logically and completely describes all elements of your celebration. It is a sequential listing of *every* task required to be performed, with detailed descriptions of who is performing the task, what they're doing, where they're doing it, and of course when it's happening (both start and finish times). A timeline is not a mandate that everything must happen precisely at the moment indicated on the document, but it does allow the wedding day festivities to proceed in an orderly manner.

If you have hired an experienced wedding planner, preparing a timeline is an important responsibility that he or she should handle for you. But if you did not hire a planner, designate a close friend or family member as the point person to interface with all of your vendors and keep tabs on their progress, to ensure your day flows smoothly. A timeline greatly aids your point person in keeping on top of things. As you're preparing your timeline, remember that it's important to clearly describe all the required tasks in detail, because someone else will be reading and relying upon this document.

Here's an example of a detailed task description that might appear on a wedding day timeline:

12:30 P.M.   Lilly Rose, florist, arrives at Ralston Hall, 500 Ralston Ave., to install decor in cocktail reception area and ballroom. To be completed by 3:30 P.M.

Cocktail Reception—Courtyard:
1 48" round escort card table with Heliotrope Topaz linen. *Centerpiece—antique pot with fuchsia and hot pink peonies mixed with a profusion of green cymbidium orchids.*
5 cocktail tables (3 wrought-iron café tables with 4 chairs and 2 kiosk tables with Kiwi Satin linen). *Centerpieces—clusters of fresh green and purple hydrangeas.*

Dinner—Ballroom:
8 60" round guest tables with Minotti Burgundy linens, Topaz Olive cushions. *Centerpieces—1 large arrangement set in Romanesque pottery and 8 round cup votives and candles for each table.*
8 54" square guest tables with Minotti Bamboo linens, Topaz Valentine cushions. *Centerpieces—3 smaller composite arrangements set in random collections of Romanesque pottery, and 8 cylinder votives and candles per table.*
1 48" square cake table with Crinkle Spice linen. *10 square votives and candles.*

Bathrooms: 2 small arrangements

Overall, your timeline must be consistent with the service times stipulated in your signed contracts. Otherwise, you may want to buy more time from your venue or vendors once you have created the timeline. In addition to the wedding day, the timeline should include important pre- and postwedding activities, such as the rehearsal, the installation of a tent, and the final pickup of rental items from the reception site.

Begin preparing the timeline now, then send a rough draft out to your venue and key vendors at least 3 weeks before the wedding to get their input. Based on their comments, make any necessary revisions, then send out the final timeline to all vendors 2 weeks before the wedding (more on that in Week 50). Your wedding party and family members should also receive an abbreviated version of the timeline, which covers only activities they are involved with.

A Timing Primer

BECAUSE NO TWO weddings are alike, I cannot give you a cookie-cutter template of a wedding day timeline that will work for your celebration. However, in the following paragraphs, I discuss typical scheduling and timing issues that frequently arise with each major player in your wedding. This information should help you to develop a timeline that fits your specific situation.

RENTAL ITEMS

TABLES, CHAIRS, DINNERWARE, and linens should be delivered as early as your reception venue allows, preferably the day before the wedding (otherwise, first thing in the morning). Your caterer should count and inspect the rental items as quickly as possible and report shortages and damage immediately to get problems fixed before guests arrive.

HAIR AND MAKEUP

THE MOST FREQUENT cause of scheduling problems on the wedding day is inadequate time allowed for hair and makeup. If the bride gets behind schedule on her hair and makeup, a domino effect results with potentially adverse impacts on the rest of the day. That's why it's important to hire experienced professionals to do this job.

If you and your attendants are having hair and makeup done professionally at home or in a hotel room, make sure you have clean dry hair and that you're wearing a shirt that buttons down the front. In setting up a schedule for hair and makeup, allow the following amounts of time for hair:

- For each bridesmaid: 60 minutes for updos or 40 minutes for regular hairdos
- For yourself: 90 minutes for an updo or 60 minutes for a regular hairdo

You should always go last so you look the freshest. It is *your* day, after all.

Makeup application follows hair styling. Allow the following amounts of time:

- For each bridesmaid: 40 to 45 minutes
- For yourself: 60 minutes

Before putting on lipstick, everyone should take a few moments to eat something (prearrange for room service if you're at a hotel).

The easiest way to put together a hair and makeup schedule on your timeline is to lay it out in a table format, as shown below:

	Hairstylist #1	Hairstylist #2	Makeup Artist #1	Makeup Artist #2
Bridesmaid #1	7:00–7:45 A.M.		7:45–8:30 A.M.	
Bridesmaid #2		7:00–7:45 A.M.		7:45–8:30 A.M.
Bridesmaid #3	7:45–8:30 A.M.		8:30–9:15 A.M.	
Bridesmaid #4		7:45–8:30 A.M.		8:30–9:15 A.M.
Bridesmaid #5	8:30–9:15 A.M.		9:15–10:00 A.M.	
Bridesmaid #6		8:30–9:15 A.M.		9:15–10:00 A.M.
Mother of Groom		9:15–10:00 A.M.		10:00–10:45 A.M.
Mother of Bride		10:00–10:45 A.M.		10:45–11:30 A.M.
Bride	9:15–10:45 A.M.		10:45–11:45 A.M.	
Flower Girl		10:45–11:30 A.M.		

LIMOUSINE/TRANSPORTATION

IF HAIR AND makeup are the most frequent sources of scheduling problems on the wedding day, then transportation is a close second. Assign someone to oversee any group transportation you have arranged. Prepare a list of passengers, check driving times on all routes being traveled, and account for likely traffic conditions. Send driving directions to the transportation companies along with your timeline, then make extra copies of directions available on the wedding day to give to the drivers.

The person you have designated to oversee transportation should "spot" vehicles—i.e., check on their arrival 15 minutes prior to the start of the contracted service time. For group transportation, have guests meet at the pickup location lobby 15 minutes before the scheduled departure. Have your coordinator check off guests against the passenger list as they board.

CEREMONY SITE

IF YOU ARE having your ceremony in a separate location from your reception, the first thing you want to know is when you and your vendors can have access to the ceremony site. Are other wedding ceremonies scheduled the same day as yours? Or, in the case of a church ceremony, does your church have other services that day? The timing of other events at your ceremony site dictates how much time your florist has for installation and how much time you have for posed photos at this location.

Regardless of when the site is available, plan for guest arrival at your ceremony site to begin 30 minutes prior to the start of the ceremony. One hour before the ceremony starts, your florist should be finished installing the ceremony flowers. You can then have about 15 to 20 minutes for photos at this location if you wish. Your ceremony musicians should arrive to set up about 45 minutes before the ceremony and begin playing prelude music 30 minutes before. Once the prelude starts, your groomsmen/ushers should be standing by, ready to escort guests to their seats.

Be sure to include your entire processional in your timeline. List everyone's first and last names in the order they will be walking down the aisle. Although you listed this information in your wedding program, when your point person is getting everyone lined up, he or she will be thankful it's in the timeline.

RECEPTION SITE

IT IS IMPORTANT to get an accurate estimate of your guests' arrival time at the reception location, as this determines when many of your vendors need to have key tasks completed. Ask your officiant for his or her best estimate of how long the ceremony will take. If your reception is at a different venue from the ceremony, tack on the driving time between the two locations to come up with an estimated earliest possible arrival time at the reception.

Ask your reception site manager when your vendors are allowed to begin setting up and when they need to finish breaking down and vacate the premises. The layout of your site dictates when certain vendors need to finish their setup. If there is a physical separation between cocktail and dining areas, the dining area setup can be completed while the cocktail hour is in progress. If not, it means that all of your setup in the dinner area must be completed before guests arrive for cocktails. If you're dancing after dinner in a separate area, your band or DJ may set up and do sound checks while your guests are dining, if they can do so quietly.

TENTING

IF YOU ARE having a tent erected for your reception, your tenting company typically needs to start installation anywhere between 2 and 7 days before the wedding. The most important issue from a scheduling standpoint is whether subflooring is required. If so, the construction can take a week. If not, the tent might go up in just a day. If local regulations require a fire marshal inspection of the tent, try to schedule this a day before the wedding.

LIGHTING

ALLOW AT LEAST 4 hours for lighting installation inside a reception room. Elevated lights must be installed as early as possible, because lifts and ladders are required, which can potentially interfere with the caterer's setup of your dining tables. If your lighting company is installing pin spot lights that are supposed to shine on the table centerpieces, have the installer come back and adjust the pin spots after the tables are set and centerpieces positioned. If you need lighting for a tented reception in the evening, it should be installed 1 to 2 days before the wedding (once the tent has been erected) and tested in the evening.

FLORIST

ON YOUR WEDDING day, the florist needs to deliver: personal flowers to the locations where you and your fiancé are dressing at least one hour before photos are being taken; set up floral arrangements at your ceremony site and perhaps remove them afterward; and install centerpieces and other items of decor at your reception location. Often, the florist needs to be in two places at once, which means that multiple crews are required.

For a church wedding ceremony, there is usually not much time available for the florist to set up, so large altar arrangements are often completed in the studio, then quickly installed when the florist arrives at the church. On the other hand, at the reception venue, florists often try to build their designs on-site. In creating their beautiful decor, a lot of ugly debris is often generated, and the florist needs to allow about 30 minutes for cleanup prior to guests entering the area.

Ask whether your florist will be returning to the reception site to pick up items immediately after the wedding. He or she usually needs to make arrangements with the venue to leave items overnight. The catering staff or wedding planner should secure items with the venue for the florist to pick up.

CATERER

TYPICALLY, YOUR CATERER needs at least 2 to 4 hours to load in and set up prior to guest arrival. If your ceremony is at the same site as the reception, the caterer may be responsible for positioning your ceremony chairs, so make sure this is one of the first things he or she takes care of.

For the cocktail reception, the caterer should be ready 15 minutes before the anticipated arrival of guests. Make sure your caterer staggers the offering of hors d'oeuvres over the duration of the cocktail reception, rather than serving them all at once.

For a seated meal, here is a typical time allowance for courses:

- 25–30 minutes for an appetizer
- 30–40 minutes for a salad
- 40–50 minutes for an entrée

Regarding vendor meals, most of your vendors want to eat while guests are eating, but it can be a challenge for caterers to serve guests and vendors simultaneously. The best solution is to have the caterer set up a buffet in a vendor break room before the guest meal service begins.

PHOTOGRAPHER

THE MOST IMPORTANT aspect of scheduling for your photographer is allowing adequate time for group photos. I mentioned this earlier, but it bears repeating: for posed photos, allow 5 minutes per group shot. As you start laying out your timeline, revisit the preliminary list of posed photos that you previously created and discussed with the photographer. You may need to change or eliminate some of the group shots in order to keep to your schedule.

You also want to allow time for your photographer to capture images of your beautifully designed reception dining tables before guests enter the area. Allow 30 minutes for these photos, so all setup should be completed in the dining area a half hour before guests enter. Have the catering staff light all candles, then clear out of the room for the photographer. Unless they are part of the decor, do not place table names/numbers on the tables until the photos are completed.

VIDEOGRAPHER

WITH DIGITAL VIDEO, setup time for the videographer is greatly reduced. For most ceremony locations, it takes less than 30 minutes to get set up, so the videographer can discreetly prepare the necessary equipment while the prelude music is playing.

WEDDING CAKE

IN MOST CASES, your cake designer should deliver the wedding cake approximately 1 hour before the cocktail reception begins. This normally gives the caterer enough time to set up the cake table and place the linen before the cake arrives. It also gives the cake designer and/or the florist enough time to decorate the cake table before the photographer comes into the reception room for photos of the decor.

However, if you're having an outdoor wedding, keep in mind that your cake needs to be kept in a cool place, because hot weather can melt a cake. It may be necessary to transport your cake into the reception area just before your guests come in, or right before the cake-cutting ceremony.

RECEPTION MUSIC

DEPENDING ON THE layout of your site, a band or DJ sometimes needs to preset hours before the actual start time for the music. Musicians can't be schlepping in equipment and performing sound checks if they're in plain view of guests setting up during the ceremony.

Cocktail reception music should be ready to begin prior to the guests' arrival. If the musicians performing during cocktail hour are also members of the band that will be playing later, have them play one 45-minute set, then move to the dining area. Guests are much less likely to miss music near the end of a cocktail hour than at the beginning. The band should be playing when guests are first invited into the dining area.

Music for dinner dances is more difficult to schedule than having dancing in a separate area after dinner. During the meal service, you want the band to be playing when guests are most likely to want to dance. So try to schedule band breaks during toasts, or when the caterer is serving a course. After dinner, whenever possible, schedule important activities like the cake-cutting ceremony during band breaks.

A well-thought-out wedding day timeline helps ensure that your special day flows effortlessly. You will be able to relax and enjoy the festivities knowing that everything has been carefully planned and all of your vendors are on the same page.

Get a License and Follow Up with Nonresponders

YOUR WEDDING DAY is about one month away! There are a couple of tasks that need to be taken care of now that are not the most romantic items on your wedding checklist but are still very important. Getting a marriage license and calling guests who have not sent their RSVPs are both vital in ensuring that your wedding is completely planned and your marriage is fully legal.

Licensing Legalities

THE RULES FOR getting a marriage license can be quite complicated and vary considerably across the country. Go online to http://marriage.about.com/cs/marriagelicenses/a/usmarlaws.htm for more information. Then contact City Hall, the town clerk, or the county clerk in the area where you are getting married to verify all current rules and requirements for getting a marriage license.

Find out how long a marriage license is valid where you will wed. In most U.S. locations, a marriage license is good for 60 days or longer, but there are a few places where you must get married within 30 days after obtaining it. (The lone exception is South Dakota, where a marriage license is valid for only 20 days.)

While blood tests were once a common prerequisite to receiving a marriage license, this requirement has been eliminated in most states. At the time of this writing, only Indiana, Mississippi, Montana, and Washington, D.C., still require blood testing. If you need to get a blood test, contact your doctor or a local medical clinic and ask for the standard "prewedding" test.

In some states, a marriage license is valid anywhere within that state. In others, you must pick up your license in the same locale where you're tying the knot. The types of pickup places can also vary. Depending on your location, it could be City Hall, the county or town clerk's office, or a marriage license bureau. In any case, both you and your fiancé need to appear personally at the appropriate place to obtain a license. Here are some things you may need to bring (but always call to confirm):

- **Proof of age**   Most places require a birth certificate, but others may allow a passport, driver's license, immigration record, or school record.
- **Photo identification**   A passport or driver's license is sufficient.
- **Proof of divorce**   If you are divorced or widowed, you may have to show a divorce or death certificate to prove you are no longer married.
- **Payment**   Some places take only cash, others prefer checks, so make sure you bring both.
- **Parental consent**   If you are under 18, a parent or legal guardian must provide written consent to your marriage. Some states allow parents to sign a consent form ahead of time in the presence of a notary public, while others require your parent to accompany you to the marriage license location.

HELPFUL HINTS

If you are having a destination wedding, set aside some time a few days before the wedding to get the license with your fiancé. If you're getting married abroad, take extra precautions, as some countries have stricter guidelines such as age requirements, residency requirements, blood tests, or an affidavit of eligibility, which shows you are legally able to marry. The embassy or tourist information bureau of the country in which you are getting married will have more information, or visit the U.S. State Department's Web site (www.travel.state.gov/law/marriage.html).

Technically a marriage license is not supposed to be signed until the wedding day, but some officiants allow your witnesses (e.g., the best man and maid/matron of honor) to sign it at the rehearsal, so there is one less thing to do on your wedding day. Verify with your officiant that he or she will mail the marriage license to the appropriate government agency shortly after your wedding.

Once the government has officially recognized your marriage in its records, you can receive an official "marriage certificate," which is essential if you intend to change your name after the wedding. Again, the rules can vary. In some states, you automatically receive a copy of your marriage certificate, while in others, you have to request a copy by fil-

ing more paperwork and paying another fee. Once you receive a mar-
riage certificate, keep it in a safe place such as a safety-deposit box, as
you will need it for various legal purposes throughout the years.

Guests Who Do Not Respond

IT IS ESSENTIAL to have an accurate count of how many guests
are coming to your wedding. You need this information, for instance, so
that your caterer knows how many meals to prepare. Furthermore, if
you're having a sit-down dinner with assigned seating, you want to know
not only how many people are coming to your party, but also everyone's
full name (with correct spelling).

Unfortunately, not all of your guests are mindful of the importance of
responding to your invitation. As a result, when the RSVP deadline on
your response cards passes, an unpleasant task you need to undertake is
contacting guests who have not replied. Other guests who did respond
may have taken handwriting lessons from their doctors. These people
may also need to be contacted to verify the spellings of their first and last
names and/or their entrée choices, if you're offering them.

The most polite way to handle a nonresponsive invitee is to telephone
him or her and graciously say something like, "I am sorry to be calling,
but we have not heard from you regarding our wedding invitation. We
need to give our caterer a final guest count soon, and were wondering if
you are going to attend. We really want you to be there, but please let me
know either way as soon as you can."

I don't recommend using e-mail in this instance, because a phone call
is more direct and personal. As uncomfortable as it may be to make the
call, your guests are more likely to respond favorably to the sound of
your well-mannered voice. Contacting an unresponsive guest in this way
may also lead him or her to be more thoughtful about future wedding invitations. Even more likely is that after planning your wedding, you will
be a much better guest at future events and always RSVP on time!

Determine Reception Seating Arrangements

AFTER YOU HAVE received all of your invitation response cards in the mail, and have contacted any nonresponsive guests, it's time to decide where your guests will sit at your reception.

Setting up a Spreadsheet

FIRST THINGS FIRST. To prepare for the table assignments, put together a new spreadsheet that lists each and every guest who has RSVP'd in a separate row on the spreadsheet. Your spreadsheet should have the following column headings:

1. First Name
2. Last Name
3. Assigned Table Name/Number
4. Assigned Table Position Number
5. Entrée Choice (if you are offering one)

Formal etiquette mavens who insist on addressing their guests with their titles (Mr., Miss, and so on) can start their spreadsheet with a "Title" column.

To help cut down on data entry time, you can copy and paste some of the information from your original guest list spreadsheet that you used for sending out invitations and tracking responses. This new spreadsheet needs more rows, because each guest is listed on a separate line. For now, leave columns 3 and 4 of this spreadsheet blank—fill them in once you make your table assignments.

Grouping Your Guests

TO MAKE IT easy for you to play around with different possible arrangements of guests, it's helpful to have each guest name listed on a separate slip of paper. One easy way to do that is to print out a copy of the spreadsheet you just created, then cut out each name with scissors. Or, if you prefer, get a big poster board and put each guest's name on a sticky note.

As you begin grouping guests together, refer to the floor plan you recently sketched out when you walked through the reception site with your caterer (see Week 45). If you haven't already done so, assign numbers or names to each of your tables now, and write them on the floor plan.

Some couples divide their guests into categories (bride's friends, groom's friends, bride's family, and groom's family) and assign tables from there. However you go about creating your chart, it is important to consider every guest's age, personality, and special needs. There are no magic guidelines that will help you devise a perfect seating arrangement, but here are some general suggestions to keep in mind:

- If you're having a dinner dance, younger guests may be happier near the dance floor and musicians, while older relatives typically prefer to be positioned where it's quieter.
- Consult with your parents about where to position guests they invited.
- Carefully consider which of your guests know each other, or at least share enough in common that they will enjoy conversing with each other.
- If you have single friends attending, try putting them at the same table—a wedding is a great place to meet someone!

Your Head Table

IF YOU HAVEN'T already thought about this while you were laying out your floor plan, there is still time to come up with a fun head table arrangement. The traditional "police lineup" head table, where the wedding party was positioned along one side of a banquet table and displayed on an elevated platform, has been mercifully put to death. (The layout of this table wasted space, stifled conversation, and made everyone feel very uncomfortable.)

Today, many brides and grooms opt to sit at the same size table as the rest of their guests. This way they feel more like a part of the celebration rather than a display piece. Couples are also choosing to invite all members of the wedding party, plus their "significant others," to the head table. To create a large enough table to hold them all, rectangular "kings" tables are placed end-to-end as needed and guests are positioned all the way around this table. To soften the sharp corners, 48-inch half-rounds (shaped like a semicircle) are sometimes used on each end, giving the entire table an oval shape. Check with your rental company to make sure they can provide the appropriate tables and linens to create the look you want.

Getting in Position

ONCE YOU'VE SETTLED on groupings of guests at various tables, determine a position location for each guest if you're having place cards at the table. (I strongly recommend this—see Week 40.). At each guest table, assign Position #1 to the person you wish to honor the most (such as a parent, grandparent, or close friend). That person is seated facing toward you. Keep in mind that with a round table of 8 people, the view from Position #8 is almost as good as Position #1, so make your seating assignments accordingly.

As for the two of you, it's best to position yourselves in the middle of your head table, facing a direction that allows you to see as many of your guests as possible. Since we're thumbing our noses at tradition, put the best man next to the groom and the maid/matron of honor next to the bride (they are your best friends, after all). Then do the boy-girl-boy-girl alternations around the rest of the table. If you are including your parents at your head table, try to place them directly across from where you are sitting. (Of course, if your parents are divorced, you probably need to seat them at other tables, away from each other.)

After you have completed your table and seat assignments, fill in the blank columns on your spreadsheet with the appropriate information. Then sort the spreadsheet (using the "Data, Sort" command in Excel) first by "Assigned Table Name/Number" and then by "Assigned Table Position Number." Send this information to your caterer when you mail out timelines next week.

Creating a reception seating chart is often a challenging process, but overall, your guests will appreciate the fact that you made this effort to make them feel more comfortable.

Send Timelines and Print Escort/Place Cards

AS YOUR WEDDING date draws closer, you've worked hard to put together the last few pieces of the puzzle. You prepared a rough draft of your wedding day timeline and received input from your key vendors. Now you can finalize your timeline and send copies to everyone involved with the wedding. Also, you have worked out the seating arrangements for your reception, which means you're ready to have your escort cards and place cards finalized.

Timelines and Accessories

ONCE YOU HAVE incorporated all comments received from your vendors, print copies of the timeline for distribution. I don't like to e-mail timelines, because I want to make sure the timeline is easily read and understood by everyone who needs it. That's why I rely on snail mail for sending them out.

Each vendor should receive, at a minimum, the portion of the timeline containing the tasks he or she is responsible for. Usually, it's helpful for a vendor to see how his or her work fits into the whole event. So I recommend that you use a highlighter to mark items on the complete timeline that a particular vendor is responsible for. That way, he or she can immediately focus on those tasks and can also refer to the rest of the timeline as needed.

In addition to the timeline, include these items in the mailings to your vendors:

- **Floor plans**   As discussed in Week 45, floor plans are necessary to indicate the correct placement of all tables, chairs, food stations, musicians, the dance floor, etc. Because you have just finished your seating assignments for the reception, make any necessary changes to the floor plan before mailing it to your vendors. Each vendor should receive floor plans for areas that he or she will be working in.

- **Vendor list** It's helpful to have a listing that identifies every vendor involved with your wedding and includes all contact information (name, address, phone number, fax, e-mail, and most important, the cell phone where they can be reached on your wedding day). This information is especially helpful for your caterer, florist, photographer, and videographer. Alongside the contact information for every vendor, I recommend that you indicate the scheduled arrival time at your ceremony and/or reception venue.
- **Driving directions** These are needed by vendors who have not been to the venue before. Do not rely on Internet directions, and don't expect your vendors to get directions online. Send them directions that you know are correct. Advise vendors of any traffic problems you are aware of, so they can plan accordingly.
- **Seating arrangements** Send a copy of your reception table assignments to your caterer, so he or she knows the number of people at each table (and the entrée choices, if applicable).
- **Posed photo list** Send your final version of this list to your photographer.

As you're printing and packaging these documents for mailing, use one copy of your vendor list as a checklist to make sure a package is mailed to every vendor. If you have not hired a wedding planner, your point person should also get copies of all these documents.

In addition to your vendors, you also want the members of your wedding party to be on schedule. Prepare an abbreviated version of the timeline for their reading pleasure. Here's an important tech tip: Before making any edits to your full timeline, create a new version for your wedding party using the "File, Save As" command (you don't want to lose that vendor timeline file you've worked so hard to create). Your wedding party needs to see only those items they are involved with—e.g. attending the rehearsal, hair and makeup, boarding limousines, giving toasts, and so on. Any unrelated tasks, such as your florist's arrival at the reception site for setup, can be deleted from their version of the timeline. If you're not providing transportation for your wedding party, send driving directions to them along with the abbreviated timeline. For your readers, enclose a copy of their readings, as well.

Escort and Place Cards

IF YOU FOLLOWED my recommendations back when you ordered your escort and place cards (see Week 40), you already know whether you'll be taking these cards to a calligrapher or printing your guests' names on them yourself.

Either way, you need to prepare a listing of your escort card assignments first. Just as you did when you sent out your wedding invitations, you want to provide one escort card per couple or family (not one per person). Now that your guest list spreadsheet is already set up in the proper configuration for creating an escort card listing, make a duplicate copy of this spreadsheet and add a column called "Table Name/Number." Then fill in the appropriate assignments. Delete the rows of people who are not coming to the wedding. Because escort cards are ultimately displayed alphabetically, sort your escort card spreadsheet by last name and first name.

Some couples prefer to address their escort cards more formally, like "Mr. and Mrs. Smith," while others use something more casual, like "John and Nancy Smith." If you addressed your invitations more formally, but prefer a more casual wording on your escort cards, you need to modify the "First Name" column on your guest list spreadsheet accordingly. Of course, if multiple Mr. and Mrs. Smiths are attending your wedding, you have to use a first name to distinguish them. Overall, the formality of your escort card dictates how you address your guests.

If you're printing names and table assignments on the escort cards yourself, back in Week 23 I discussed how to use the "Mail Merge" utility in Microsoft Word to address envelopes. You can use the same process to print the appropriate names and table assignments on your escort cards/envelopes. Use the "File, Page Setup" command to set the size of your card, as well as the appropriate margins on the page.

For the place card names, use the table assignment spreadsheet that you put together last week. Again, if you're printing the place cards yourself, you can use the "Mail Merge" function in Microsoft Word to transfer the names from your spreadsheet into a Word document. If you're offering a choice of entrée for your meal and using ink colors to designate these choices, you have to manually select the appropriate ink color for each guest name in the document you have created.

Give Final Counts, Get Prepared, and Make Payments

AT THE END of next week you will officially be husband and wife! But don't let the anticipation throw you off track, because you still have some important things to do in order to ensure a smooth wedding day experience.

Contact Vendors with Final Counts

FIRST, YOU NEED to communicate with your vendors about the "final" number of guests attending your wedding.

CATERER (FOOD AND BEVERAGE)

YOUR CATERER NEEDS a final head count "guarantee" anywhere from 3 to 14 days before the wedding, so that appropriate amounts of food and beverages can be purchased. Check your contract for the exact date the "guarantee" is required. Count up the number of people who have accepted your invitation, then figure out the split between adults and children (ages 3 to 10). And don't forget to include yourself and your fiancé in the total!

Of course, if you're having a sit-down meal with a choice of entrée, you need to give your caterer a breakdown of quantities for each entrée. In addition, the caterer wants a breakdown of meal choices for each guest table, so that the service can be efficient and gracious.

Also, you need to give your caterer a count of vendor meals needed during the reception. Typically, the vendors needing a meal include your photographer and his or her assistant, your videographer(s), your DJ or band members, and your wedding planner.

RENTAL COMPANY

IF YOU ARE renting anything, this is the week to verify with the rental company the numbers of each item you need. Make sure that everything—chairs, tables, linens, napkins, china, flatware, stemware, etc.—is coming in the correct quantities. Confirm also that the rental company will set up tables and chairs if that is stipulated in your contract.

Once you have determined your final head count, you should know exactly how many tables you need at your reception—especially if it's a sit-down meal. Your florist needs to know the precise number of tables during this week so he or she can determine the amount of flowers to purchase for making the correct number of centerpieces, chair arrangements, and/or any other necessary design pieces. Again, check your contract to reconfirm when your florist requires this information.

Preparing for Your Honeymoon

MANY COUPLES ARE SO excited about their wedding they don't spend enough time getting ready for their honeymoon. Here are some tips for a smooth getaway:

- Confirm reservations and recheck departure/arrival times with your travel agent, airline, and/or hotel.
- Before you depart, arrange for a bridesmaid or family member to pick up the bridal gown for cleaning; also arrange for a groomsman to pick up the groom's tuxedo to return to the rental shop. Have someone pick up any other belongings from the wedding that you don't want to take along with you.
- Arrange transportation to your departure airport.
- Pack passports and airline tickets in an easily accessible carry-on bag, and put photocopies of them in your suitcase.
- Get traveler's checks/foreign currency from your bank.
- Prepare a list of phone numbers for doctors, credit card companies, and emergency contacts.
- Arrange for someone to house-sit pets and water plants.
- Attach identification tags to every piece of luggage.
- Buy locks for all suitcases (not for flying but for leaving bags in hotel rooms).
- Put health insurance cards in wallet if not there already.
- Refill prescriptions.

As I discussed in Week 38, bring clothes that are versatile and appropriate for the climate. Consider how much you will have to carry your suitcases, and pack light!

Wedding Day Emergency Kit

MISHAPS ARE ALWAYS a possibility on your wedding day. The real horror story occurs when you're not prepared if things go wrong. If you have hired a wedding planner, he or she routinely carries an "emergency kit." Otherwise, I strongly recommend you put together a bag of emergency supplies and assign someone to be in charge of it throughout the day. Here are some things to include:

- Band-Aids
- breath mints
- brushes and combs
- chalk (to cover up any last-minute stains)
- clear nail polish
- energy bars
- extra pair of contacts (if you wear them) and contact solution
- eye drops
- hairpins, bobby pins
- hair spray
- hand towelettes
- medicine—aspirin, cold and cough tablets, antacid
- safety pins, preferably large
- sewing kit
- spot remover
- sunscreen
- tampons
- tissues
- toupee tape (helps dresses stick to skin if they need to)
- tweezers
- water
- wrinkle remover (you may consider even bringing a steamer to get out any last-minute wrinkles in bridesmaids' dresses)

Open Checkbook, Start Writing!

THIS IS THE last painful task you need to perform before your wedding. Since you have just given your caterer, rental company, and florist your final head counts, they should be supplying you with final pricing—which means it's time to start making your final payments.

Review all of your vendor contracts to determine which vendors want to receive their final payments before the wedding, and which ones ask to be paid on the wedding day. Also note which vendors take credit cards, and use plastic whenever possible. Mail out any checks that need to be paid in advance. For those vendors that don't require payment until services are rendered, such as ceremony musicians, write those checks now, put them in labeled envelopes, and give them to your wedding planner, point person, or the best man to distribute on the day of the wedding. When you call those vendors next week to confirm all logistics and arrangements (see next week for more), advise them who is in charge of payments so they won't be bothering you about it.

In addition to giving vendors their final payments, you may be wondering whether a tip or gratuity is appropriate. Check your vendor contracts, especially catering and transportation. Many times, there is a gratuity charge of 17 to 22 percent already added to the contract. Gratuities are mandatory charges, while tips are discretionary. If you believe a vendor has delivered exceptional service, beyond what was contractually promised, then a tip is always a lovely (and greatly appreciated) gesture. Put your tip into an individual envelope with the vendor's name on it and give it to your wedding planner or point person. It should be distributed on the day of the wedding only after services are rendered.

While writing all those checks may not be the most pleasant experience, look forward to next week: Your wedding is going to be fabulous, and you've got only a few little things to do before you can start the celebration!

Reconfirm All the Details

DURING THOSE FINAL days before a wedding, the news media love to portray the image of a bridezilla going ballistic in a fit of frenzy. You'll have none of that nonsense, thanks to this book. Everything about your wedding has been carefully planned, and all but the last little details are taken care of. There are just a few items that need your attention this week. Otherwise, your primary job is to relax and enjoy this wonderful time in your life.

Check In with Vendors and Your Wedding Party

CALL ALL OF your vendors 2 or 3 days before the wedding to reconfirm all arrangements and logistics. Make sure they received a copy of your timeline, then go over the relevant portions and driving directions with each vendor. Recheck to make sure you have their correct cell phone numbers for the day of the wedding.

If your attendants and family members aren't already excitedly calling you, check in with them to reconfirm the time and location of your rehearsal and rehearsal dinner. Remind them to arrive at your rehearsal location 15 minutes earlier than the official start time.

Deliver Essentials to the Caterer

THERE ARE A number of items you have picked out for your reception that you should bring to your catering manager 2 or 3 days before your wedding, so that they can be properly positioned on your wedding day: your escort cards, guest book and pens, place cards, table names/numbers, menus, favors, toasting glasses, and cake knife/server. (If you hired a wedding planner, give these items to him or her instead.)

If you are providing wines and/or other beverages for the reception, bring these to your beverage caterer.

Drop Off Welcoming Gifts

BEFORE YOUR OUT-OF-TOWN guests begin to arrive at the hotel where you have blocked rooms, deliver the gifts and welcoming notes that you have prepared for them. Call the hotel first and speak to the catering sales manager to make arrangements for your delivery. There may be a charge for the hotel staff to put welcome gifts in the guest rooms. Also reconfirm the guests who are staying at the hotel and when they are scheduled to arrive. Make sure you clearly label each gift with the guests' full names, and place each welcoming note in a labeled envelope.

Pamper Yourselves and Your Attendants

DEVOTE THE DAY before to really relaxing and luxuriating. In the morning, take your bridesmaids to a day spa for a massage, manicure, and pedicure, then enjoy a luscious lunch at your favorite restaurant. Your groom and his groomsmen can get into the swing of things with a round of golf in the morning, followed by burgers and beer on the clubhouse patio.

Rehearse

GET TO YOUR rehearsal a bit early, but before you jump in your car, make sure you bring along the following items:

- your wedding programs and any decorative tray or basket that they will be placed in
- extra copies (in case anyone forgot theirs) of
  - wedding party timelines
  - readings
  - driving directions to the reception
- your marriage license
- any remaining vendor payments (put in labeled envelopes)

Give the programs and vendor payments to your wedding planner or point person for safekeeping overnight. Give the marriage license to your officiant if he or she is attending the rehearsal, and request that it be signed now by your witnesses and officiant, rather than waiting until the wedding day. If your officiant is not attending the rehearsal, give the marriage license to your planner/point person, who is responsible for getting the necessary signatures before the ceremony.

The purpose of your wedding rehearsal is to rehearse for the wedding. I know that sounds like I'm belaboring the obvious, but believe me, when the members of your wedding party first arrive at your ceremony location, rehearsing is often the farthest thing from their minds. Instead, the scene generally resembles a family reunion, where all your attendants are hugging and kissing and catching up on the latest news in their lives.

Unfortunately, there may not be a lot of time for idle chitchat at this point. At many popular ceremony sites, you have an hour or less to conduct the rehearsal before the next wedding party is given access to the premises. You need to get down to business quickly and save the socializing for the rehearsal dinner. If there isn't a "church lady" on site to act as your drill sergeant, your wedding planner or point person should assume this role.

First of all, give your groomsmen guidance on how to be effective ushers—their most important role. They should be positioned at the entrance to the ceremony area, ready to warmly welcome your arriving guests. Your groomsmen should also learn where the restroom facilities are located, because they will invariably be asked for this information.

To escort arriving guests down the aisle, the groomsmen offer their right arm to unescorted females. But when escorting couples, they simply lead the couple to their seats. Traditionally, there was a "bride's side" and "groom's side" for seating, and the groomsmen had to ask whether the guest was a friend of the bride or the groom. Nowadays, other than the first couple of rows that may be reserved for parents and close family members, the groomsmen typically fill in the subsequent rows without regard to the guest's relationship to the couple. That way, there are roughly equal numbers of people on both sides of the aisle.

Rehearse the processional and recessional at least twice. I like to first line everyone up starting at about the fourth row of seats from the front, then have them process to their appropriate places on the altar. (For more information on processional/recessional formations and positions, refer to Week 34.) It's much easier for everyone to understand what they're supposed to do if they initially practice processing over a shorter distance. Then they can recess all the way out of the ceremony area and process back in again from the real starting point. When getting into formation for the processional, everyone should make a mental note of who is standing in front of them—they will all find their places much faster when it's showtime.

You can ask your ceremony musicians to attend the rehearsal so that your attendants can hear the songs they're supposed to walk down the aisle to. However, this is likely to cost you just as much as securing their services for your wedding day. If you hired a wedding planner, there is really no need to practice with the processional music you have selected. Your planner cues your attendants and musicians to play their parts at the appropriate time. If you really want your attendants to hear the music beforehand, you can record your ceremony songs and bring a portable CD player or an iPod/MP3 player with portable speakers to the rehearsal.

It is important to go over all parts of the ceremony requiring the participation of your rehearsal attendees, such as readings or candlelighting rituals. Also, make sure your maid/matron of honor understands that she will be holding your bouquet (and your gloves, if you are wearing them) during the exchange of vows and rings. She will give them back to you just before the recessional.

When the rehearsal is complete, let the celebration begin at the rehearsal dinner! With all of the hard work you have put into planning your wedding, you are probably more than ready to party. But don't overdo it this evening. After all, you have a pretty big day ahead of you tomorrow!

Wedding Day: Relax and Enjoy

WHEN YOU WERE a child, what special occasion did you look forward to with great anticipation? For many, it might have been your birthday, and for others, the excitement of Christmas. Now multiply this excitement by ten and you'll get the feeling of what it's like on your wedding day!

Try to get at least 8 hours of sleep the night before. Take a leisurely shower or soothing bath, then put on your wedding dress foundation, hosiery, and a button-front white shirt. This way, once your hair and makeup are done, all you have to do is slide into your slip and gown.

Don't forget to nosh a little before the bridesmaids arrive—preferably, plan a breakfast or brunch ahead of time. If you're staying at a hotel, make this easy on yourself and order room service for you and your bridesmaids to dine together. If you are dressing at home, perhaps your mom can get takeout from the neighborhood gourmet grocery.

Fresh fruits, yogurts, light cheeses, and delicious breads, with plenty of water and juice, make for a filling meal. Stay away from garlic, salty snacks, caffeine, tuna, and other foods with lingering odors. Avoid alcohol or any sedatives that you think you might need to relax you. The best form of relaxation is confidence—knowing that you have followed the chapters in this book and planned a perfect wedding.

Meanwhile, your groom and his guys should also be meeting to have their own get-him-to-the-church-on-time bonding session. This could be an early jog in the park followed by brunch with the boys—and don't forget to include the dads as well.

All of your bridesmaids should arrive with their dresses, undergarments, shoes, two pairs of stockings, makeup, correct jewelry, toothbrush, and any other personal items they might need.

As you finish your brunch, the hairstylist and makeup artist should be arriving, unless you are scheduled to go to their salon. Remember, the bride goes last, so just relax and have fun with your dear friends. Once it is your turn to be pampered, enjoy! You have the right to feel like royalty on your wedding day.

After your hair and makeup are complete with veil and all, you will be transformed into a glamour queen. Your photographer and videographer show up just about this time if you asked them to get photos of the final finishing before stepping into your gown.

Visit the ladies' room, so your mom and maid/matron of honor can assist you in stepping into your slip and gown. In fact, put the slip into the gown and make it one step. Just don't cry. It will spoil your makeup. Everyone is going to let you know what a beautiful bride you are. It's an inner beauty as well as a joyous outer elation. Don't forget your shoes and jewelry, but leave the watch behind.

As you walk down the aisle, take it slow and easy, and savor every second. Remember why so many family members and friends have gathered in your honor—in case you have a case of temporary amnesia, the answer is standing at the end of the aisle, waiting for you!

Your reception should and will take on a life of its own, but keep in mind that you set the tone. If you want everyone to dance the night away in celebration, plan to spend some quality time on the dance floor too. Your guests will follow your lead. But don't forget to sit down and enjoy the meal. Your caterer has created a delicious culinary experience, which is an important part of your wonderful wedding day memories (besides, you need the nourishment). End your festivities on a high note, either with a favorite song for your last dance, or a grand getaway.

I feel blessed to have had this opportunity to share my approach for planning a perfect wedding with you. I know that you have worked long and hard to make it a perfect day. Rest assured that my approach has worked every time with hundreds of brides and grooms whose weddings I have had the honor of designing and planning. I know that your celebration will also be sensational!

Finally, don't forget that your wedding is just a day, while your marriage is for a lifetime. From this day forward, may you love and cherish each other forever. Please accept my congratulations and best wishes for a wonderful life together!

Subject	Resource	Web site
All	Condé Nast Bridal Group: *Brides, Elegant Bride,* *Modern Bride*	www.brides.com, www.elegantbride.com, www.modernbride.com
	The Knot	www.theknot.com
	The Wedding Channel	www.weddingchannel.com
Bridesmaid Dresses	Aria Dress	www.ariadress.com
Calligraphy	Association for the Calligraphic Arts	www.calligraphicarts.org
	Identifying a font	www.identifont.com
	Identifying a font	www.myfonts.com
Caterers	International Caterers Association	www.icacater.org
	Leading Caterers of America	www.leadingcaterers.com
Churches	Worship Here	www.worshiphere.org
Design Trends	Daily Candy	www.dailycandy.com
	Splendora	www.splendora.com
Engagement Rings	Better Business Bureau	www.bbb.org
	Gemological Institute of America	www.gia.edu
	International Gemological Institute	www.igi-usa.com

Favors	Favor Favor	www.favorfavor.com
	My Wedding Favors	www.myweddingfavors.com
Florists	American Institute of Floral Designers	www.aifd.org
	California Cut Flower Commission	www.ccfc.org
	Society of American Florists	www.aboutflowers.com
Gifts for Out-of-Town Guests	Bags & Bows	www.bagsandbowsonline.com
	Gift Basket Superstore	www.gift-basket-superstore.com
	Global Gift Network	www.globalgiftnetwork.com
	Harry and David	www.harryanddavid.com
	Nashville Wraps	www.nashvillewraps.com
	Paper Mart	www.papermart.com
	VeriPack	www.veripack.com
	Wine Country Gift Baskets	www.winecountrygift baskets.com
Group Travel	American Automobile Association	www.aaa.com
	Groople	www.groople.com
	Travel Manager	www.travelmanager.com
	Trip Advisor	www.tripadvisor.com
Honeymoon-Hawaiian Shirts	Paradise Found	www.paradisefound hawaiianshirts.com
	Shirts of Hawaii	www.shirtsofhawaii.com
Honeymoon Registries	The Big Day	www.thebigday.com
	Honey Luna	www.honeyluna.com
	The Honeymoon	www.thehoneymoon.com

Honeymoons	American Society of Travel Agents	www.astanet.com
	Creative Travel Adventures	www.creativetravel adventures.com
	Honeymoon Consultants	www.honeymoon consultants.com
	Honeymoons, Inc.	www.honeymoonsinc.com
	Just Honeymoons	www.justhoneymoons.net
	The Travel Institute	www.thetravelinstitute.com
	U.S. State Department	www.travel.state.gov
	Unforgettable Honeymoons	www.unforgettable honeymoons.com
Mailing	U.S. Postal Service	www.usps.com
Marriage Laws and License Information	U.S. Marriage Laws	marriage.about.com/cs/ marriagelicenses/a/ usmarlaws.htm
Music	American Disc Jockey Association	www.adja.org
	American Federation of Musicians	www.afm.org
Officiants	National Association of Wedding Ministers	www.aministry.net
	National Association of Wedding Officiants	www.nawoonline.com
		www.weddingministers.com
		www.weddingofficiants.net
Photo- graphers	Professional Photographers of America	www.ppa.com
Registries	I Do Foundation	www.idofoundation.org
		www.findgift.com
		www.myliferegistry.com

Rentals	American Rental Association	www.ararental.org
Stationery	9spotmonk Design	www.9spotmonk.com
	Bella Figura	www.bellafigura.com
	Clip Art	www.clipart.com
	Creative Intelligence	www.creative-intelligence.com
	A Day in May Design	www.adayinmay.com
	Elizabeth Hubbell Letterpress Studio	www.elizabeth hubbellstudio.com
	My Gatsby	www.mygatsby.com
	Pantry Press	www.pantrypress.net
	Paper Source	www.paper-source.com
	Peculiar Pair Press	www.peculiarpairpress.com
	Purgatory Pie Press	www.purgatorypiepress.com
	Twig & Fig	www.twigandfig.com
	Twinrocker	www.twinrocker.com
Toasting Glasses & Cake Knives/ Servers	Exclusively Weddings	www.exclusively weddings.com
Transportation	National Limousine Association	www.nlaride.com
Veils	Veil Shop	www.veilshop.com
	Wedding Veil	www.weddingveil.com
Videographers	Professional Videographer Association of America	www.pva.com
	Wedding and Event Videographers Association	www.weva.com
Wedding Planners	International Special Events Society	www.ises.com

ACKNOWLEDGMENTS

I AM INDEBTED to numerous experts in the wedding industry who generously provided insights and perspectives in their areas of expertise. I offer my heartfelt thanks to the following professionals for their input:

- Robert Allen, Robert Allen Videojournalist, New York, www.robert allenvideo.com
- Alex Angelle, Gemological Institute of America, www.gia.edu
- Jennifer Angilello, All about the Dress, San Francisco, www.aboutthe dress.com
- Peter Berliner, Innovative Entertainment, San Francisco, www.inn-entertainment.com
- Marcy Blum, Marcy Blum Associates, New York, 212-929-9814
- Hillary Clark, Blush Beauty, San Francisco, www.blushbeauty.com
- Fred Cueller, Diamond Cutters International, Houston, www.dia mondcuttersintl.com
- Lauri Dorman, Paula LeDuc Fine Catering, Emeryville, California, www.paulaleduc.com
- Jerry Ehrenwald, International Gemological Institute, www.igiworld wide.com
- Jeni Fong, Grace Image, San Francisco, www.graceimage.com
- Sam Godfrey, Perfect Endings, Napa, California, www.perfectend ings.com
- Dr. Joe Goldblatt, Temple University School of Tourism and Hospitality Management, Philadelphia, www.temple.edu/STHM
- John A. Green, Lux Bond & Green, West Hartford, Connecticut, www.LBGreen.com
- Bill Hansen, Bill Hansen Catering / Leading Caterers of America, Miami, www.billhansencatering.com, www.leadingcaterers.com
- Eliot Holtzman, Eliot Holtzman Photography, San Rafael, California, www.eliotholtzman.com
- Richard Horne, Shreve & Co., San Francisco, www.shreve.com

- Susan Kidwell, Classic Party Rentals, Burlingame, California, www.classicpartyrentals.com
- Brian Merkley, Merkley Kendrick Jewelers, Louisville, 502-895-6124
- Susan Morgan, Elegant Cheese Cakes, Half Moon Bay, California, www.elegantcheesecakes.com
- Dan Ohrman, Denon & Doyle Entertainment, Pleasant Hill, California, www.djay.com
- Richard Olsen, Richard Olsen Orchestras, Sonoma, California, www.bigbandswing.com
- Dorcas Prince, Low's Bridal, Brinkley, Arkansas, www.lowsbridal.com
- Rob Puccinelli, California Parking, San Francisco, 415-447-1700
- Denis Reggie, Denis Reggie Photographers, Atlanta, www.denisreggie.com
- Wendy Maclaurin Richardson, Wendy Maclaurin Richardson Photography, San Francisco, www.wmrphoto.com
- Chuck and Jewel Savadelis, Savadelis Films, Sunnyvale, California, www.savadelis.com
- Mel Wasserman, Zwillinger & Company, San Francisco, www.zwillinger.com

I owe a debt of gratitude to Kirk Kazanjian at Literary Productions for believing in me and asking me to write this book. You were always thoughtful and patient with me and helped make a dream come true. I would also like to thank Sheila Curry Oakes, my editor at St. Martin's Press, for "keeping me in the present," and everyone else at St. Martin's Press who has labored behind the scenes to make this book a reality.

"We are still reminiscing about your fabulous wedding day. What fun it was! We would love to turn back the clock a few weeks and celebrate with you all over again." That was a thank-you note I received from a guest who attended my wedding on June 19, 1994. Although I would love to repeat the most magical day of my life, part of what made my wedding so special is that it truly was a once-in-a-lifetime superlative experience.

I had the most fun planning my wedding with my handsome and debonair husband, Dana Becker. It was not the norm for grooms to be so involved back then, but I soon realized that I wasn't just planning a wedding. I was planning a marriage with a man whom I knew would be by my side supporting me throughout my life.

There were so many wonderful little details of our wedding: the "Sheikh" exotic Moroccan rehearsal dinner, the Prenuptial Picnic in the park where we invited guests to "Barbecue Your Buns Off, Run Rapid Relay Races, Suck Down Suds, and Soak Up Sun"; and then "The Main

Event" that made it so *perfect* (my favorite word). Echoes of sounds from my childhood permeated St. Brigid's Church (the same church where my parents were married in June 1937) as the Golden Gate Boys Choir and Bellringers performed songs from my Catholic school days. The cocktail reception at the Mark Hopkins Hotel included a surprise video featuring all our guests as the stars. A gracefully timed four-course dinner was served with romantic tunes and dancing between the courses. At sunset, the band kicked into Motown and everyone went crazy on the dance floor.

I remember every moment as if it were yesterday! It wasn't just a passing blur as so many wedding couples have described their wedding day to be. I truly believe the reason I recall everything so vividly is because it was planned with precision. We were extremely organized, left nothing to chance, and truly enjoyed our day. I have no regrets about the wedding day, nor the man I married. Dana has been my best friend, my greatest cheerleader, my confidant. To you, Dana, I am forever grateful for all the many sacrifices you have made for me.

To my loving parents, Ines Scardina and Tony Scardina, your presence was surely felt on my wedding day and every day thereafter, as I continue to feel your strength. Mom, you were a lady of grace and style managing a household of four children. You raised ironing to an art form, never a wrinkle in my beautifully pressed organza dresses from I. Magnin's department store. I now appreciate the attention I received from strangers who stopped me on the street admiring the perfect bows you tied on the backs of my dresses. Little did you know how those perfect bows would influence my life and the students I teach.

A first-generation Italian-American grocer with a sixth-grade education, my dad was a magnanimous man, "bigger than life," and so respected in his community. He used to say to me in that fatherly tone of voice, "I'd like to see you when you get to be my age." Well, Dad, I am your age now, and so grateful for inheriting your entrepreneurial genes.

To my loving siblings, Gerry Benson, Diane Hollister, and Bob Scardina, and to their spouses for the examples they have set for living happily ever after in their marriages of thirty-five years and more. Thank you for giving me the opportunity to be in your weddings at such a tender age. Little did we know that those experiences would turn into a passion and vocation for me.

To dear Lauretta Vogelheim Parker, "The Wedding Secretary" on Post Street in San Francisco, a heartfelt thank-you for your inspiration.

To students and friends along the way, without whose journalistic input I never would have whipped this book into shape. For their editorial efforts, I am most grateful to Joanie Cesano, a former student whose wit, charm, and stylistic talents have become invaluable to me and Events of Distinction; to Lee Cordon, a recent graduate of the wedding consulting certificate program who will surely be a success in the wedding industry; and to dear Molly Frankforter, a longtime friend who was with me the day I met my husband . . . your prince too will come!

To my wedding consultant certificate students past and present, I am always energized when I walk into the classroom to share my knowledge and joy of teaching with you. May you learn well and teach others. You are tomorrow's leaders in this most remarkable industry.

Finally, to all the wonderful brides and grooms who have given me the honor of planning their weddings over the many years: May you live your dreams of a joyful marriage now and forever.

WHETHER DESIGNING IN the classical, eclectic, or modernist mode, Joyce Scardina Becker produces unique, timeless weddings that transcend style. Internationally acclaimed for innovative design and meticulous planning, Scardina Becker is president of Events of Distinction in San Francisco, where she has reigned since 1995 as a premier wedding designer in one of the world's most exquisite yet competitive wedding environments.

Scardina Becker is a celebrated wedding expert with more than twenty-five years of event-management experience, strengthened with professional credentials as a Certified Wedding Consultant (CWC) and Certified Meeting Professional (CMP). A cross between an interior designer, floral designer, and event designer extraordinaire, she has planned and produced hundreds of dazzling weddings and special events that have literally left guests awestruck.

Scardina Becker received her bachelor's degree from San Francisco State University, where she excelled in hospitality management and education. At City College of San Francisco, she earned a prestigious degree in retail floristry and mastered the art of design, color, and texture. Scardina Becker is founding director of the first Wedding Consultant certificate program at a university. Nationally recognized by students and wedding professionals, this program is now offered at California State University, East Bay.

Scardina Becker served as the prestigious "Northern California Expert" for *TheKnot.com* Web site and was a contributing editor for *The Knot Weddings Northern California* magazine. She was selected by KGO-TV (ABC) in San Francisco to work closely with the producer in creating several "ABC 7 Wedding Guide" television programs, and dispensed expert advice on the abc7news.com wedding Web page. As the wedding expert for the Leading Caterers of America Web site, Scardina Becker provides valuable nuptial tips to couples and caterers alike. Her ideas and works have appeared in countless publications, including *Brides, Modern Bride, Wedding Bells, Bridal Guide,* the *Chicago Tri-*

bune, the *Los Angeles Times, The Boston Globe,* and *The Miami Herald.* The International Special Events Society has honored her as one of the top wedding producers in the United States with the prestigious WESTIE Award.

She has been an active member of the International Special Events Society since 1993 and has served on the board of directors for its Northern California chapter and as vice president of education in 1996, 1997, 1998, 2002, 2003, and 2004—a fitting position for a consummate scholar.

Joyce Scardina Becker can be reached through her Web site at www.eventsofdistinction.com.